Possible Selves and Higher Education

Drawing together example studies from international contexts, this edited collection provides a new and cross-disciplinary perspective on the concept of the possible self, exploring its theoretical, methodological and empirical uses with regards to Higher Education. Building on research which examines the ways in which possible selves are constructed through inequalities of class, race and gender, the book interrogates the role of imagined futures in student, professional and academic lives, augmenting the concept of possible selves, with its origins in psychology, with sociological approaches to educational inequalities and exclusionary practices.

Possible Selves and Higher Education considers both the theoretical and methodological frameworks behind the concept of possible selves; the first section includes chapters that consider different theoretical insights, while the second section offers empirical examples, exploring how the possible selves concept has been used in many diverse higher education research contexts. With each chapter considering a different aspect of the structural barriers to or within education, the examples provided range from the experiences of students and teachers in the language learning classroom, to graduates entering employment for the first time, and refugees seeking to rebuild lives through engagement with education.

Offering a broad and diverse examination of how concepts of our future selves can affect and limit educational outcomes, this book furthers the sociological dialogue concerning the relationship between individual agency and structural constraints in higher education research. It is an essential and influential text for both students and academics, as well as anyone responsible for student services such as outreach and widening participation.

Holly Henderson is an ESRC-funded doctoral researcher at the School of Education, University of Birmingham, UK.

Jacqueline Stevenson is Professor of Education Research and Head of Research at the Sheffield Institute of Education, Sheffield Hallam University, UK.

Ann-Marie Bathmaker is Professor of Vocational and Higher Education at the University of Birmingham, UK and Visiting Professor at the Centre for Development Studies, University of the Free State, South Africa.

The Society for Research into Higher Education (SRHE) is an independent and financially self-supporting international learned Society. It is concerned to advance understanding of higher education, especially through the insights, perspectives and knowledge offered by systematic research and scholarship.

The Society's primary role is to improve the quality of higher education through facilitating knowledge exchange, discourse and publication of research. SRHE members are worldwide and the Society is an NGO in operational relations with UNESCO.

The Society has a wide set of aims and objectives. Amongst its many activities the Society:

* is a specialist publisher of higher education research, journals and books, amongst them *Studies in Higher Education, Higher Education Quarterly, Research into Higher Education Abstracts* and a long running monograph book series.

The Society also publishes a number of in-house guides and produces a specialist series "Issues in Postgraduate Education".

* funds and supports a large number of special interest networks for researchers and practitioners working in higher education from every discipline. These networks are open to all and offer a range of topical seminars, workshops and other events throughout the year ensuring the Society is in touch with all current research knowledge.

* runs the largest annual UK-based higher education research conference and parallel conference for postgraduate and newer researchers. This is attended by researchers from over 35 countries and showcases current research across every aspect of higher education.

SRHE *Society for Research into Higher Education*
Advancing knowledge Informing policy Enhancing practice

73 Collier Street
London N1 9BE
United Kingdom

T +44 (0)20 7427 2350
F +44 (0)20 7278 1135
E srheoffice@srhe.ac.uk

www.srhe.ac.uk

Director: Helen Perkins
Registered Charity No. 313850
Company No. 00868820
Limited by Guarantee
Registered office as above

Society for Research into Higher Education Series
Series Editors:
Jennifer M. Case
University of Vermont, USA

Jeroen Huisman
University of Ghent, Belgium

This exciting new series aims to publish cutting edge research and discourse that reflects the rapidly changing world of higher education, examined in a global context. Encompassing topics of wide international relevance, the series includes every aspect of the international higher education research agenda, from strategic policy formulation and impact to pragmatic advice on best practice in the field.

Titles in the series:

Changing Pedagogical Spaces in Higher Education
Diversity, Inequalities and Misrecognition
Penny Jane Burke, Gill Crozier and Lauren Ila Misiaszek

Access to Higher Education
Theoretical Perspectives and Contemporary Challenges
Edited by Anna Mountford-Zimdars and Neil Harrison

Religion and Higher Education in Europe and North America
Edited by Kristin Aune and Jacqueline Stevenson

Reconstructing Relationships in Higher Education
Celia Whitchurch and George Gordon

Possible Selves and Higher Education
New Interdisciplinary Insights
Edited by Holly Henderson, Jacqueline Stevenson and Ann-Marie Bathmaker

Enhancing the Freedom to Flourish in Higher Education
Participation, Equality and Capabilities
Talita Calitz

For more information about this series, please visit: www.routledge.com/Research-into-Higher-Education/book-series/SRHE

Possible Selves and Higher Education

New Interdisciplinary Insights

Edited by Holly Henderson,
Jacqueline Stevenson and
Ann-Marie Bathmaker

LONDON AND NEW YORK

First published 2019
by Routledge
2 Park Square, Milton Park, Abingdon, Oxon OX14 4RN

and by Routledge
711 Third Avenue, New York, NY 10017

Routledge is an imprint of the Taylor & Francis Group, an informa business

© 2019 selection and editorial matter, Holly Henderson, Jacqueline Stevenson and Ann-Marie Bathmaker; individual chapters, the contributors

The right of Holly Henderson, Jacqueline Stevenson and Ann-Marie Bathmaker to be identified as the author of the editorial material, and of the authors for their individual chapters, has been asserted in accordance with sections 77 and 78 of the Copyright, Designs and Patents Act 1988.

All rights reserved. No part of this book may be reprinted or reproduced or utilised in any form or by any electronic, mechanical, or other means, now known or hereafter invented, including photocopying and recording, or in any information storage or retrieval system, without permission in writing from the publishers.

Trademark notice: Product or corporate names may be trademarks or registered trademarks, and are used only for identification and explanation without intent to infringe.

British Library Cataloguing-in-Publication Data
A catalogue record for this book is available from the British Library

Library of Congress Cataloging-in-Publication Data
A catalog record has been requested for this book

ISBN: 978-1-138-09799-5 (hbk)
ISBN: 978-1-138-09803-9 (pbk)
ISBN: 978-1-315-10459-1 (ebk)

Typeset in Galliard
by Apex CoVantage, LLC

Contents

About the contributors ix

1 Introduction: why possible selves and higher education? 1
HOLLY HENDERSON, ANN-MARIE BATHMAKER AND
JACQUELINE STEVENSON

SECTION 1
Theorising possible selves 11

2 Potentials and challenges when using possible selves
in studies of student motivation 13
MARTIN G. ERIKSON

3 Borrowed time: a sociological theorisation of possible
selves and educational subjectivities 27
HOLLY HENDERSON

4 Extending the analytical scope of theories of
'possible selves' 41
SUE CLEGG

SECTION 2
Using the possible selves concept empirically 57

5 A discursive approach to understanding the role of
educators' possible selves in widening students'
participation in classroom interaction: language
teachers' sense making as 'acts of imagination' 59
MAGDALENA KUBANYIOVA

6 Shaping possible selves: the role of family in constructing higher education futures for students with dyslexia 78
ANGELA MURPHY

7 Unintended imaginings: the difficult dimensions of possible selves 93
MATT LUMB

8 Transitions from higher education to employment among recent graduates in England: unequal chances of achieving desired possible selves 111
VANDA PAPAFILIPPOU AND ANN-MARIE BATHMAKER

9 Imagining a future: refugee women, possible selves and higher education 127
JACQUELINE STEVENSON

Index 151

About the contributors

Ann-Marie Bathmaker is Professor of Vocational and Higher Education at the University of Birmingham, UK, and Visiting Professor at the Centre for Development Studies, University of the Free State, South Africa. Her research focuses on questions of equity and inequalities in vocational, post-compulsory and higher education, particularly in relation to issues of social class. She has a particular interest in the role of further education colleges and their international equivalents in the provision of education and training. Her recent research includes a study of higher education, social mobility and social class (the Paired Peers project), a study of the role and purposes of vocationally-oriented University Technical Colleges for 14–19-year-olds in England, and research examining constructions of knowledge in general vocational qualifications. She was the specialist advisor to the House of Lords Select Committee on Social Mobility School to Work (2015–2016).

Sue Clegg is Emeritus Professor of Higher Education Research at Leeds Beckett University and Visiting Professor at University of the Arts London. She was a Mellon Visiting Scholar at the University of Cape Town in 2014 and Visiting Professorial Scholar at the University of Newcastle NSW in 2016. Her research draws on critical realism and feminist theory. She has been involved in theorising the nature of curriculum and researching extracurricular activity and the formation and recognition of social and cultural capital. She has written on temporality in higher education and is currently working on the significance of powerful knowledge in higher education and its implications for theorising equity and diversity. She was Editor of *Teaching in Higher Education* from 2006 to 2014. She plays a major role in the *Society for Research into Higher Education* and chairs their Publications Committee.

Martin G. Erikson is Associate Professor of Psychology at University of Borås, Sweden. He completed his PhD in Psychology in 2006 at Lund University, Sweden, with a thesis about possible selves, and has since done further research on possible selves in applied settings. His research is currently focused on various aspects of higher education, particularly in relation to quality enhancement, and he is Chair of the Research and Education Board at the University of Borås.

Holly Henderson is an ESRC-funded doctoral researcher at the School of Education, University of Birmingham. Her PhD project is exploring student experiences of HE in FE, conceptualising HE in FE students as on the boundaries of provision in terms of the local and the national, the academic and the vocational. She is particularly interested in theorising subjectivities in relation to space, time and narrative, and the methodological challenges related to these theorisations. Her previous research focused on the construction of teacher professional identities with relation to sexualities and gender.

Magdalena Kubanyiova is Professor of Educational Linguistics at the University of Leeds. Her research interests concern language teacher development, additional language learning and use, classroom interaction, and ecological approaches to research, including research ethics. She has worked with researchers and language educators internationally, including in Slovakia, China, Greece and Japan. She is author of *Teacher Development in Action: Understanding Language Teachers' Conceptual Change* (Palgrave, 2016), and her book *Motivating Learners, Motivating Teachers: Building Vision in the Language Classroom* (co-authored with Zoltan Dörnyei; Cambridge University Press, 2014) was highly commended for the HRH Duke of Edinburgh English Language Book Award.

Matt Lumb is with the Centre of Excellence for Equity in Higher Education (CEEHE) at the University of Newcastle in Australia. His commitment to more socially just communities was founded through diverse experiences as a classroom teacher in remote Australian high schools, as a community development professional working on projects in Australia and in parts of Asia and Africa, and as a 'Widening Participation' (WP) outreach practitioner at the University of Newcastle. He is currently enrolled in a PhD with CEEHE, investigating the concealed impacts of outreach connections by exploring sociological understandings of modern psychological constructions. Matt also has an interest in the ways sophisticated participatory methodologies have the potential to make evaluative practices more productive, and to deliver nuanced and contextualised understandings of the underlying mechanisms that produce programme impact.

Angela Murphy completed her Professional Doctorate at Leeds Beckett University. She is an occupational therapist and has practised within the National Health Service with people with long-term conditions such as Chronic Fatigue Syndrome and Neurological conditions such as Multiple Sclerosis. More recently Angela has been teaching occupational therapy at Leeds Beckett University as a Senior Lecturer and has developed an interest in dyslexia and how people achieve their potential and reach desired possible selves as a result of teaching and personal experiences of dyslexia.

Vanda Papafilippou is Lecturer in Human Resource Management in the Faculty of Business and Law, University of the West of England. Since being awarded a PhD at the University of Bristol (Graduate School of Education, funded by the ESRC), she has worked as a Teaching Associate at the University of Bristol, a Regional Facilitator for Action Tutoring (Registered Charity Number 1147175) and as a Research Associate on the Paired Peers Moving On Up project. Her research interests revolve around sociology of work and higher education, women in male-dominated sectors (especially in engineering), identity construction as well as alternative research methodologies/epistemologies.

Jacqueline Stevenson is Professor of Education Research and Head of Research in the Sheffield Institute of Education, Sheffield Hallam University. She is a sociologist of education with a particular interest in policy and practice relating to equity and diversity in higher education, widening participation, access and student success, pedagogic diversity and the stratification and marketisation of higher education. Key areas of interest are the social and academic experiences of religious students, the access, retention and success of refugees in higher education, and Black and Minority ethnic students' degree attainment and success.

Chapter 1

Introduction
Why possible selves and higher education?

Holly Henderson, Ann-Marie Bathmaker and Jacqueline Stevenson

Just over thirty years ago, Hazel Markus and Paula Nurius (1986), two psychologists working in the USA, published a paper that offered a new way of thinking about a long-standing issue. Their work was located in the field of social psychology and they proposed the concept of possible selves to describe the ways in which the future is imagined as embodied and personalised, and how this imagining of the future impacts upon behaviour in the present. They explained:

> Possible selves are the ideal selves that we would very much like to become. They are also the selves we could become, and the selves we are afraid of becoming.
>
> (Markus and Nurius, 1986, p. 954)

Thirty years after their paper was first published, we have put together this volume, because we believe that the concept has the potential to help us think in still newer ways about temporality and the self. More specifically, we argue that the concept can be put to use in addressing key issues in the current context of an increasingly globalized field of higher education (HE). In this introduction, we first highlight a number of these contemporary issues, showing where the possible selves concept is useful in theorising and researching HE. We then outline where the concept intersects with other theoretical or methodological approaches, and where its potential pitfalls might be, using the responses we received to the question 'Why possible selves?' from contributing authors in this volume. We conclude by summarising the structure of the book and the chapters that follow.

Since the proposal of possible selves by Markus and Nurius, the concept has been widely used in the discipline of cognitive psychology in the US, in research literature and in the development of programmes of educational intervention for school-age students, especially adolescents (see, for example, Oyserman, Terry and Bybee, 2002; Pizzolato, 2007). Over time, the concept has been used outside of these specific geographical, disciplinary and empirical parameters. In relation to HE, possible selves has been used to address contexts as diverse as English Language learning in Iranian universities (Khajavy and Ghonsooly, 2017), sexual identity and university experience in the US (Anders, Olmstead and Johnson, 2017), and teacher education in Turkey (Dalioglu and Adiguzel, 2016). The range of these uses of the possible selves concept demonstrates its dynamism and its endurance as a way of thinking about the future, and the role that 'future' plays in current HE practices. Particularly important for us, as researchers with disciplinary backgrounds in the sociology of HE, is to acknowledge that the possible selves concept has its origins in the field of social psychology, and is used to study the role of cognition in educational contexts, but that its application can be usefully augmented with sociological analysis. The project of writing for and editing this volume has therefore been in part an exploration of the reasons we and our contributing authors are drawn to the concept, and in part an argument for its applicability and relevance in multi-disciplinary analyses of HE. Our subtitle 'New Interdisciplinary Insights' points to how different authors in the book bring to bear ideas and thinking from sociology in particular, but also from educational linguistics (Chapter 5), occupational health (Chapter 6) and widening participation practice (Chapter 7), and how the book as a whole foregrounds discussions of disciplinary interactions.

Possible selves and higher education: why now?

The current unprecedented increase in rates of participation in HE across the globe is, as Marginson (2016) argues, driven by the associations between degree education and the maintenance or upward revision of social class positions. Participation in undergraduate education is indivisible from the expected outcomes of that education; the implied graduate future is ever-present, and all the more powerful where the costs of tuition are increasingly being passed on to students themselves, as is the case in the UK. This graduate future is drawn upon by school career services and university marketing materials (Duggan, 2017; Symes and Drew, 2017), as well as by undergraduate curricula and extra-curricular activities that focus on career futures and employability (Baker and Henson, 2010).

One of the key reasons for using the possible selves concept in HE research, therefore, is that *it is already there*. It is there in the ways that students are guided towards university education through schools-based outreach activities, and there in the ways that they are required to navigate through and beyond HE, including those employability initiatives which start at the point when students arrive in HE. Beginning with an acknowledgement that the possible selves concept describes HE's future-oriented present (see Clegg, 2010) allows the concept to be put to work in important ways. Most crucially, it enables a focus on how access to imagined futures in HE might differ along lines of privilege and disadvantage (Stevenson and Clegg, 2011). As the chapters in this volume highlight, using the possible selves concept means thinking about what is *impossible* as well as, and sometimes over and above, what is *possible*. In turn, thinking about what is impossible requires that the imagined future is understood in the context of the ever-present legacy of the past.

In an example of the ways that HE possible futures are caught up in past impossibilities, Corbett's (2007) analysis of rural school leavers' ambitions for the future in Canada argues that:

> The ability to think into future scenarios and to construct imaginary 'project selves' (Giddens, 1991, pp. 32–34) that involve 'realistic' or what Bourdieu (1990) called 'coherent and convenient' (p. 86) mobility trajectories is differentially distributed along social class lines.
>
> (Corbett, 2007, p. 785)

From a Canadian context in which participation in HE requires geographical mobility, Corbett argues that this requirement has an underlying and often unseen prior condition – access to that mobility as an imagined future. We have taken access to imagined futures as an important focus in this volume, exploring the multiple ways in which structures within and outside of HE constrain the ways that futures can be imagined. While social class is one of the structures that these chapters address, we also look at factors such as race, disabilities and immigration status as markers of inequality that enable and limit particular kinds of HE futures. Just as Corbett uses the work of Giddens and Bourdieu in his discussion of imagined futures in the above quotation, throughout this volume the different authors work to conceptualise possible selves alongside other theoretical tools. In doing so, we create a dialogue that seeks to open future possibilities for social research into HE, just as it illuminates the role of the possible future in our current research contexts.

Possible selves and higher education: why possible selves?

It is to this dialogue that we now turn, drawing on the words of our contributing authors. We asked each of them the question, 'Why possible selves?', and their responses pick up a range of important aspects of working with the concept, each of which is explored further in the chapters that follow.

> Possible selves are about the individual idiosyncratic meaning given to goals, beyond motivational models with generalized goal-conceptions where individual variance is lost.

This response, from Martin G. Erikson (Chapter 2), highlights both the unique nature of the concept, in its attention to the individual rather than the general, and the concept's potential problems in social research contexts. After all, most authors in this volume are not seeking to focus on the individual to the exclusion of the social, but, as Angela Murphy (Chapter 6) puts it, to use possible selves to:

> Highlight injustices when sociological and occupational injustices obstruct perceptions of possible selves and/or prevent meaningful actions.

This dialectic, between the focus on the individual and the critique of sociological injustices that shape and limit what is possible for the individual to imagine, is important to all our authors. Jacqueline Stevenson (Chapter 9) and Vanda Papafilippou and Ann-Marie Bathmaker (Chapter 8) argue that the concept of possible selves 'allows researchers to bring into consideration both structure and agency' (J. Stevenson). It is this comment, with its focus on *how researchers use* the possible selves concept, that is crucial to the chapters in this volume, and to the reasons that the contributing authors have continued to work with and wrestle with the concept.

Martin G. Erikson further argues:

> No other theory of motivation I am aware of (even in a broad sense) offers such a broad scope, particularly when it comes to bringing in cultural and social factors. The drawback is that the complexity at the same time gives rise to methodological challenges, not the least because subjectivity is at the core of the model, but the theoretical advantages make it worth struggling with the methodological issues.

As Erikson's response points out, there are complex methodological consequences involved when setting out to research what is, by definition, in the abstract of the imagined. Engaging with a concept that deliberately seeks to explore complexity, drawing together understandings of subjectivity and structure, agency and motivation, requires a constant critical re-examining of theoretical and methodological assumptions in research. There are important questions to be asked of how the concept can be used in research methodologies. What questions, for example, can we ask about what students imagine, without implicitly suggesting what they *should* imagine? If, as suggested above, the possible selves concept also attends to the impossible, how can the impossible be researched? How can lost or un-imagined possible selves be present enough in data to be analysed? And, perhaps most importantly, how can such analysis move beyond the tendency to situate such absence in the failures and deficits of individuals, rather than in the structures that shape them? What Jacqueline Stevenson argues is that the possible selves concept can 'help illuminate broad patterns of disadvantage across social groups', because it can put emphasis on how the past influences the present and imagined future. While the material present of HE contexts relies so heavily upon the future and while both present and future are so consequentially linked to advantages and disadvantages in educational pasts, the methodological struggle involved in a critical approach to these temporalities is worth it.

The broad themes elucidated by our contributing authors of the interplay between structure and agency in social research, of the dialectic between abstract theorisation and empirical methodology, of narrative temporality and its place in HE contexts and HE research, are touched upon in multiple ways by the chapters in this volume. In the chapters in Section 2, which demonstrate the uses of possible selves in empirical work, there are studies which include the experiences of healthcare students, training and practising teachers, recent graduates from HE and refugees in the UK. While this deliberately demonstrates the diversity of contexts in which the possible selves concept may be applied, the chapters also serve to further the volume's central project of adapting the concept to sociological thinking about HE. Each study separately takes as its subject an aspect of the structural barriers to or within education. By applying the possible selves concept as a theoretical and methodological framework, the studies both individually and as a whole further the sociological dialogue concerning the relationship between individual agency and structural constraints in HE research.

The book: an overview

The book is divided into two sections. In the first section, three chapters offer different theoretical insights into the possible selves concept and its potential for use in HE research contexts. The second section is empirically driven, and each of the chapters shows how the possible selves concept has been used in different and diverse HE research contexts.

Section 1: theorising possible selves

Chapter 2, by Martin G. Erikson, summarises and challenges the ways that the possible selves concept has been used in studies of student motivation in HE. Arguing strongly for a specific and elaborated definition of 'motivation', Erikson explores the language associated with the possible selves concept, focusing on positive and negative valence and on the important distinction between possible selves and life tasks. The chapter then sets out a development of the possible selves concept which includes the notion of 'possible others', necessitating a shift away from the individual and towards social context and social construction. Throughout the chapter, Erikson discusses and problematises the ways in which studies of student motivation frequently assume a collective understanding of the broader purposes of HE.

Chapter 3 sustains the focus on interrogating the language of the possible selves concept, in order that the concept can be used critically and productively. This chapter, by Holly Henderson, suggests that while the possible selves concept originates in the field of cognitive psychology, it can be theorised sociologically. In order for this theorisation to be productive, the chapter argues, a thorough conceptualisation of narrative temporality and subjectivity is necessary. Henderson therefore works through these conceptualisations, looking first at the discursive structures of possible selves if they are positioned as narratives, and then at the role played by narratives of possible selves in the construction of educational subjectivities. Finally, the chapter uses these conceptualisations to question how useful the concept of possible selves can be in addressing and analysing inequalities in HE contexts.

Chapter 4, by Sue Clegg, interrogates the purposes of extending the reach of the possible selves concept from its original disciplinary field, looking at uses of social theory in the field of HE research. This chapter situates the concept of possible selves among theories of the 'middle range' (Merton, 1968), which offer a way of negotiating between theoretical abstraction and the analysis of empirical data. This discussion argues for more attention to be paid to the practices of theorising in educational research, and suggests that the possible selves concept is unusual in both opening up avenues for further theoretical work, and offering the tools for meaningful data analysis and dissemination. Like the first two chapters, this third chapter is structured around the importance of thoroughly defining conceptual terms. The chapter positions the possible selves concept within discussions of temporality and HE more broadly, before offering a definition of the sociological self through ideas of agency and reflexivity.

Section 2: using the possible selves concept empirically

In the empirically driven second section, Chapter 5 applies the possible selves concept to the language-learning classroom, arguing that the possible selves created in these contexts have a direct impact upon HE futures. Magdalena Kubanyiova addresses methodological questions around the concept of possible selves in this chapter, showing how her grounded theory ethnographic approach to data collection allows discourses of future temporalities to emerge from qualitative data analysis. This methodology therefore works against the perception that representations of possible selves are found only when explicitly targeted by data collection methods. Instead, Kubanyiova's methodological approach further emphasises the ubiquity of discourses of future temporality in educational contexts. The chapter uses data from both classroom observation and teacher interviews to focus on one case study, which explores the ways in which language teachers' actions in the classroom are reflective of past and present imaginings of their future selves as teachers. As Kubanyiova goes on to highlight, these actions then shape what is possible for students and teachers to imagine, in language learning and in educational contexts more broadly.

Chapter 6 by Angela Murphy also offers methodological and empirical insights into the possible selves concept. The chapter presents narrative data using an innovative theatrical structure of scenes from a play, which allows for the creation of dialogue between multiple narratives and invites the reader to interact directly with the narratives of the participants. Focusing on experiences of Master's level healthcare students with dyslexia, Angela Murphy's chapter sets out an important development of the possible selves concept. The scenes presented destabilise the association of possible selves with individuals, instead suggesting that these narratives are shared and inherited in and through family structures. The chapter shows how vital a role families play in the sharing and development of academic possible selves that enable access to HE despite the barriers experienced as a result of disability. In emphasising how familial narratives of the future are often determining factors in the academic successes of students with dyslexia, the chapter also highlights how precarious these HE futures are.

Chapter 7 offers a problematisation of widening participation outreach programmes in Australia that draws out both the dangers and the potential of using the possible selves concept in this HE context. Looking at two stages of a particular outreach project working with historically under-represented groups, Matt Lumb shows how the first stage of the project might be seen from a critical perspective. Positioning the project as part of a discourse of deficit, Lumb suggests that the prospective students involved were required to produce or perform possible selves with HE aspirations that were deemed to be acceptable or valuable. By contrast, Lumb explores how the second stage of the project was used to reflect on these performances of aspiration with the participants, and to explore more complex and more difficult imaginings of the future with them. As well as highlighting how a discourse of possible futures is endemic to programmes of outreach and widening participant, Lumb's chapter shows how this discourse can be mobilised in more critical and productive ways.

Chapter 8 shifts the focus from progression into HE to progression beyond degree-level study. Drawing on data from a longitudinal qualitative study of students' progression into and through HE in England (the Paired Peers project), Vanda Papafilippou and Ann-Marie Bathmaker use the concept of possible selves alongside Bourdieu's conceptual tools in order to examine the transition from undergraduate study to the labour market. The chapter looks at the experience of three participants in the study who aspired to work in the finance and accountancy sectors, and discusses the implicit and explicit requirements of gaining entry into these employment sectors. The analysis provides insights into the interaction of cultural, structural and social processes that contributed to the development of the career identity and future work selves of these young graduates. The chapter produces a working dialogic theorisation of the possible selves concept that shows how a strong possible career self could be viewed as a form of capital in its own right (Bourdieu, 1977). Seen as a form of capital, the career possible self is both a product of unequal access to valued resources, and further reproduces advantages and disadvantages in realised and unrealised graduate futures.

In the volume's final chapter, by Jacqueline Stevenson, the concept of possible selves is put to a difficult test as it is applied to the context of refugee women in the UK who are participating in educational projects and seeking to reframe their career possible selves. The narrative data in this chapter illuminate how structural barriers such as unemployment, poverty, ill health and a lack of recognition of existing qualifications affect refugees' ability to think about their futures, or put strategies in place to attain them. At the same time, Stevenson asks in this chapter how the possible selves concept can be used to account for the loss and fracturing of futures, as well as for the more familiar questions of hoped for and feared futures. The chapter offers a fitting conclusion to our exploration of the possible selves concept, emphasising how the impossible must be theorised alongside the possible, and the lost future understood as lived alongside the process of re-building imagined futures. Stevenson concludes by arguing a need for the possible selves construct to be reframed, to take account of the sociological and not just the psychological.

As the chapters in this book each highlight in different ways, the possible selves concept allows an acknowledgement of the powerful role played by personalised, imagined, hoped for and feared futures (Markus and Nurius, 1986), but it also runs the risk of situating educational problems with the individual, thereby ignoring social and structural issues. Rather than dismiss the concept for this reason, the contributors to this volume instead use the opportunity to foreground discussions of the struggle between endemic discourses of individualisation and vital interruptions that highlight structural constraints on educational possibility. Each grappling with this important dialogue in different ways, the studies in this collection demonstrate new ways of thinking about the kind of work required of future of HE research, that engages with both individual hopes and desires and with the structures that frame and constrain the realisation of possible selves.

References

Anders, K. M., Olmstead, S. B. and Johnson, E. I. (2017) The sexual possible selves and strategies of first-semester college students: What do they hope for and fear and how do they plan to get there? *The Journal of Sex Research*, 54, 6: 728–740.

Baker, G. and Henson, D. (2010) Promoting employability skills development in a research-intensive university. *Education and Training*, 52, 1: 62–75.

Bourdieu, P. (1977) *Outline of a theory of practice*, Cambridge: Cambridge University Press.

Clegg, S. (2010) Time future: The dominant discourse of higher education. *Time & Society*, 19, 3: 345–364.

Corbett, M. (2007) Travels in space and place: Identity and rural schooling. *Canadian Journal of Education*, 30, 3: 771–792.

Dalioglu, S. T. and Adiguzel, O. C. (2016) Teacher candidates' self-efficacy beliefs and possible selves throughout the teaching practice period in Turkey. *Asia Pacific Education Review*, 17, 4: 651–661.

Duggan, S. (2017) Understanding temporality and future orientation for young women in the senior year. *Discourse: Studies in the Cultural Politics of Education*, 38, 6: 795–806.

Khajavy, G. H. and Ghonsooly, B. (2017) Predictors of willingness to read in English: Testing a model based on possible selves and self-confidence. *Journal of Multilingual and Multicultural Development*, 38, 10: 871–885.

Marginson, S. (2016) The worldwide trend to high participation higher education: Dynamics of social stratification in inclusive systems. *Higher Education*, 72, 4: 413–434.

Markus, H. and Nurius, P. (1986) Possible selves. *American Psychologist*, 41, 9: 954–969.

Merton, R. K. (1968) *Social theory and social structure*, London: Simon and Schuster.

Oyserman, D., Terry, K. and Bybee, D. (2002) A possible selves intervention to enhance school involvement. *Journal of Adolescence*, 25, 3: 313–326.

Pizzolato, J. E. (2007) Impossible selves: Investigating students' persistence decisions when their career-possible selves border on impossible. *Journal of Career Development*, 33, 3: 201–223.

Stevenson, J. and Clegg, S. (2011) Possible selves: Students orientating themselves towards the future through extracurricular activity. *British Educational Research Journal*, 37, 2: 231–246.

Symes, C. and Drew, C. (2017) Education on the rails: A textual ethnography of university advertising in mobile contexts. *Critical Studies in Education*, 58, 2: 205–223.

Section 1

Theorising possible selves

Chapter 2

Potentials and challenges when using possible selves in studies of student motivation

Martin G. Erikson

Introduction

Regardless of whether we want to understand the challenges facing individual students, or the working of student groups, *student motivation* is a core theme for anyone involved in higher education. However, student motivation is a notion that has to be handled with caution, not the least because the concept *motivation* in itself covers such a wide array of psychological mechanisms (e.g. Weiner, 1992). First, motivation is about mechanisms behind the mere activation of an individual, whatever direction behaviour will take (though this perspective receives comparably little interest in the present day). Second, it is about the direction of behaviour once the individual is activated, and third it is about persistence and striving for achievement. In fact, motivation covers such a broad field of phenomena that almost any psychological theory can be adopted for a discussion of some aspect of motivation. Further, motivation can be discussed on every level of analysis from neurology to cultural structures. In other words, the concept of motivation covers so much that it can say very little: we cannot discuss motivation without selecting a particular aspect of human behaviour that we want to understand, with a precise set of questions, and adopting a particular theory to help us structure our understanding.

Would delimitation to *student* motivation be feasible as such a more specific aspect? It would not, as motivations for student behaviour covers such a broad set of behaviours that they cannot be handled as a whole. Student motivation covers the motivation to engage in higher education at all, to select an educational programme, to persist and graduate; it covers levels of ambition in the long and short term; it covers classroom and reading behaviour as well as social interaction and the acceptance of, or resistance to, personal development. So, any discussion of student motivation calls for strict delimitations, where the right choice of theoretical perspective can help structure our understanding and answer the questions we are interested in.

One such theoretical delimitation is to discuss student motivation in terms of *possible selves*. This theory can explicate the workings of the individual, idiosyncratic meaning given to students' goals, which is an advantage over models of generalized goal-conceptions where individual variance is lost. The theory of possible selves can also help us understand both negative and positive conceptions of the future and bring their interdependency into motivation theory. Further, the theory of possible selves provides a theoretical link between motivation and the self-concept, as well as between motivation and the social and cultural structures in which the individual is embedded. Thus, the purpose of this chapter is to explore some possibilities and challenges of the possible selves model when adopted for the study of student motivation in higher education.

Beyond the need for theoretical delimitations, student motivation is a complex notion also because it must be related to students' goals. Unless we have a clear idea about what students should be motivated to achieve, it would be meaningless to discuss students' motivation and it would be impossible to discuss how we can support students' motivation. On the most general level, this is a question about the purpose of higher education, which of course is an ideological issue (as are all discussions of quality of higher education; see, for example, Lindsay, 1992; Filippakou, 2011). I will eventually return to this ideological issue of purpose in relation to possible selves, but it is important to keep this caveat in mind: student motivation cannot be seen as some isolated psychological phenomena without cultural or social context, and therefore educational purposes cannot be left out. As a consequence, regardless of what purpose we want to promote, the importance of purposes also makes it reasonable to adopt a *goal-focused* theory of student motivation. A goal-focused theory explains motivation in terms of goals to be attained, and not, for example, in terms of needs that these goals would satisfy once attained – the latter would be called a *need-focused* theory. The value of a goal-focused theory, which can help us understand what students are striving for, is a further reason to adopt the theory of possible selves, as the approach to motivation is clearly focused on goals in terms of futures to achieve or avoid.

I will start with an outline of the basics of the possible selves theory. Thereafter, I will outline three areas of possibilities and challenges when adopting the theory of possible selves for student motivation, both in relation to research and to various aspects of supporting students. These possibilities and challenges will be both theoretical and methodological in their nature.

The theory of possible selves

The theory of possible selves places discussions of motivation in a context of the self-concept, which from the outset has been emphasized as an advantage of the theory (Markus and Nurius, 1986). Following Markus (1977, 1990), the self-concept is seen as a set of knowledge structures covering an individual's generalized assumptions and knowledge about herself or himself. The more elaborated of these structures are known as *self-schemata*, with a reference to the cognitive models of schemata, being mental representations guiding the selection and processing of stimuli from the environment – a core model of cognitive psychology (e.g. Rumelhart et al. 1986; Schank and Abelson, 1977).

The self-concept is regarded as paramount in our orientation and understanding of the world around us. Here Markus (1990, p. 242) argued that the self is "the front and centre of the meaning making process". This cognitive approach to the self is not only a matter of how we define ourselves today but covers also visions of ourselves in the future: possible selves are about futures that we hope for, fear or are indifferent about. Explicating the original definition of possible selves by Markus and Nurius (1986), Erikson (2007, p. 356) defined possible selves as

> conceptions of our selves in the future, including, at least to some degree, an experience of being an agent in a future situation. Possible selves get vital parts of their meaning in interplay with the self-concept, which they in turn moderate, as well as from their social and cultural context.

By being part of the self, possible selves become part of the meaning-making process described by Markus (1990). They determine what we see as opportunities as well as threats, and one person's threat might be another's opportunity. One person's desires and ambitions are another person's feared venture into scary uncertainties in strange worlds. And here is the point: only the individuals themselves can define which is which.

Beyond the situational content or end-state, there are four aspects of possible selves in relation to motivation highlighted in the literature. Emotional valence is the first; the extent to which the idea of the end-state evokes positive and/or negative emotions that are related to the emotions the individual assumes would be experienced in such a future situation. The second motivational aspect is the extent to which the individual believes she or he can control if the possible self can be attained or avoided: the higher the perceived controllability of a possible self, which is regarded as important by the individual, the more the individual is inclined to strive to attain or avoid it. The third motivational aspect is the probability that the possible self can be realized. The fourth motivational aspect is the salience or availability of the possible self, as a possible self readily imagined appears more probable, whereas an end-state less easy to imagine in detail appears more improbable. When we state that a possible self influences the motivation (as well as meaning-making) of the individual it is through the combined effects of these four features (e.g. Markus and Kunda, 1986; Markus and Nurius, 1986; Markus and Ruvolo, 1989; Norman and Aron, 2002). Oyserman et al. (2004) used the metaphor of the roadmap when describing how possible selves provided a link between now and the future – the possible selves are associated with assumptions about strategies that might lead to the realization of the end-state and it is in assessing these strategies that the individual puts the motivational function of possible selves into play. This also includes an assessment of the probability of realizing the end-state and the extent to which it is within the individual's own ability to do so.

The full experience of a possible self is shaped by the four motivational aspects of emotional valence, probability, salience and perceived control. In other words, the meaning of a possible self is not constituted by the experience of the future situation as such (the end-state) but by the total experience of the end-state and the ensuing four motivational aspects. It is only by looking at the individual experience of this totality that we can make assumptions about any motivational power in a possible self. These factors are in turn influenced by social norms and cultural assumptions and beliefs. It is in the shape of this complete experience that we can talk about the meaning of a possible self. The end-state alone does not cover more than a part of the possible self's meaning. We can exemplify this with a student with a possible self of a future higher education graduate as an end-state. Is this future probable and is it a future that she or he can influence? Is this possible self emotionally positive and/or negative? These are the questions we must answer if we want to use possible selves as a theoretical approach to student motivation.

Possibilities and challenges in the research and application of possible selves

It can be suggested that three areas are particularly interesting to explore further when possible selves is adopted as a theoretical approach to student motivation in higher education, for both theoretical and methodological reasons. These are (1) the complexity of emotional valence in possible selves, (2) the theoretical distinction between possible selves and more general strivings or life tasks, and finally (3) the notion of 'possible others'. I will discuss the three of them in turn before reaching some final considerations.

The complexity of emotional valence in possible selves

Many theories of motivation have a tendency to make assumptions about general goals, shared among a large number of individuals. The theory of possible selves can help us gain a more nuanced picture of individual motivation, first by including a broader set of futures than such general goals, and second by explicating the importance of understanding the personal nature of these expectations (or lack of expectations). Markus and Nurius (1986) pointed out that when a possible self is activated, it evokes emotions relating to how the individual believes it would feel to be in that future situation. Traditionally, the idea has been that possible selves representing desirable futures have a positive valence whereas possible selves representing unwanted futures are seen as negative (e.g. Markus and Nurius, 1986; Markus and Ruvolo, 1989; Vignoles et al., 2008). However, the findings of Erikson (2006) suggest that this is an oversimplification (see also Erikson, Hansson and Lundblad, 2012, 2014). Instead, these findings indicate that possible selves are often emotionally complex and that many possible selves have both negative and positive connotations, even if one of them dominates.

Dissolving the sharp dichotomy between positive and negative possible selves implies that we should be careful to avoid too simple interpretations or assumptions about how people perceive their futures. Such a view also calls for empirical investigations taking this added complexity into account, as has been done by, for example, Erikson, Hansson and Lundblad (2012, 2014). Such approaches are also supported by the arguments of Godley, Tchanturia, MacLeod, and Schmidt (2001), which suggest that it might be a misconception to see positive and negative emotions as opposing ends of a continuum. Instead, it might be more correct to consider them being the effect of the working of two separate systems: one cognitive-affective system that operates with positive emotions and another that operates with negative emotions, both possibly contributing to the experience of a particular possible self.

Even if the dichotomy between either 'positive' or 'negative' possible selves is too crude to capture a nuanced understanding of the role of emotions in motivation, there are of course many possible selves that are clearly on the emotionally positive or negative side. Here, the findings of Oyserman and Markus (1990a, 1990b) suggested that a positive possible self has its biggest influence on motivation when balanced by a negative possible self, where the latter shows what might happen if the positive possible self is not reached (e.g. Oyserman, Gant and Ager, 1995; Oyserman et al., 2004; Oyserman and Markus, 1990b). A simplified example could be an expected possible self about getting a degree, relating to other possible selves of longs hours of structured studies, balanced by a negative possible self about failing, related to possible selves of pleasurable frivolities instead of studies. However, the empirical findings relating to the motivational power of positive and negative possible selves is also inconclusive, as reviewed by Oyserman, Destin and Novin (2015), who suggest that the motivational power of possible selves is context dependent. In other words, the motivational power is determined by how the individual sees his or her current situation (see also Smith et al., 2014). As Oyserman, Destin and Novin (2015) argue, contexts can be associated with failure or success. Oyserman, Destin and Novin give the example of a university department where students are known to fail to meet expected standards or find it difficult to be employed in desired positions after graduation. For a new student at such a department, the context becomes more failure-likely. As well as such external factors, individual factors, such as a pessimistic disposition, can also make a context more failure-likely. In their study, Oyserman, Destin and Novin (2015) found that undesired possible selves are more motivating in a failure-likely context whereas desired possible selves are more motivating in a success-likely context.

It should once more be mentioned that we must be careful not to assume that we are dealing with clear-cut positive or negative possible selves. When a youth, unfamiliar with academia, is contemplating a future with both alluring potentiality and frightening mysteries, it is difficult to assume that there are such emotionally clear positive or negative possible selves that the motivational models presume. In fact, such a potential student might not even know which part of an imagined future to regard as positive or to regard as negative, seeing potential threats in all of them. If even primarily positive and probable possible selves about student life are emotionally complex, there is a higher threshold to pass before entering an educational programme compared with a situation where the possible selves are clearer in their positive valence. This shows how important it is to challenge the dichotomy between positive and negative possible selves.

It is reasonable to suggest that supporting students or future students to develop possible selves is a matter of making their possible selves less emotionally complex and more manifestly positive, for example by making the possible selves more detailed in their situational content and more related to an understanding of individual abilities that will help with realizing this future. We cannot know what individual students' possible selves look like but we can create situations where they have the opportunity to form positive possible selves about future education, graduation and career which are elaborated, validated and confirmed by peers and others whose opinions matter to them (e.g. Oyserman, Terry and Bybee, 2002). For example, Pizzolato (2006) showed that students need salient and detailed possible selves about being admitted to university, including what it takes to get that far. There is also a risk of backlashes to consider: if futures that parents or teachers regard as positive are represented as unrealistic possible selves by the youth (see Chapter 6 in this volume), we might not only have a possible conflict but also added negative valence to the possible self. The individual might agree that the end-state is desirable but the possible self gets negative valence by bringing with it the pressure of something the individual regards as unattainable. A further source of potential complexity is how conceptions of individual-focused futures are valued by youths from cultural backgrounds with more focus on family or community (e.g. Loveday, Lowell and Jones, 2016). This calls for further research, particularly in relation to widening participation.

Possible selves and life tasks

Cantor et al. (1986) made an important distinction between possible selves and *life tasks*. They argued that: "Life tasks refer to the problems that people see them selves as working on and devoting energy to solving at a particular period in life" (pp. 97–98). These life tasks get their personal meaning through the possible selves that are evoked in relation to them. For example, striving for a higher education degree is a life task, whereas seeing oneself participating in a seminar is a possible self. Most people would probably agree that a degree or a good job is something positive. Still, unless there are predominantly positive, realistic and attainable possible selves in relation to the life tasks, there is very little motivational power in these life tasks, if any. To adopt a life task means that the life task has been interpreted, where existing possible selves and the self-concept at large serve as the interpretative framework. So, for high school students, the idiosyncratic possible selves of becoming a university student, as well as those referring to alternative paths, will taken together influence the likelihood of adopting a life task of going to university or planning for a career after graduation (see also Oyserman, Gant and Ager, 1995). Strauss, Griffin and Parker (2012) showed that detailed, readily available positive and probable possible selves accentuated discrepancies between the present and hoped-for futures, enhancing motivation. As Griffin, Parker and Mason (2010) argued, without a desirable future to strive for, there is little reason to be proactive. An interesting example is Early (2017), who let adolescent girls interview female scientists and found that the interviews provided a tool for the girls to formulate images of themselves being involved in science in the future. In terms of possible selves, the adolescent girls were given an opportunity to form possible selves of working as scientists, which might result in a life task of becoming a scientist or at least to strive for a higher degree.

Theoretically, the relation between life tasks and possible selves is rather straightforward but it leads us to the perhaps most prominent methodological challenges relating to possible selves. The problem is easy enough to define: to what extent can we actually distinguish possible selves in our data, and to what extent are we instead investigating life tasks (or even just general hopes and fears)? This is a particular challenge when participants are asked to generate possible selves themselves. The self-reported "I can see myself graduating" can be a description of a possible self, perhaps even including a very specific conception of receiving a diploma from the dean, but it can also be a life task with only a few vague possible selves connected with it. This methodological problem can to a certain degree be handled by giving concrete instructions to the participants. However, further investigation is needed to see if such instructions influence the participants 'selection' of possible selves to report – for example in terms of time-frames. Therefore, any research on possible selves making use of possible selves generated by participants must be interpreted in relation to this issue. The alternative is to offer participants pre-defined possible selves to react to, but this approach also has challenges in that possible selves are so subjective in their nature. If we make these pre-defined conceptions of the future too general, we are back to the problem that they might be understood as life tasks rather than possible selves (because our participants don't understand this theoretical difference). If we make them too detailed, it becomes more difficult to assume that the description of a future we offer actually represents a possible self that the participants have had before contemplating the item offered in the data collection. In general, individuals have a range of positive possible selves to report when asked to, but that does not mean that they have given much thought to them or are motivated by them – in other words the dimension of the possible selves' salience (King and Raspin, 2004; King and Smith, 2004). On the other hand, anyone wishing to investigate possible selves has a further dimension to investigate here: in a study of student possible selves with pre-defined descriptions, can we get the participants to report whether these are detailed as well as previously considered conceptions, or whether the responses to these conceptions are formed in the situation of data collection and therefore do not represent possible selves that have formed their decisions to date? This would be important knowledge if we want youths to engage in higher education – do they actually have the possible selves we hope to support as part of the understanding of a life task or are the possible selves isolated or induced in a different framework? In that context, also relating to widening participation, such findings would help us understand how possible selves can be induced or activated in order to support students.

In terms of supporting students or future students, the concept of life tasks helps identify the importance of not having just possible selves but also a broader goal to strive for, which gets its meaning from the possible selves associated with it. For engaging in higher education, it is thus not enough to have positive possible selves about being a student and succeeding in getting a grade. There is also the need for a life task about what to do after graduation, with associated possible selves. Previous research also shows general advantages with strong possible selves when it comes to academic achievement. As Niedenthal, Setterlund and Wherry (1992) showed, individuals with more detailed and elaborated possible selves, covering a broader set of assumptions about the future, were less vulnerable to criticism, as well as more secure in assessing and adapting to criticism. In other words, it is reasonable to suggest that strong, probable, detailed and elaborated possible selves relating to academic achievement can support critical thinking and the willingness to engage in intellectual discussions also with those holding opposing opinions. This is further supported by Cross and Markus (1994), who argued that "the more vivid and elaborate the possible selves that can be created in preparation for a performance, the better the performance, because many of the routines required for the performance are already engaged through the processes of anticipation and simulation" (p. 424). To sum this up, the distinction between life tasks and possible selves are vital for the understanding of possible selves; it is through the possible selves that motivation to achieve a life task gets its power and it is through the obstacles to the life task manifest in possible selves that we see how fears and negative expectations counterbalance a striving for a different future.

Possible selves and possible others

The connection between the self-concept and possible selves provides a link between motivation and the social and cultural structures the individual is involved in. Several factors affect the development of possible selves, and one of the most influential is perceived membership of social groups (e.g. Oyserman, 2007; Oyserman and Fryberg, 2006; Oyserman and James, 2009; Oyserman et al., 2004). Possible selves are constructed and shaped in social interaction with others – for students it is others such as old friends, other students, parents or professors. In these interactions, the validity of the individual's possible selves is conformed or undermined. So what we think we can become or not become, want to become and not become, is adjusted by group norms and standards (Cameron, 1999; Oyserman, Gant and Ager, 1995; Markus and Nurius, 1986; Wurf and Markus, 1991; Oyserman and Fryberg, 2006). In many instances, possible selves can actually be seen as joint projects created in cooperation with others, voluntarily or involuntarily (Marshall, Young and Domene, 2006). However, there is a further dimension to this: such social interactions take place in the imagined future situations constituting possible selves. In the original paper defining possible selves, Markus and Nurius (1986) showed that possible selves provide a future social context for the individual, adding to the meaning of the possible selves.

This social dimension in the theory of possible selves can be expanded through the concept of *possible others*. Here, the concept of possible others refers to the other persons imagined in a possible self, to a greater or lesser extent influencing us through their behaviours and attitudes (as assumed by us). The concept of possible others has previously been used in relation to possible selves, but only sparingly.[1] Murphey et al. (2014) argued that possible others could guide behaviour, and Miller and Read (1991) argued that our imaginations of possible others can be complex, where our presumptions about their personality and other traits will influence how we think about interacting with them.

However, whereas the presence of possible others is implicit in much of the literature on possible selves, an explicit approach opens the door for a wider set of empirical and theoretical work. As to the research questions that can be asked in relation to possible others, three general aspects can be suggested. The first aspect concerns the presence of possible others in the possible selves, where it would be of interest to investigate both who is present and who is absent in these conceptions of the future. This includes such variables as the extent to which these individuals are known today, or are new acquaintances such as other students or professors to be met in a future as a student. The second aspect is the kinds of social interaction with possible others assumed in the possible selves, for example about cooperation or competition, or about being accepted into a group or not, or about being alienated from old friends. The third aspect is the assumed behaviour (or lack of such) of the possible others: what actions are they taking and what attitudes are they showing or assumed to have (supportive, inviting, disapproving, etc.)? Taken together, these aspects of possible others would influence factors such as emotional valence and perceived controllability, and thus motivational functions of possible selves.

I also suggest that two methodological approaches are viable for the study of possible others. The first is to include possible others as a new dimension in interview guides or inventories – either where participants are asked to generate possible selves or asked to respond to pre-defined possible selves. The second approach is to take possible others as the point of departure for the data collection. Asking participants to "imagine a future situation where you are a university student and interact with others at university" could be an example. The interesting point about this latter approach is that it makes it easier to have the students reporting conceptions concrete enough to actually be possible selves according to our theoretical delimitation, and not just life tasks, as discussed above. Regardless of approach, the concept of possible others can help us get a more nuanced understanding of possible selves in terms of the future social context discussed by Markus and Nurius (1986). This might also be a fruitful addition if we want to expand studies of possible selves into neighbouring areas of social cognition. One example of the latter could be the study of independent and interdependent self-concepts in students with different cultural backgrounds (e.g. Downie et al., 2006; Markus and Kitayama, 1991).

It has previously been found that the social process around the construction of possible selves is a matter of validation, when the possible self is 'tried out'. Wurf and Markus (1991, p. 44) wrote: "To foster personal growth, possible selves need to be expressed." This is dependent on a social context where the possible self in question can be validated and supported. Also in this process, we can assume the working of possible others within possible selves: in this case, there is the meta-level of a possible self about being able to express another and important possible self. Expectations of others' reactions, as imagined as possible others, will influence whether the individual dares to validate potentially controversial possible selves. It is easy to imagine social contexts where a possible self of attaining a degree or moving on in life is seen as out of place or even threatening to others, and an individual afraid to lose support from significant others might easily visualise their lack of support in a possible self. In other words: possible selves with possible others reacting to one's hoped-for future might hamper or support the validation of possible selves about the future. The implications become obvious in the example of widening participation. For example, black youths from low-income backgrounds have been found to see commitment to educational success as a 'sell-out' of their culture (e.g. Milner, 2002; see also Pizzolato, 2006; Yowell, 2000, 2002). Murphey et al. (2014) also showed that simple interventions based on students' own descriptions of ideal classmates could facilitate possible selves of how they supported other students. This is one of the few studies that has explicitly used the concept of possible others.

Finally, the notion of possible others can be given a further function if we want to describe possible selves in terms of narratives about the future, adding a narrative element which explicates future social interaction. However, the meta-level of possible selves about divulging important possible selves to possible others shows another complexity, going beyond the notion of possible selves as narratives. Here, we can talk about clusters of possible selves, posing methodological challenges, but where the notion of possible others at the same time can help us understand the mechanisms of these clusters. Beyond possible others, further aspects of possible selves can also be determined and would benefit from further attention. For example, Prince (2014) showed that the future physical environment assumed in a possible self could influence motivation through feelings such as aversion, belonging or entrapment.

Implications and conclusions

The more we want students to have detailed and salient negative and positive possible selves in balance as a guide to the future, the more important it will be to develop ways of supporting students by influencing their sense of purpose.

We have seen that this also involves the assumed educational context and that conceptions of possible others can be an interesting addition to the model. Still, motivation is not formed in a cultural vacuum. This brings us back to the initial discussion of the purpose of higher education. Without a clear notion of what we want our students to achieve, there is little we can do about student motivation. Here, we can use the classical purposes of higher education as a guide, such as the need for personal development and the need to become active citizens in a democratic society. However, we must also know how these conceptions of the future fit in with the students' self-concept, as this will be the filter helping the formation of possible selves. It is easy enough to say that we want to create positive possible selves about being a student, but before we can do that we need a view of what it means to be a student and what it would take to make that positive for the individuals we want to support. For example, do we want our students to form possible selves where they see themselves as customers or consumers, regarding their education as a commodity, or do we want to create possible selves where the students regard themselves as victims, with the right to expect protection from the harsh workings of academia, and the right to remain in their comfort zones? Or do we want them to adopt possible selves of themselves as members of an academic community, taking responsibility for expanding their minds and seeking knowledge, more in line with the notion of higher education expressed by Jaspers (1959) where the students are seen as free adults (see also Macfarlane, 2016)? This can actually be a matter of how senior scholars, as represented as possible others in our students' possible selves, are motivating them or putting them off higher education.

The dimensions of possible selves presented in this chapter help us explicate the complex matter of student motivation, showing that the self-concepts of the students are embedded in cultural preconceptions of higher education, including ideological assumptions underlying higher education. In other words, studies of possible selves are not only a road towards a better understanding of student motivation, but can also be a tool for the investigation of the ideological assumptions embedded in students' possible selves. Beyond student motivation, we must not forget that senior academics also have possible selves, and that the possible selves of the university teachers are a factor when it comes to supporting the possible selves of students, as well as understanding how ideological assumptions about higher education are manifest in the possible selves of academics. If reflexivity is regarded as important for teachers' development, we can even try some reflexivity in relation to our own possible selves, where students as well as colleagues are our possible others.

Note

1 There have also been different definitions: Howard and Hollander (1993) used the notion of possible others for all conceptions of the futures of others, regardless of their being part of the own possible self or not.

References

Cameron, J. E. (1999) Social identity and the pursuit of possible selves: Implications for the psychological well-being of university students. *Group Dynamics: Theory, Research, and Practice*, 3, 3: 179–189.

Cantor, N., Markus, H. R., Niedenthal, P. and Nurius, P. (1986) On motivation and the self-concept. In R. M. Sorrentino and E. I. Higgins (eds) (1997) *Handbook of motivation and cognition*, New York: Guilford Press, pp. 96–127.

Cross, S. E. and Markus, H. R. (1994) Self-schemas, possible selves, and competent performance. *Journal of Educational Psychology*, 86, 3: 423–438.

Downie, M., Koestner, R., Horberg, E. and Haga, S. (2006) Exploring the relation of independent and interdependent self-construals to why and how people pursue personal goals. *The Journal of Social Psychology*, 146, 5: 517–531.

Early, J. S. (2017) This is who I want to be! Exploring possible selves by interviewing women in science. *Journal of Adolescent & Adult Literacy*, 61, 1: 75–83.

Erikson, M. G. (2006) *Our Selves in the Future: New Angles on Possible Selves*. Diss., Department of Psychology, Lund University, Lund.

Erikson, M. G. (2007) Towards a more specific definition of possible selves. *Review of General Psychology*, 11, 4: 348–358.

Erikson, M. G., Hansson, B. and Lundblad, S. (2012) The possible selves of adult women with anorexia nervosa. *Eating Disorders*, 20, 4: 288–299.

Erikson, M. G., Hansson, B. and Lundblad, S. (2014) Desirable possible selves and depression in adult women with eating disorders. *Eating and Weight Disorders*, 19, 2: 145–151.

Filippakou, O. (2011) The idea of quality in higher education: A conceptual approach. *Discourse: Studies in the Cultural Politics of Education*, 32, 1: 15–28.

Godley, J., Tchanturia, K., MacLeod, A. and Schmidt, U. (2001) Future-directed thinking in eating disorders. *British Journal of Clinical Psychology*, 40, 3: 281–296.

Griffin, M. A., Parker, S. K. and Mason, C. M. (2010) Leader vision and the development of adaptive and proactive performance: A longitudinal study. *Journal of Applied Psychology*, 95, 1: 174–182.

Howard, J. A. and Hollander, J. A. (1993) Marking time. *Sociological Inquiry*, 63, 4: 425–443.

Jaspers, K. (1959 [1946]) *The idea of the university* (H. A. T. Reiche and H. F. Vanderschmidt, Trans.), Boston, MA: Beacon Press.

King, L. A. and Raspin, C. (2004) Lost and found possible selves, subjective well-being, and ego development in divorced women. *Journal of Personality*, 72, 3: 603–632.

King, L. A. and Smith, N. G. (2004) Gay and straight possible selves: Goals, identity, subjective well-being, and personality development. *Journal of Personality*, 72, 5: 967–994.

Lindsay, A. (1992) Concepts of quality in higher education. *Journal of Tertiary Education Administration*, 14, 2: 153–163.

Loveday, P. M., Lowell, G. P. and Jones, C. M. (2016) The best possible selves intervention: A review of the literature to evaluate efficacy and guide future research. *Journal of Happiness Studies*, advance on-line publication. doi:10.1007/s10902-016-9824-z

Macfarlane, B. (2016) *Freedom to learn*, Abingdon, UK: Routledge.

Markus, H. R. (1977) Self-schemata and processing information about the self. *Journal of Personality and Social Psychology*, 35, 2: 63–78.
Markus, H. R. (1990) Unresolved issues of self-representation. *Cognitive Therapy and Research*, 14, 2: 241–253.
Markus, H. R. and Kitayama, S. (1991) Culture and the self: Implications for cognition, emotion, and motivation. *Psychological Review*, 98, 2: 224–253.
Markus, H. R. and Kunda, Z. (1986) Stability and malleability of the self-concept. *Journal of Personality and Social Psychology*, 51, 4: 858–866.
Markus, H. R. and Nurius, P. (1986) Possible selves. *American Psychologist*, 41, 9: 954–959.
Markus, H. R. and Ruvolo, A. (1989) Possible selves: Personalized representations of goals. In L. A. Pervin (ed) *Goal concepts in personality and social psychology*, Hillsdale, NJ: Erlbaum, pp. 211–241.
Marshall, S. K., Young, R. A. and Domene, J. F. (2006) Possible selves as joint projects. In C. Dunkel and J. Kerpelman (eds) *Possible selves: Theory, research, and application*, Huntington, NY: Nova, pp. 141–161.
Miller, L. C. and Read, S. J. (1991) On the coherence of mental models of persons and relationships: A knowledge structure approach. In G. J. O. Fletcher and F. D. Fincham (eds) *Cognition in close relationships*, Hillsdale, NJ: Lawrence Erlbaum, pp. 69–99.
Milner, H. R. (2002) Affective and social issues among high achieving African American students: Recommendations for teachers and teacher education. *Action in Teacher Education*, 24, 1: 81–89.
Murphey, T., Falout, J., Fukuda, T. and Fukada, Y. (2014) Socio-dynamic motivating through idealizing classmates. *System*, 45, 1: 242–253.
Niedenthal, P. M., Setterlund, M. B. and Wherry, M. B. (1992) Possible self-complexity and affective reactions to goal-relevant behavior. *Journal of Personality and Social Psychology*, 63, 1: 5–16.
Norman, C. C. and Aron, A. (2002) Aspects of possible self that predict motivation to achieve or avoid it. *Journal of Experimental Social Psychology*, 39, 5: 500–507.
Oyserman, D. (2007) Social identity and self-regulation. In A. W. Kruglanski and E. T. Higgins (eds) *Social psychology: Handbook of basic principles*, New York, NY: Guilford Press, pp. 432–453.
Oyserman, D., Bybee, D., Terry, K. and Hart-Johnson, T. (2004) Possible selves as roadmaps. *Journal of Research in Personality*, 38, 2: 130–149.
Oyserman, D., Destin, M. and Novin, S. (2015) The context-sensitive future self: Possible selves motivate in context, not otherwise. *Self and Identity*, 14, 2: 173–188.
Oyserman, D. and Fryberg, S. A. (2006) The possible selves of diverse adolescents: Content and function across gender, race and national origin. In C. Dunkel and J. Kerpelman (eds) *Possible selves: Theory, research, and applications*, Huntington, NY: Nova, pp. 17–39.
Oyserman, D., Gant, L. and Ager, J. (1995) A socially contextualized model of African American identity: Possible selves and school persistence. *Journal of Personality and Social Psychology*, 69, 6: 1216–1232.
Oyserman, D. and James, L. (2009) Possible selves: From content to process. In K. D. Markman, W. M. P. Klein and J. A. Suhr (eds) *Handbook of imagination and mental stimulation*, New York, NY: Psychology Press, pp. 373–394.
Oyserman, D. and Markus, H. R. (1990a) Possible selves and delinquency. *Journal of Personality and Social Psychology*, 59, 1: 112–125.

Oyserman, D. and Markus, H. R. (1990b) Possible selves in balance: Implications for delinquency. *Journal of Social Issues*, 46, 2: 141–157.

Oyserman, D., Terry, K. and Bybee, D. (2002) A possible selves intervention to enhance school involvement. *Journal of Adolescence*, 25, 3: 313–326.

Pizzolato, J. E. (2006) Achieving college student possible selves: Navigating the space between commitment and achievement of long-term identity goals. *Cultural Diversity and Ethnic Minority Psychology*, 12, 1: 57–69.

Prince, D. (2014) What about place? Considering the role of physical environment on youth imagining of future possible selves. *Journal of Youth Studies*, 17, 6: 697–716.

Rumelhart, D. E., Smolensky, P., McClelland, J. L. and Hinton, G. E. (1986) Sequential thought processes in PDP models. In J. L. McClelland, D. E. Rumelhart and The PDP Research Group (eds) *Parallel distributed processing*, Cambridge, MA: The MIT Press, pp. 7–57.

Schank, R. C. and Abelson, R. P. (1977) *Scripts, plans, goals and understanding*, Hillsdale, NJ: Erlbaum.

Smith, G. C., James, L., Varnum, M. and Oyserman, D. (2014) Give up or get going? Productive uncertainty in uncertain times. *Self and Identity*, 13, 6: 681–700.

Strauss, K., Griffin, M. A. and Parker, S. K. (2012) Future work selves: How salient hoped-for identities motivate proactive career behavior. *Journal of Applied Psychology*, 97, 3: 580–598.

Vignoles, V. L., Manzi, C., Regalia, C., Jemmolo, S. and Scabini, E. (2008) Identity motives underlying desired and feared possible future selves. *Journal of Personality*, 76, 5: 1165–1200.

Weiner, B. (1992) *Human motivation: Metaphors, theories, and research*, London: Sage Publications.

Wurf, E. and Markus, H. R. (1991) Possible selves and the psychology of personal growth. In D. J. Ozer, J. M. Healy, Jr. and A. J. Stewart (eds) *Perspectives in personality* (Vol. 3), London: Jessica Kingsley, pp. 39–62.

Yowell, C. M. (2000) Possible selves and future orientation: Exploring hopes and fears of Latino boys and girls. *Journal of Early Adolescence*, 20, 3: 245–280.

Yowell, C. M. (2002) Dreams of the future: The pursuit of education and career possible selves among 9th grade Latino youth. *Applied Developmental Science*, 6, 2: 62–72.

Chapter 3

Borrowed time

A sociological theorisation of possible selves and educational subjectivities

Holly Henderson

Introduction

Possible selves is one of a myriad ways of understanding temporality and education, and therefore requires careful definition, as well as a clear rationale for its use. This chapter sets out to explain what the possible selves concept brings to contemporary educational research, with a particular focus on theorising the concept sociologically. After defining the concept, and then summarising current uses in a variety of research contexts, the chapter turns to an interrogation of possible selves using theorisations of narrative and subjectivity. The terms of the concept itself signify these tools as particularly relevant. The word 'possible' works to signal the potential future, therefore evoking a narrative sequence that moves from the present towards that future. As the chapter argues, this narrative sequence is often implicit in uses of the possible selves concept, and there is much to be gained from a more explicit discussion of narrative and temporality. Because the word 'self' carries the weight of multiple popular and theoretical definitions, it is important to develop a clear theoretical engagement with processes of self-making. This chapter defines the self using writing on subjectivation, in order to draw out the potential of the possible selves concept to address experiences of systemic inequality in higher education (HE). As the chapter progresses, the stages of this theorisation are set out in detail, and lead to a reflection on its implications for educational research and the researcher in future uses of the possible selves concept.

The possible selves concept is particularly applicable to education contexts because of the strong relationship between education and temporality. It is not difficult to make the argument that formal education is structured through measurements of linear temporality, such as the start and completion dates of a course, or the annual divisions between terms and semesters. There is also an expectation that formal education is organised on a temporal, sequential basis, so that the level or topic of previous study prepares the student for present or future study. Even in this self-evident understanding, however, temporality and education are intertwined in a way that is more than simply organisational. Instead, the very purpose of education is understood temporally, as a progression from past to future. Within this more complex understanding of education and temporality are discourses that describe, for example, students' *uses of time* as more or less successful, as part of the already-temporal context of the progression from past to future that is expected of them (Bennett and Burke, 2017). As with Clegg's (2010) discussion of 'time future' as the 'dominant discourse of higher education', Bennett and Burke show the seeming neutrality of time to be in fact highly complex, multi-layered and reproductive of the relationships of power and status that structure educational contexts.

My theorisation of the possible selves concept in this chapter focuses on the future as experienced in the present of HE, as a critical response to precisely the dominant discourse of the future described by Clegg (2010). For example, a 'discourse' of employability (Boden and Nedeva, 2010) has become central to UK HE in the 21st century, in the context of university marketing materials (Christie, 2016), curriculum and pedagogy (Tymon, 2013), and broader issues of access, inclusion and the purposes of HE (Brown, Hesketh and Wiliams, 2003; Delaney and Farren, 2016; McCaig, 2015; McQuaid and Lindsay, 2005). Where it is understood to signify the relationship between studying HE and gaining employment both beyond and as a consequence of that study, the discourse of employability also implies a temporal relationship. This temporal relationship is one in which the present of HE cannot be experienced without the anticipation of the future for which the present is a preparation (see Chapter 8 in this volume). As well as prescribing a purely instrumental purpose for HE study, this discourse also ensures that the future is experienced as an integral part of the present, rather than being temporally divided from it. This is even more the case in terms of institutional marketing materials, which often draw upon employability rankings and statistics to advertise successful employability markers to prospective students (Christie, 2016). The prospective student is therefore understood as one who makes their choice of place to study based on the future that place offers them beyond study. However, as analysis of students' strategies for the future has shown, not all students negotiate the demands of 21st century HE in the same way (see, for example, Bathmaker et al., 2016; Hodkinson and Sparkes, 1997). Given the embedded nature of future temporality within HE study, then, I argue that it is vital to develop the theoretical resources to critically analyse students' multiple and diverse experiences of temporality. In particular, as I go on to argue, it is important that sociological tools be developed in order to explore structural constraints that work to enable some student futures, and limit others. The following section looks at the original definition and subsequent uses of the concept of possible selves, before detailing the process of my theoretical engagement with the concept.

Possible selves: definitions and uses

The concept of possible selves was introduced in 1986 by Markus and Nurius, researchers working in the US in the discipline of social psychology. They define possible selves as:

> [h]ow individuals think about their potential and about their future. Possible selves are the ideal selves that we would very much like to become. They are also the selves we could become, and the selves we are afraid of becoming.
>
> (Markus and Nurius, 1986, p. 954)

There are several key elements of this definition that have informed subsequent work using possible selves, and which I will go on to discuss in this section. First, however, I want to highlight what I see as unique to the possible selves concept, with the awareness that the concept is by no means the only theorisation of student futures in HE. Breen and Goldthorpe (1997) for example use Rational Action Theory to argue that classed differences in educational choices are at least in part logical responses to perceptions of risk and reward. Woodman (2011) explores literature on young people planning (or not) for the future, and Duggan (2016) discusses the 'future orientation' of young people in Australia making choices about further and higher education. Neither Woodman nor Duggan use the concept of possible selves, and both show how students' progression through systems of education requires them to occupy future temporalities at the same time as experiencing the present. Similarly, Hodkinson and Sparkes (1997) develop a theorisation of career decision-making that uses Bourdieu's notion of horizons for action to articulate tensions between structure and agency. However, as the following quotation from Markus and Nurius (1986) suggests, what is unusual in the possible selves concept is the personalised nature of the imagined future:

> The assistant professor who fears he or she will not become an associate professor carries with him or her much more than a shadowy, undifferentiated fear of not getting tenure. Instead, the fear is personalized, and the professor is likely to have a well-elaborated possible self that represents this fear.
>
> (p. 954)

Using the possible selves concept therefore explicitly requires an engagement with the embodied self, both in the present and in the imagined future. I will go on in later sections to explore how the individualised 'selves' of the discipline of cognitive psychology might be thought of alongside sociological theorisations of 'subjectivity'. Here, I want to highlight that using and developing the possible selves concept is important because the concept describes the kind of imagining of futures in which students of HE are routinely encouraged to participate. The 'personalised' rather than the 'shadowy, undifferentiated' imagined future is precisely the most powerful and most popularly understood version of the future in educational experience. This can be seen in a range of future-oriented educational activities, such as HE outreach programmes that are based on familiarising prospective students with the university environment so that they are better able to imagine themselves there in the future, or employability initiatives that encourage participation in work so that students can better imagine themselves as future professionals.

In the body of research that has followed the introduction of the possible selves concept, a crucial aspect of its definition is the connection between imagined future and present behaviour. Markus and Nurius' (1986) definition signals this relationship when it describes imagined selves as selves 'we would very much like to become' or 'are afraid of becoming'. The concept has therefore been used to explore how the hope and/or fear that is related to the imagined future acts as a motivating factor, changing current behaviour (Strahan and Wilson, 2006). Much of this research has taken place in educational contexts in the US, with the main focus being on schools. For example, Hock, Deshler and Schumaker (2006) argue that student motivation can be improved if students are encouraged to identify and work towards positive academic possible selves. Similarly, Oyserman, Terry and Bybee (2002) develop a 'possible selves intervention' programme, which aims to work with school students to develop the relationship between their imagined future and their current behaviour. A study by Pizzolato (2007) looks at 'career possible selves' as influencing students' participation in extra-curricular activity in schools. In particular, Pizzolato asks how students respond when they encounter experiences that threaten or endanger the likelihood of achieving their career possible selves. As can be seen in Erikson's work (Chapter 2 in this volume), the concept of motivation is highly complex in itself; it is nevertheless an integral part of the possible selves concept's original definition and subsequent uses. As Markus and Nurius (1986) write, '[t]he concept of possible selves allows us to make a more direct connection between motives and specific actions' (p. 961).

A further important element of Markus and Nurius' definition of the possible selves concept is the description of possible selves as 'elaborated', as in their example earlier of the professor who fears not achieving promotion. Markus and Nurius argue that, in this example, the professor is 'likely to have a well-elaborated possible self' (1986, p. 954). For Markus and Nurius, this elaboration would be seen in the detail with which the professor imagines their future: 'the self as having failed, as looking for another job, as bitter, as a writer who can't get a novel published' (ibid.). The relationship between the imagined future and current behaviour is therefore seen as influenced by the detail with which the possible self is imagined. This aspect of the possible selves concept has been important, both in the research interventions cited above, and in research that has taken the possible selves concept beyond schools. For example, the concept has been used in researching professional education contexts such as nursing education (Eaton and Donaldson, 2016) and teacher training (Dalioglu and Adiguzel, 2016; Hamman et al., 2013; Hamman et al., 2010). These studies argue that trainee professionals with more elaborated, positive possible selves form robust and secure professional identities in the present experience of their training, and that these professional identities enable them to better negotiate the challenges of their early careers.

Bak's (2015) use of the concept in the context of psychotherapy moves further beyond the educational setting, but similarly argues that the more detailed a client's imagining of positive possible futures, the more easily and quickly they are able to work towards those futures. Dark-Freudeman and West (2016) looks at possible selves in relation to chronic illness, finding that patients who are able to imagine a detailed version of themselves as healthy are more likely to behave in ways that will achieve improved health. Offering the reverse perspective, Abrams and Aguilar's (2005) research on the imagined futures of juvenile offenders in the US finds that their participants' lack of clear strategies for moving towards positive futures is integrally connected to the vagueness with which they imagine such futures. They argue that the participants are likely to have detailed fears of the negative futures they imagine, so that the elaboration of their feared possible selves counters the lack of elaboration of their hoped-for possible selves. As a result, Abrahams and Aguilar argue, their behaviour shifts more easily towards a realisation of the negative than the positive of their imagined futures.

As Abraham and Aguilar's study in particular shows, there are differences in the level of elaboration with which certain people or groups of people imagine the future. Often, these differences relate to the available resources that can be drawn upon in the process of projecting an embodied sense of self into the future. Many of the studies that use the possible selves concept address this complexity, which again is first set out in Markus and Nurius' original definition: 'These possible selves are individualised or personalised, but they are also distinctly social' (1986, p. 954). Approaches to exploring the social construction of possible selves often focus on particular groups that are seen to be less likely to have strongly elaborated positive possible selves. Oyserman, Gant and Ager's (1995) study of African American students is an example of this approach, as is Oyserman and Fryberg's (2006) study of 'diverse adolescents', which takes into account differences of 'gender, race and national origin'. In other studies of gender (Knox, 2006), age (Frazier and Hooker, 2006; Stevenson and Clegg, 2013), race (Stevenson, 2012) and 'culture' (Rathbone et al., 2016), the selves that are possible to imagine and the detail in which it is possible to imagine them are shown to be affected by these intersecting identity characteristics. Focusing on HE specifically, Stevenson's (2012) study of minority ethnic students in UK universities looks at the societal, systemic and structural influences and barriers that affect minority ethnic students' imagined futures as successful students, and that therefore impact upon these students' current academic behaviour and performance.

As signalled by Markus and Nurius in their depiction of possible selves as 'distinctly social', the concept brings together theorisations of both the individual and the social. All the studies cited above are examples of the ways in which these theorisations can be negotiated differently. In using the concept for sociological research, it is important to emphasise the social construction of possible selves. Because the concept can be used to argue that individuals are more or less successful in their creation of detailed and elaborated imagined futures, there is otherwise a risk that it can create or contribute to discourses of individual deficit. In these discourses, the individual could be seen to lack the resources or abilities that might allow them to imagine a successful future and adapt their behaviour accordingly. If the social construction of possible selves is given more emphasis, however, the concept can be used instead to identify where there are inequalities of available resources, and the analysis therefore focuses on systemic inequalities, rather than on individual lack.

In order that the possible selves concept be developed to emphasise social construction, it is important to accurately theorise and define the terms of the concept. As Erikson (2007) argues, the 'selves' that the concept refers to can be used to encompass a range of disciplinary theorisations of self and subjectivity, each of which influences the way the concept is used in research and each of which should therefore be clearly defined and explicated. I see this slippage between definitions of self and subjectivity as an important part of the possible selves concept, and one that has provoked useful theoretical work for me. I have found, for example, that bounded, knowable 'academic selves' or 'professional selves' do not readily align with a sociologically informed understanding of subjectivity and subjecthood. Nevertheless, I am also aware that the self as knowable, as complete and coherent, is the self of popular understanding and therefore of the educational discourses in which HE students are versed. My understanding of possible selves therefore veers between these two understandings of self/subjectivity. It requires an ongoing dialogue between conceptualisations of the individual, the social, structure and agency that can never be entirely resolved but is perpetually useful. In order to develop this dialogue further, I now develop a narrative theorisation of possible selves/subjectivities, asking what happens to a concept as it is adapted across disciplinary fields.

Possible selves and narrative

Although the possible selves concept lends itself to narrative research, its potential has yet to be fully explored in this area (Erikson, 2007; see also Whitty, 2002). There are, however, some studies using possible selves that adopt narrative methods. Segal (2006), for example, asks his undergraduate participants to write 'anticipated life histories', which narratively represent their futures as they imagine them to be. Hamman et al.'s (2013) study of possible selves in beginning teachers' professional identities uses the method of 'anticipatory reflection', to record participants' responses to their imagined teaching practice. The use of both of these methods foregrounds the sequential, narrative temporality implied by the possible selves concept. Seen in this way, the argument that the present is peopled with imagined embodiments of future selves is also an argument that these selves are part of narratives in which we progress sequentially from the present towards that future. In Segal's and Hamman et al.'s use of narrative methodologies, the sequential nature of this temporal narrative is both explored and reversed. Their participants' imagined futures are recorded in order that their present behaviour be understood, which reverses the linear working of time from present to future. At the same time, these futures are seen as useful insights into the present precisely because present behaviours are then understood as working towards the future. In a further temporal and methodological complexity, these methodologies require that the participants imagine their future as past, in the narrative genre of history or reflection. The method therefore suggests that the anticipation of the self or selves in the future is powerful because it is also an anticipation of the future as it will be seen or understood when it is the past.

I have begun this section with a discussion of the complexity of possible selves and narrative method because these examples highlight both the importance and the difficulty of pinning down the possible selves concept and its relationship to narrative temporality. I now step back from research methodology to further establish the conceptual context for understanding possible selves in relation to narrative. Ricoeur's (1980, 1992) work on narrative, temporality and subjectivity is useful here because it theorises the processes through which narratives are created. This theorisation de-naturalises some of the familiar aspects involved in the telling and re-telling of narratives, drawing out some of the contradictions highlighted above. Ricoeur argues that when a narrative is received, the listener checks that each event in the sequence of the narrative logically follows from the next, and logically anticipates the narrative's conclusion. This checking appears to work along a linear understanding of temporality, with the listener progressing temporally forward with each narrative event. However, the checking process also requires that the listener checks the newest narrative event against the previous one, and therefore also, and simultaneously, moves backwards in their listening to the narrative. The narrator, in response to this collective awareness of the requirements of narrative structure, must create a narrative whose events are causally linked to one another, and therefore stand up to the listener's scrutiny. This causal linking, Ricoeur argues, is applied after the events have taken place, in order that they can be recounted narratively. Ricoeur (1992, p. 142) describes this retrospective causal linking as 'the paradox of emplotment' that 'inverts the effect of contingency'. The 'contingency' in a narrative, that suggests that each new event is a consequence of the previous event, is therefore reversed for narrator and listener, who must look back to establish *how* the previous event can be understood as having caused the subsequent event.

One consequence of this theorisation of the narrative process is that, while asserting the role of narrative in human experience, the theorisation also de-naturalises the temporal workings of producing and receiving narratives. It shows these workings to be difficult and complex, rather than given and logical. The theorisation allows analysis of temporality and narrative that moves beyond narrative content, and also takes into account narrative form. This is particularly important in working with the possible selves concept using narrative methods, because the methods outlined above further exaggerate already complex narrative processes. Using Ricoeur's theorisation to look at the method of anticipated life history, for example, the narrator of the anticipated life history can be seen to create a narrative emplotment within which the imagined events of the future are causally connected to the present, anticipating the future in which this causality will be applied retrospectively. This temporal narrative logic echoes the double temporal manoeuvre of the prospective student whose decision to attend an institution in the future is based on the possibility of a future in which there will be a *retrospective causal connection* to be made between future educational institution and future employment. The method of collecting anticipated life histories is premised on the idea that the present is experienced, and can only be understood, within a self-narration that both looks to the future and looks to how the future might be seen when it is past. Ricoeur's theorisation, which explicates these complex processes of narrative production, draws attention to the work done by the producer of such a narrative, in order that they make themselves understood narratively.

Using the possible selves concept alongside a theory of narrative such as Ricoeur's ensures that future temporalities are theorised as a part of narrative processes. The complexities of the above theorisation also push the possible selves concept in different ways than it has yet been used. For example, as set out above, much of the research that uses the possible selves concept is focused on behaviour. In particular, it is focused on the imagined future as it acts or does not act as a motivating factor in present patterns of behaviour. A theorisation of narrative such as Ricoeur's shifts attention towards the discursive production of possible selves as narratives, as well as seeing them as explanatory of current behaviour. This approach therefore has the potential to be useful in exploring the conditions in which narratives of the future are produced, and the discourses that are drawn upon in the narratives' production. In educational contexts, using the possible selves concept in this way means asking questions of both (i) how the imagined future prompts particular educational behaviours and (ii) how particular futures are important to the ways that educational subjects understand and narrate their experiences of education.

Thus far, I have referred to the process of narrative production, and therefore to the narrator as 'producer' of narratives. Inherent to Ricoeur's theorisation of narrative, however, is the connection between narrative and subjectivity. Because Ricoeur sees narrative as the mode through which human experience is both understood and related, narrative is therefore a formative condition of subjectivity. This goes some way towards explaining why the complexities of narrative logic are usually conformed to, in and despite all of their complexity. To conform to such complexities is a condition of making oneself understood as a subject, as I will go on to explore further in the next section. In the context of researching HE, these conditions of subjectivity must be extended further to encompass the specific conditions of educational subjectivities. It is in understanding the conditions of educational subjectivities that the possible selves concept is particularly useful. As outlined above, the 'self' of the possible selves concept accords with the linear, future-oriented coherence that is required of participants in formal education. In England, these participants are required, for example, to apply to HE while still taking the courses on which their entry to HE depends. They are encouraged, in their choice of HE course and institution, to imagine themselves in a future of employment to which their future course of HE is integral. In order that it can be used in the context of HE, then, the possible selves concept requires a theorisation of subjectivity that takes into account the conditions in which educational subjectivities are formed, and in which they come to be narrated as both temporally complex and causally robust. The following section sets out a theorisation of subjectivity that uses insights from Butler's *Excitable Speech* (1997) to further push the possible selves concept in sociological ways.

Possible selves and subjectivity

Butler's theorisation of performative subjectivity in *Excitable Speech* (1997) builds upon the Foucauldian concept of subjectivation. This concept understands subjectivity as in part an involuntary submission to societal norms, through the obeyance of which the subject is made recognisable and legitimate as a subject to themselves and others. In the chapter on censorship ('Implicit Censorship and Discursive Agency' pp. 129–164), Butler shows how processes of speech and censorship are an important part of subjectivation. She argues that there are two kinds of censorship. The first is the more familiar, explicit censorship, in which particular kinds of writing or speech are illegal or made dangerous. The second kind of censorship is less easily or usually recognised as such, precisely because it is largely unconscious. This kind of censorship marks the difference between intelligible and unintelligible speech, and determines the norms through which a subject makes their speech recognisable as such to others:

> The question is not what it is I will be able to say, but what will constitute the domain of the sayable within which I begin to speak at all. To become a subject means to be subjected to a set of implicit and explicit norms that govern the kind of speech that will be legible as the speech of the subject.
> (Butler, 1997, p. 153)

Here, Butler argues that limitations on what it is possible to say do not come from the individual's ability or inability to speak, or to voice particular words. Instead, there are structural limitations that determine what is understood, either to speaker or to listener, as 'the domain of the sayable' within which a subject can make themselves recognisable as a subject. Butler sees subjectivation as performative because it is through repeated acts of obeyance and conformity to norms, such as the norms of speech, that the subject continues to constitute themselves as a subject. Subjectivity is therefore not a static, achieved status, but one which is perpetually negotiated and re-affirmed through performative acts. These performative acts include speaking from within that which is 'sayable'.

This theorisation of subjectivity and Ricoeur's theorisation of narrative have in common an analysis of the terms that govern legibility. Seen together, the processes through which narratives are constructed and understood, as theorised by Ricoeur, can be seen as examples of the 'norms that govern the kind of speech that will be legible' (Butler, 1997, p. 153). In other words, if narrative is understood as integral to the experience of the subject, then narrative structures and processes are some of the norms which must be obeyed if the subject is to make themselves understood.

These narrative structures are particularly relevant to the experience of educational subjects. I use the terms 'educational subjects' and 'educational subjectivities' with care, acknowledging the difficulty of defining the boundaries of 'educational subjectivity'. Formal processes of education echo and exaggerate the processes through which subjects are interpellated into and recognised in discourse. In educational contexts, there are explicit and implicit norms and terms of recognition that are both particular to educational contexts and indivisible from the more general subjective experience of which Butler writes. The narration of an academic or career future, for example, might be encouraged within and outside of formal education, but is particularly required in order to progress through the linear education system. Because formal schooling begins after the subject's entry into discourse, the processes of subjectivation may be more consciously understood, but their compulsory nature makes them equally non-negotiable if the subject is to be made comprehensible. The subjectivation processes of formal schooling do not begin or end with the parameters of the educational institution, but instead blur in complicated ways with the ongoing constructions of subjectivity beyond them. Discussions of subjectivity in educational contexts are therefore likely to include experiences of subjectivity that reach temporally and spatially beyond the educational context. Despite this difficulty of definition, I refer to 'educational subjectivity' in order to draw attention to the specific requirements of subjectivation in educational contexts. In particular, I see the emphasis on linear, future-oriented narratives as a particular requirement of educational subjectivation.

The possible selves concept, then, describes precisely the kind of future-focused, causally coherent narratives of subjectivity that are a condition of the construction and maintenance of a legible educational subjectivity. Such narratives of the subject in the future are therefore in themselves a performative negotiation of the boundaries of the 'domain of the sayable'. The detail, or 'elaboration' (Markus and Nurius, 1986, p. 954), of the imagined future is further revelatory of inequalities between the different kinds of futures that are 'sayable' within particular contexts. An example of the particularity of context can be seen in Prince's (2014) research, which looks at place as a contextual factor that determines which possible selves are imaginable. Her analysis of previous studies of young people in juvenile detention centres in the US shows how these studies could have explored the impact of place to far greater effect. In particular, she argues, these studies interviewed young participants while they were within the walls of the detention centres in which they were incarcerated, but neglected to think through the ways in which such a place might limit what was possible for the participants to imagine. In an almost literal way, though Prince does not use a Butlerian theorisation herself, the walls of the detention centres can be seen to surround the domain of what is 'sayable' about the imagined future.

As Prince's study shows, the circumstances in which the future is imagined limit what is possible to imagine. In using the possible selves concept in the HE context, it becomes important to ask how the limits around the domain of the sayable are formed differently for students whose circumstances differ. In the UK, where the HE system is hierarchically stratified (Bathmaker et al., 2016), and where access to HE is heavily influenced by factors such as class and race (Boliver, 2016; Reay, David and Ball, 2005), experiences of structural inequality shape and limit imagined futures in unequal ways. Rather than focusing on the individual student's capacity to imagine an elaborated future as a participant in HE, this conceptualisation instead asks what has been made impossible for them to imagine as well as what is possible: which educational futures are unspeakable, to the extent that speaking them might threaten the subject's integrity and intelligibility? Questions of this kind also allow for analysis of structures that render the future difficult or impossible to imagine. Using this theorisation of possible selves and educational subjectivity, students who do not coherently imagine a future are seen as doubly excluded. They are first excluded from access to the resources that might enable an imagined future, and secondly from the legitimate, recognisable educational subjectivity for which an imagined future is a condition.

Conclusion

The question of how to use the possible selves concept sociologically is closely related to the question of why to use it. There are potential problems that come with the possible selves concept, particularly regarding its focus on the individual. If the concept is not used carefully, this focus risks undermining sociological analyses of educational structures that have drawn attention away from individual deficit and towards systemic inequalities. I have argued in this chapter that this risk is a reason to use the concept thoughtfully, rather than a reason to dismiss it; it is the concept's echoing of popular understandings of the individual and of temporality that make it difficult to disregard. To use the possible selves concept is to acknowledge the powerful nature of this narrative of self that pervades educational structures and institutions. It is to wrestle with the same understanding of self that students of HE take for granted. A critical use of the concept does not ignore this popular understanding, but rather engages with and resists it.

In this chapter, I have taken the possible selves concept and worked it through a theorisation of narrative and subjectivity that shifts the concept from its original discipline of social psychology. This theorisation requires a complex balancing, between the sociological demands of the concept as it is applied to the structures of educational inequalities, and the integrity of the original concept that risks becoming blurred beyond the point of recognition. What is lost from the original theorisation is the sense, in Markus and Nurius' (1986) definition, that possible selves are knowable, malleable and bounded, with a clear and linear link between imagined future and current behaviour. This sociological re-deployment of the concept is messier, as are the methods for conducting research that uses it. The perpetual re-negotiation of the concept is then also a re-negotiation of what it is possible to do with a concept without moving too far beyond it, and it is hard to know when the boundaries have been breached. This chapter has proposed that the concept remains useful as long as it includes this kind of questioning, of research processes as well as research subjects. If this questioning is thorough, the concept can both acknowledge and disrupt accepted understandings of educational subjectivities, and of the structures that shape futures in educational settings.

Acknowledgements

This research was funded by the ESRC (grant number ES/J50001X/1). The author would like to thank Professor Ann-Marie Bathmaker, Professor Jacqueline Stevenson and Dr. Emily F. Henderson for their comments on early drafts of the chapter.

References

Abrams, L. S. and Aguilar, J. P. (2005) Negative trends, possible selves, and behavior change: A qualitative study of juvenile offenders in residential treatment. *Qualitative Social Work*, 4, 2: 175–196.

Bak, W. (2015) Possible selves: Implications for psychotherapy. *International Journal of Mental Health and Addiction*, 13, 5: 650–658.

Bathmaker, A.-M., Ingram, N., Abrahams, J., Hoare, A., Waller, R. and Bradley, H. (eds) (2016) *Higher education, social class and social mobility: The degree generation*, London: Palgrave Macmillan.

Bennett, A. and Burke, P. J. (2017) Re/conceptualising time and temporality: An exploration of time in higher education. *Discourse: Studies in the Cultural Politics of Education*, 1–13.

Boden, R. and Nedeva, M. (2010) Employing discourse: Universities and graduate 'employability'. *Journal of Education Policy*, 25, 1: 37–54.

Boliver, V. (2016) Exploring ethnic inequalities in admission to russell group universities. *Sociology*, 50, 2: 247–266.

Breen, R. and Goldthorpe, J. H. (1997) Explaining educational differentials: Towards a formal rational action theory. *Rationality and Society*, 9, 3: 275–305.

Brown, P., Hesketh, A. and Wiliams, S. (2003) Employability in a knowledge-driven economy. *Journal of Education and Work*, 16, 2: 107–126.

Butler, J. (1997) *Excitable speech: A politics of the performative*, London and New York: Routledge.

Christie, F. (2016) The reporting of university league table employability rankings: A critical review. *Journal of Education and Work*, 1–16.

Clegg, S. (2010) Time future: The dominant discourse of higher education. *Time & Society*, 19, 3: 345–364.

Dalioglu, S. T. and Adiguzel, O. C. (2016) Teacher candidates' self-efficacy beliefs and possible selves throughout the teaching practice period in Turkey. *Asia Pacific Education Review*, 17, 4: 651–661.

Dark-Freudeman, A. and West, R. L. (2016) Possible selves and self-regulatory beliefs: Exploring the relationship between health selves, health efficacy, and psychological well-being. *The International Journal of Aging and Human Development*, 82, 2–3: 139–165.

Delaney, L. and Farren, M. (2016) No 'self' left behind? Part-time distance learning university graduates: Social class, graduate identity and employability. *Open Learning: The Journal of Open, Distance and e-Learning*, 31, 3: 194–208.

Duggan, S. (2016) Understanding temporality and future orientation for young women in the senior year. *Discourse: Studies in the Cultural Politics of Education*, 1–12.

Eaton, J. and Donaldson, G. (2016) Altering nursing student and older adult attitudes through a possible selves ethnodrama. *Journal of Professional Nursing*, 32, 2: 141–151.

Erikson, M. G. (2007) The meaning of the future: Toward a more specific definition of possible selves. *Review of General Psychology*, 11, 4: 348–358.

Frazier, L. D. and Hooker, K. (2006) Possible selves in adult development: Linking theory and research. In C. Dunkel and J. Kerpelman (eds) *Possible selves: Theory, research and applications*, New York: Nova Science Publishers, pp. 41–60.

Hamman, D., Coward, F., Johnson, L., Lambert, M., Zhou, L. and Indiatsi, J. (2013) Teacher possible selves: How thinking about the future contributes to the formation of professional identity. *Self and Identity*, 12, 3: 307–336.

Hamman, D., Gosselin, K., Romano, J. and Bunuan, R. (2010) Using possible-selves theory to understand the identity development of new teachers. *Teaching and Teacher Education*, 26, 7: 1349–1361.

Hock, M. F., Deshler, D. D. and Schumaker, J. B. (2006) Enhancing student motivation through the pursuit of possible selves. In C. Dunkel and J. Kerpelman (eds) *Possible selves: Theory, research and applications*, New York: Nova Science Publishers, pp. 205–222.

Hodkinson, P. and Sparkes, A. C. (1997) Careership: A sociological theory of career decision making. *British Journal of Sociology of Education*, 18, 1: 29–44.

Knox, M. (2006) Gender and possible selves. In C. Dunkel and J. Kerpelman (eds) *Possible selves: Theory, research and applications*, New York: Nova Science Publishers, pp. 61–78.

Markus, H. and Nurius, P. (1986) Possible selves. *American Psychologist*, 41, 9: 954–969.

McCaig, C. (2015) The impact of the changing English higher education marketplace on widening participation and fair access: Evidence from a discourse analysis of access agreements. *Widening Participation and Lifelong Learning*, 17, 1: 5–22.

McQuaid, R. W. and Lindsay, C. (2005) The concept of employability. *Urban Studies*, 42, 2: 197–219.

Oyserman, D. and Fryberg, S. (2006) The possible selves of diverse adolescents: Content and function across gender, race and national origin. In C. Dunkel and J. Kerpelman (eds) *Possible selves: Theory, research and applications*, New York: Nova Science Publishers, pp. 17–40.

Oyserman, D., Gant, L. and Ager, J. (1995) A socially contextualized model of African American identity: Possible selves and school persistence. *Journal of Personality & Social Psychology*, 69, 6: 1216–1232.

Oyserman, D., Terry, K. and Bybee, D. (2002) A possible selves intervention to enhance school involvement. *Journal of Adolescence*, 25, 3: 313–326.

Pizzolato, J. E. (2007) Impossible selves: Investigating students' persistence decisions when their career-possible selves border on impossible. *Journal of Career Development*, 33, 3: 201–223.

Prince, D. (2014) What about place? Considering the role of physical environment on youth imagining of future possible selves. *Journal of Youth Studies*, 17, 6: 697–716.

Rathbone, C. J., Salgado, S., Akan, M., Havelka, J. and Berntsen, D. (2016) Imagining the future: A cross-cultural perspective on possible selves. *Consciousness and Cognition*, 42: 113–124.

Reay, D., David, M. E. and Ball, S. (eds) (2005) *Degrees of choice: Class, race, gender and higher education*, Stoke-on-Trent: Trentham Books.

Ricoeur, P. (1980) Narrative time. In M. McQuillan (ed) (2000) *Narrative reader*, Abingdon: Routledge, pp. 255–261.

Ricoeur, P. (1992) *Oneself as another*, Chicago: University of Chicago Press.

Segal, H. G. (2006) Possible selves, fantasy distortion, and the anticipated life history: Exploring the role of the imagination in social cognition. In C. Dunkel and J. Kerpelman (eds) *Possible selves: Theory, research and applications*, New York: Nova Science Publishers, pp. 79–96.

Stevenson, J. (2012) An exploration of the link between minority ethnic and white students' degree attainment and views of their future 'possible selves'. *Higher Education Studies*, 2, 4: 103–113.

Stevenson, J. and Clegg, S. (2013) My past is a double edge sword: Temporality and reflexivity in mature learners. *Studies in Continuing Education*, 35, 1: 17–29.

Strahan, E. J. and Wilson, A. E. (2006) Temporal comparisons, identity, and motivation: The relation between past, present and possible future selves. In C. Dunkel and J. Kerpelman (eds) *Possible selves: Theory, research and applications*, New York: Nova Science Publishers, pp. 1–16.

Tymon, A. (2013) The student perspective on employability. *Studies in Higher Education*, 38, 6: 841–856.

Whitty, M. (2002) Possible selves: An exploration of the utility of a narrative approach. *Identity*, 2, 3: 211–228.

Woodman, D. (2011) Young people and the future. *Young*, 19, 2: 111–128.

Chapter 4

Extending the analytical scope of theories of 'possible selves'

Sue Clegg

Introduction

In this chapter I will make an argument for extending the analytical scope of theories of possible selves, from their original location in psychology linking self-concept to motivation (Markus and Nurius, 1986; see also Chapter 2 in this volume), to encompass more sociologically informed notions of the self and temporality. There is a danger of course that adopting theory from a different intellectual tradition simply nullifies its power (Clegg, 2012a). There need to be good reasons for extending the scope of a theory, in this instance as an additional resource with which to theorise the complex interactions in higher education which involve both structure and agency (Ashwin, 2009). The notion of possible selves is potentially productive in theorising because it points to the importance of the self and agency as key concerns in understanding student and others' behaviour and the ways these are shaped and understood in policy. The idea of possible selves is fruitful because it highlights the significance of future imaginings in the experiences and interpretation of actors' lived presents and pasts. Possible selves also lends itself to thinking more sociologically because, while it is firmly rooted in the psychological literature, its proponents recognise that what is possible to imagine is shaped by agents' life circumstances, by what options are known and seem feasible, and by what is feared and to be avoided. In other words structural considerations are built in. One of the motivations in advocating extending the scope of the theory is that it seems to offer a way of bringing together some themes about temporality and the self in ways that illuminate empirical work.

In order to elaborate this overall line of reasoning the chapter will explore a number of arguments linked to the author's own empirical work. The first section will discuss the need for theory and attempt to clarify its role. Theory here is understood as being an active process of theorisation, not a process of validation by citation (Clegg, 2012a). The second section will outline the argument for greater attention to theories of the self and temporality which resulted from a concrete need to make sense out of student data. The third and fourth sections will explore the broader ramifications of temporality and theories of the self in structure/agency relations which provide the context for my sociologically inscribed reading of the concept of 'possible selves'. The final section will show how this is a productive and legitimate move and prepares the way for subsequent chapters in this volume whose authors illustrate the different ways they have drawn on the theory in their own empirical work.

On theorising

My move to a consideration of theories of possible selves is an example of theory development impelled by empirical work and by the gap between prior conceptualisations of the objects of study and the analysis emergent from multiple data sources and studies over time. I have reflected elsewhere on the problem of theorising in higher education and argued for the importance and power of theorisation in making sense of empirical research while at the same time cautioning against reified notions of theory (Clegg, 2012a). In the latter case the necessarily messy and difficult work of theorising is glossed over and theory can appear as no more than an appeal to sanctified theorists, all too often male, as a way of validating an author's particular claims. Anxiety over the role of theory in higher education research appears to have been particularly prevalent and is undoubtedly related to the relative newness of the area, its interdisciplinary nature, contestation over whether it can be seen as a distinct field, and legitimation and status issues associated with its positioning alongside academic development and education studies which have themselves struggled to assert their intellectual and professional authority (Clegg, 2012b). Haggis (2009) has criticised higher education researchers for an overly narrow focus on particular theories and notably the dominance of phenomenographic research at a time when the social sciences more generally were extending the scope of their theories. While it is true that phenomenographic research, uniquely in higher education, was influential in the approaches to learning and teaching literature particularly from a cognitive perspective (Tight, 2008), the dominance of this tradition has arguably waned. Both Tight (2004), another critic of higher education research, and Haggis (2009) rely on a relatively limited range of journals and they did not read full papers, so while their concerns are legitimate they do not add much to the diagnosis of what is impeding theory development in higher education research.

More recently Ashwin (2012) has approached the matter from a slightly different angle emphasising the issue of theory development and the lack of conceptualisation of the object of research in the reporting of research findings. This takes us closer to the heart of the issue of theorising as theory development rather than seeing theory as a thing. In particular, Ashwin is interested in the nature of the changing lenses through which we view our research, an argument which is central to my claim that extending the scope of theories of possible selves is a productive move. Ashwin draws on Bernstein's (2000) distinction between the internal and external language of description. The internal language of description is about seeing the object of research in particular ways, in other words how we are conceptualising the object under scrutiny – the theoretical framing adopted. The external language is provided by the empirical evidence which is generated in a particular study. Crucially what Ashwin argues is that there must be a 'discursive gap' between the two if the reasoning is to be non-circular and for there to be theoretical development. While I have not adopted Ashwin's Bernsteinian distinction as my framing for this chapter I am interested in the 'discursive gap', that is the ways in which the empirical analysis provides challenges to our initial ways of conceptualising the object of study.

My view of knowledge practices and meaning making has also been influenced by a review I undertook of papers published in *Teaching in Higher Education* 2005–2013 (Clegg, 2015). Unlike Tight and Haggis I undertook a full reading of all the papers. I was interested in *how* higher education researchers were developing and deploying theory and by what they took theory to be, rather than relying on a summary of what the paper was 'about' or the theorists cited. These can usually be gleaned from titles and abstracts but reveal little about the meaning making processes authors adopt. Based on a fuller reading I detected a series of strategies: description, personal reflection and reflexivity, explicit theorisation and data-driven analysis. Interestingly the first two categories would probably have been categorised as a-theoretical in the reviews described above and not all would have met the criteria of identifying a productive discursive gap, but close description is an important element of what Ashwin (2012) describes as the external language of description. Based on this work, therefore, I came to an understanding of theorisation and theory development as a process of meaning making involving multiple knowledge practices which are not reducible to findings, or to the initial framing in the work of particular theorists. The relationship between theorisation and empirical research is rather a dialectical one.

The final strand of thinking that has gone into making up the 'assemblage' (Hey, 2006) of ideas for interrogating the process of theory development (in this case theories of possible selves) are insights gleaned from the classical sociologist Robert Merton (1968). He describes the importance of 'theories of the middle range' – that is theory that enables the proper conceptualisation of empirical research, which he contrasts with grand or abstract theories which are often too remote from the actual research to be of concrete intellectual use. This resonates strongly with Ashwin's ideas of theory development, my own insights from attempting to do this as part of my own research and my observations on how authors contributing to *Teaching in Higher Education* approached meaning making in their writing about the framing of teaching, teaching practices and more broadly structure and agency relations in higher education. So my answer to the question of what is theory for is that it is about the multiple, non-reductive, dialectal, messy intellectual process whereby we attempt to come to better understandings of conceptually informed empirical research (broadly understood) through theory development.

Engaging with 'possible selves' – from research findings to theorisation

In their classical statement Markus and Nurius (1986) define self-knowledge in the domain of possible selves as:

> [the] type of self-knowledge [that] pertains to how individuals think about their potential and their future. . . . They are also the selves we could become and the selves we are afraid of becoming . . . they provide the essential link between the self-concept and motivation.
>
> (Markus and Nurius, 1986, p. 954)

The two core ideas are a sense of futurity as experienced in the present, hence my concern with temporality, and the sense of self and its influences on potential actions. In order to explain how I came to appreciate the relevance of this conceptualisation I am going trace my concerns with temporality and selfhood which arose out of a particular empirical investigation. This research was not conceived of in terms of possible selves but provides an example of the ways in which empirical research exceeded the prior conceptualisation and framing of a study (Clegg, 2012a). The 'topic' was Personal Development Planning (PDP), a process which was designed to give all higher education students, including at Doctoral level, the opportunity to reflect on their learning and engage in purposeful planning – a process which in many areas was expected to extend beyond education and into professional life (Clegg and Bradley, 2006; Clegg and Bufton, 2008). As such the research was policy and practice led in the context of curriculum innovation in English higher education. It became apparent, however, that PDP was a chaotic conception involving multiple processes and practices (Clegg, 2004). The first stages of the research, framed in terms of pedagogic practices, was based on data from staff interviews and revealed a complex and non-intuitively obvious relationship between disciplines/courses and approaches to developing a PDP curriculum (Clegg and Bradley, 2006). From this I came to an understanding of PDP as part of a broader restructuring of higher education. This process has involved a move away from the introverted singulars of academically controlled disciplines to what Bernstein has described as the 'projectional' and 'generic' – that is the development of curricula which look outwards from the academy. My PDP data could be understood in relation to this broader projectional project. This move to theory is an example of where my original conceptualisation was insufficient to the task of making sense of the data. The discursive gap between data and initial conceptualisation necessitated a move to further theorisation, in this case drawing on theories derived from Bernstein.

The second phase of the project which led to thinking about temporality and self was based on student data (Clegg and Bufton, 2008). The empirical data collection was conceptualised in terms of a series of puzzles about the mechanisms involved in reflective practice and the processes involved in the development of meta-cognitive abilities which were posited by academic staff as underpinning a particular PDP innovation. The specific context was a well-theorised implementation of a PDP curriculum on a first-year sociology course. The colleagues involved were distressed to find that the assessed work was of poor quality with what were seen as low-level descriptions of time management problems rather than higher-level reflections displaying a meta-cognitive awareness of the students' own learning. The study was therefore framed in terms of student learning and the mechanisms involved.

The study was explicitly not aimed at course evaluation. Course evaluations, like most programme evaluations, tell us little about what the underlying mechanisms are at work, merely telling us whether in a specific case something (in this instance a first-year PDP curriculum intervention) did or did not work. Influenced by a critical realist interest in underlying mechanisms, not just a reductive 'what works' approach, the decision was made to interview final-year students with the aim of exploring how students understood their own learning. In the interviews, therefore, we explored what influenced their understandings and whether these had changed over time. Only towards the end of the interview did we probe about whether or not they had drawn on (or even remembered) their experiences of the first-year PDP input. The three themes as described in the original paper were: 'Time and retrospective meaning making'; 'Narratives of the self'; 'Understandings of support/autonomy and independence' (Clegg and Bufton, 2008). The first two themes were the ones that led me to elaborate on temporality and theories of the self and are the ones described in this chapter. All three themes challenged our original conceptualisation of the data collection as being primarily about the mechanisms involved in student learning. The students' reflections seemed to go much deeper to their core beliefs about the self and their understandings of time. The third theme also demanded more theorisation and was subsequently developed in relation to theories of care and kindness influenced by feminist critiques of higher education (Clegg and Rowland, 2010).

The journey to thinking about temporality and the self was, therefore, rooted in the discursive gap between the initial conceptualisation of the study and our empirical analysis. The initial attempts at theorising involved a (re)reading and revisiting of work on temporality and the self – ideas with which I was already to a degree familiar but which I came to with a new interest because of our empirical data. As I will show in the subsequent sections, however, while this theorising was productive it remained at quite a high level of abstraction. The move to theories of possible selves represented a move to the 'middle range' and also to an area of theory which had already explicitly linked the two areas of the self and the future (temporality). It is important to note, however, that I came to read the possible selves literature only after immersion with other more sociologically and philosophically informed theory. My possible selves explorations, therefore, entailed extending the analytical scope beyond psychology and was also designed to act as a conceptual framing for new phases of empirical work.

Temporality and possible selves

The move to thinking about temporality was necessary because it was apparent from our data that experiences of time were extremely fluid and ideas of future time and personal futures were frequently absent from the students' accounts (Clegg, 2010). The significance of events was processed through retrospective meaning making, and the assumed policy time of future-focused planning envisaged in PDP was at best problematic in relation to their experiences. Our empirical research was therefore pointing us in the direction of seeing time not as a singular but as a complex set of relations. Our findings resonated with the work of Barbara Adam (1995, 2004), who has been at the forefront of the movement to take time seriously in social analysis. Adam (1995) distinguishes different aspects of time and challenges the assumption that we all live in a linear 'Western' time frame, which can be seen in contrast with the cyclical rhythms of an anthropological past. She argues for the co-existence and intermingling of different dimensions of time as co-present: time as linear divisible clock time; temporality as our being in time; timing as in 'when' time; and tempo the intensity of time. In our data and indeed in subsequent studies we have found evidence of the interplay of these different timescapes. In thinking about being in time Araújo (2005) points to the ways in which present time is created between past, present and future. The 'phase' (Araújo, 2005) of the students' lives in our research could, therefore, be understood as a passage between school and becoming a graduate, in which the 'present' was lived differently in relation to past and a possible imagined post-graduate future. We can also see the ways in which other aspects of time create tensions and contradictions in the time of higher education. Tempo and intensity vary over the academic year, and the divided clock time of years of study is often out of joint with lived existential time, while timing creates pressures at odds with the slow time which Ylijoki and Mäntylä (2003) characterise as the 'timeless time' necessary for academic life, reflection and learning. In contrast the pressured time of 'time management' is highly normative 'clock time' and in the dominant pedagogic discourse positions students as lacking (Burke et al., 2017; Bennett and Burke, 2017), which limits the scope for autonomous thinking developing slowly over time.

More fundamentally, however, the work of Adam and Groves (2007) challenges us to think about time as entailing the future. Futures according to Adam and Groves have been imagined and managed in historically different ways. They distinguish the ways historically futures have been 'told' (through divination), 'tamed' (for example through ritual) and 'traded' (as time becomes commodified). Crucially they point out that contemporary ideas of the future which they describe as 'futures transformed' involve the subjugation of time to human will whereby the future is presented as open:

> Emptied of content and meaning, the future is simply there, an empty space waiting to be filled with our desire, to be shaped traded or formed according to rational plans and blueprints, holding out the promise that it can be what we want it to be.
>
> (Adam and Groves, 2007, p. 11)

This sort of time has become the dominant time modality imagined in higher education and as we will see presents some challenges to the ways futures are conceptualised in theories of possible selves (see Chapter 3 in this volume). In presenting the future as empty, human will and agency are imagined as having the potential to transform the future in ways which transcend the structural liabilities of the past and present. This is the dominant social mobility narrative of higher education where historic inequalities are ignored despite the evidence that structural inequalities shape future opportunities (see Chapter 8 in this volume). Moreover capital is constantly and relentlessly restructuring future possibilities based on the underlying imperative of competitive accumulation. These mechanisms stretch into the future and render it unpredictable and unreadable. Students are being exhorted to orientate towards a future and 'plan' towards it as if it were open when in fact the future is already on the way. Another way of thinking about this is of the future as non-factually but actually entailed in the present (Bhaskar, 2008). Underlying mechanisms stretch into the future and shape it – perhaps the most frightening examples of this come in the form of the long-lasting consequences of actions past and present which are producing global warming.

Adam and Groves (2007) present a compelling critique of the present future and argue it inhibits our thinking and produces a moral vacuity in thinking about possible futures. In contrast they argue a case for the idea of a 'future present' which 'as a standpoint . . . positions us with reference to the deeds and processes already on the way' (Adam and Groves, 2007, p. 196). 'Future present' practices and knowledge involve care towards future generations whose futures are already entailed in the actions of the present. This critique resonates with Shahjahan's (2015) argument that the dominant colonial and western conceptions of time, of time traded and futures transformed, forcibly erase other notions of time. Indigenous and subaltern peoples are denigrated as lazy and their conceptions of time and customs and ways of knowing are presented as anachronistic. One implication of this is that it is important not to read Adam and Groves as offering a neutral periodisation of historical ways of thinking about the future. Different conceptualisations of the future are also a site of struggle and power. We should be open in empirical work, therefore, to questions about the co-existence of different forms of subjectivity and temporality which have implications for seemingly neutral pedagogical categories such as 'planning' with its already inbuilt imaginary of the present future. Manathunga (2014) has also argued that issues of temporality are highly significant in thinking about research into higher education on the global 'south'. Temporal and spatial relations are entwined and historically entailed. There is good reason, therefore, as Bennet and Burke argue, to see time in relation to power:

> Time does not exist apart from context, and it is not neutral. Time is embedded in the social and cultural dynamics of power and inequality.
> (Bennett and Burke, 2017, p. 3)

As researchers we should, therefore, be questioning and critical in our use of the term 'future' including the notion of future possible selves. If we return to the Markus and Nurius (1986) quote at the beginning of the previous section, 'how individuals think about their potential and their future' appears much more problematic. The concept of the future is not only socially and politically framed but is also philosophically contested. The 'selves we could become and the selves we are afraid of becoming' are positioned in the dominant ideology as empty and fully open to the imposition of human agency, and as I have argued this is not the case.

Sociological theories of the self[1]

The other area of theorisation which emerged most forcefully from the PDP project, and also evident from other studies, was the need to think more deeply about theories of the self and the implications of these for research. This might be easier territory for psychological theory, as in theories of possible selves, but theories of personhood have had a more chequered history in sociology. In the broader social sciences and humanities the influence of poststructuralist or postmodernist theory has resulted in understandings of the self as discursively (re)enacted and instantiated over time – a process of subjectification. This has proved a powerful resource in thinking about the fluidity of the self/selves and about gendered and racialised identities in all their plurality, but the sense of the self 'who is me' so evident in our data is rendered problematic in these accounts. While the anti-essentialism and rejection of the idea of a unified human subject in postmodernism is undoubtedly well founded, human agency is at best under-theorised in these accounts of subjectivity. In arguing the case for a more sociologically informed version of possible selves, therefore, it is important to articulate a more coherent sociological theory of the self.

One key sociological theory of the self in contrast is to be found in the work of Margaret Archer (1995, 2000, 2007, 2012). Her theorisation of self and human agency is part of her project of theorising structure agency relations which, as I argued in the introduction, is key for higher education research. Archer's arguments concern the avoidance of what she calls upwards, downwards and central conflation in social theorising, all of which prevent us recognising the real emergent powers of persons and the foundations of human agency. Downwards conflation involves the over-socialised personhood whereby persons are conceived of as no more than 'society's being', as being discursively formed, and consequently having no real agency as in poststructuralism. Conversely, the upward conflation of methodological individualism or 'modernity's man' reduces society to the individual and denies any emergent powers at the societal or cultural level. The seemingly more sophisticated option offered by Giddens and his structuration theory is, according to Archer (1995), an example of central conflation whereby structure is only evidenced in its enactment. In this version it is impossible to analyse social change as the world is only instantiated in the actions of the present. In response she argues for an analysis which recognises emergent, stratified natural kinds with causal powers at both the level of person and of society:

> both humanity and society have their own *sui generis* properties and powers, which make their interplay the central issue of social theory.
> (Archer, 2000, p. 17)

Archer's arguments are ontological, not merely epistemological; being is not anthropocentrically reduced to knowing. In insisting on the ontological status of persons she is claiming that they have real powers. In *Being Human* (2000) Archer argues that the conflations, outlined above, are incapable of sustaining agency. The thin flat logocentrism of modernity's man provides an inadequate basis for understanding human action, reducing as it does the motive power of human action to rationality. She argues that the alternative versions based on the Vygotskyan ontology developed by Harré, in which inter-subjectivity precedes intra-subjectivity, are also inadequate. This account subsumes naturalised being into social being whereas Archer insists that:

> The properties and powers of the human being are neither seen as *pregiven*, nor as *socially appropriated*, but rather these are emergent from our relations with our environment. As such they have relative autonomy from biology and society alike, and causal powers to modify both of them.
> (Archer, 2000, p. 87)

Archer argues that we should recognise the embodied nature of human beings and the primacy of practice – Marx's 'continuous practical activity in a material world' (Archer, 2000, p. 122). Species being with natural potentials creates the conditions for the emergence of the self in its necessary relations with the environment. In this she distinguishes between concepts of the self which are necessarily social, and a sense of the self. So that while there are discursively produced subjectivities, there is also an embodied sense of self continuous through the history of a particular life. Her argument does not deny that we are confronted by the reality of society, but she argues that a coherent account of the development of agents and social actors needs to be grounded in the non-discursively formed continuous sense of self. Archer's account analytically distinguishes and charts the development of the 'full range of personal powers (PEPs) – those of *self, agent, actor*, and *particular person*' (Archer, 2000, p. 295). Her model of personal and social identity is thus one in which individual and collective agents have the resources to act creatively in the world, thus creating conditions for transformation and change as well as social stasis. She argues that we can distinguish between the I, Me, We and You: the self, primary and corporate agents, and what kind of you to project into the future. None of these are necessarily emergent from the other. The development of a particular kind of agent, both primary (personal) and collective, is emergent in concrete historical circumstances and is based on the inner conversation:

> The 'inner conversation' is how our personal emergent powers are exercised on and in the world – natural, practical and social – which is our triune environment. This 'interior dialogue' is not just a window on the world, rather it is what determines our being in the world, though not in times and circumstances of our choosing. Fundamentally, the 'inner conversation' is constitutive of our concrete singularity. However, it is also and necessarily a conversation *about* reality. This is because the triune world sets us three problems, none of which can be evaded, made as we are. It confronts us with three inescapable concerns: with our physical well-being, our performative competence and our self worth.
>
> (Archer, 2000, p. 318)

The idea of the internal conversation adds a critical dimension to how people come to make judgements about their future possible selves and crucially incorporates the idea of them being *about* reality (albeit fallibly so). The temporally prior conditions 'not of our own choosing' are an important aspect of how people come to make judgements about what is and is not possible.

The ways people deliberate about the world are not all the same. Based on her empirical work Archer distinguishes four forms of reflexivity: 'communicative reflexives' who remain anchored in their natal social context; 'autonomous reflexives' who adopt strategic stances towards constraints and become socially upwardly mobile; and 'meta-reflexives' who are 'contextually incongruous'. This latter group are 'subversive towards social constraints and enablements, because of their willingness to pay the price of the former and to forfeit the benefits of the latter in the attempt to live out their idea' (Archer, 2007, p. 98). She also describes a state of fractured reflexivity where people are unable to form and act on their central projects or cares. I have argued that higher education, both in policy and pedagogy, privileges autonomous reflexivity (Clegg, 2010) and an orientation to the future as empty and open.

The forms of reflexivity represent different dominant personal orientations to being in the world. More recently, however, Archer has also suggested that we can distinguish the dominant forms of reflexivity which characterise different historical periods (Archer, 2012). The present period is characterised by accelerated morphogenesis (change) both structurally and culturally, which makes it harder to read and predict what is happening. She argues that the intensification of morphogenesis, at both cultural and structural levels, presents actors with 'contextual incongruity'. This renders communicative reflexivity, which relies on confirmation of our views from others and ties people to their natal origin, and the rational calculation of autonomous reflectivity which underpins social mobility, more problematic. Communicative reflexivity, which might have once formed a basis for inter-generational learning, is less powerful as the challenges facing younger students and academics are more uncertain. Similarly, autonomous reflectivity becomes more difficult as it becomes less clear what the routes to academic success and social mobility are (Brown, Lauder and Ashton, 2011). At a system level Margaret Archer argues that meta-reflexivity becomes the dominant orientation (although not necessarily the most common in a numeric sense). Meta-reflexivity generates greater capacity for the navigation of contextual ambiguity and meta-reflexives are less dependent on the linear trajectories of either staying put or social mobility. When we come to think about possible selves, therefore, not only do we need to take account of different forms of reflexivity, we also need to recognise that the ability to make judgements about what is possible are profoundly influenced by the structural conditions and rates of morphogenesis. For example, the contextual incongruities faced by students in 2017 might be considerably more profound than those confronting students in 1986 when Markus and Nurius were writing (see Brown, Lauder and Ashton, 2011).

It is clear that Archer's ideas link to the temporal concerns outlined in the previous section, because people are making judgements about their own commitments and futures based on their assessment of external conditions of existence. In making these links between temporality and the self, however, I have drawn on theoretical work at quite a high level of abstraction. In the section on theorising I made an argument for theories of the middle range and suggested that theories of possible selves could perform this function especially when, as suggested above, they are read through a more sociologically informed lens. It seemed obvious, therefore, to start a new phase of research by directly conceptualising the research in these terms. Theories of possible selves appeared to meet the criteria of being a theory of the middle range concerned with concrete mechanisms and processes rather than the more philosophical deliberations outlined above. So, in the final section, having assembled my analytical resources, I will illustrate how in new phases of research I have drawn on and simultaneously extended the scope of theories of possible selves.

Extending theories of possible selves

In bringing together the themes of self and temporality we (Stevenson and Clegg, 2013) explicitly looked to theories of future possible selves in a number of studies, and in particular one which asked mature further education students about how they envisaged possible futures in higher education. We wrote in our first working draft:

> The possible selves construct offers a useful framework 'for understanding adult learning as the medium through which change, growth, and goal achievement occur throughout the life course' (Rossiter, 2003, 5). Possible selves are future representations of the self (Markus and Nurius, 1986) including those that are desired and those that are not. They can be experienced singly or multiply, and may be highly elaborated or unelaborated.

> They may relate to those selves we desire to become or those we wish to avoid. Possible selves play both a cognitive and an affective role in motivation, influencing expectations by facilitating a belief that some selves are possible whereas others are not and, by functioning as incentives for future behaviour, providing clear goals to facilitate the achievement of a desired future self, or the avoidance of a negative one. More significantly the possible selves construct holds that individuals actively manage their actions in order to attain desirable selves and evade less-desirable selves. As representations of the self in possible future states, possible selves give form, specificity and direction to an individual's goals, aspirations, or fears (Markus and Nurius, 1986).
>
> (revised published version Stevenson and Clegg, 2013)

This usage represented a conscious decision to frame the analysis of our empirical work in terms of a theory of the middle range. In other words we were viewing possible selves as a mechanism for understanding how a particular group of learners viewed their futures and how they were able/unable to use their imaginings to actively shape their present actions.

However, our approach was tempered by our more sociologically informed interpretation and the need to question the culturally specific nature of conceptions of the future and the self that are normalised in the possible selves literature. For example Markus and Nurius (1986), in their original paper, report on their use of an instrument containing 150 listed possibilities for the self, but even a quick review of the items as they report them would suggest that this is far from neutral. The first item they report in the table showing percentages of respondents endorsing selected self items lists under 'personality' the terms 'happy', 'confident', 'depressed' and 'lazy' as descriptors that can be 'used to describe you now' and in response to the question 'have you ever considered this a possible self?'(Markus and Nurius, 1986, p. 959). A more sociological reading based on the sources cited above, however, would suggest that these descriptors erase significant and stratified valuations of these characteristics – 'lazy' for example is highly racialised in a context where the dominant mode of temporality valorises 'managing' time and efficiency (Shahjahan, 2015). Similarly under 'physicality': 'sexy', 'in good shape', 'wrinkled' and 'paralysed' are listed – a sociologically informed critique of this item would point to the gendered dynamics of any personal attribution of the self as 'sexy', the ageist implication of 'wrinkled' and assumptions about the body, ability and disability which might be attached to 'paralysed'. These cultural and specifically North American assumptions can also be seen in the list under 'general abilities' which includes 'speak well publically, make your own decisions, manipulate people, cheat on taxes', which have classed and gendered assumptions built in and an individualised conception of power and selfhood. There are two points here. One is methodological and the use of this sort of questionnaire-based study as against more qualitative approaches. Qualitative data enable a more nuanced exploration of values and how they come to be expressed and this is the approach we have taken in our studies. The other argument is that this way of exploring possible selves erases and naturalises power in the valorisation of the items listed. It becomes very difficult, if not impossible, to know how respondents understand their presumed possible self. We cannot tell for example whether the imaginary future of 'wrinkled' is a defiantly feminist recognition of the aging self or an acceptance of the dominance of certain beauty standards. One way of reading the instrument is that it tacitly endorses both a temporality of the 'present future' and the reflexivity of autonomous reflexivity. Meta-reflexivity as a stance is effectively erased. I am not suggesting that Markus and Nurius (1986) are entirely unaware of these problems; they do for example extend their research using 'an open ended format' and also argue the need to analyse the 'nature and valance of possible selves' (Markus and Nurius, 1986, p. 965). But a sociologically informed framing brings these issues more clearly into focus. In our research we found that respondents were able to come to clear judgements about the reality of the world they confronted and position themselves in relation to it in ways that reflected their own values. Our respondents displayed both communicative reflexivity and meta-reflexivity and rarely the autonomous reflexivity that can be inferred from the wording of the original Markus and Nurius (1986) instrument.

An explicit and theorised recognition that temporality and the future are not neutral terms greatly strengthens the use of possible selves as a framing for research. It opens up the discursive gap between how individuals think and talk about their futures in relation to their actions in the present, and the ways this cannot be discursively neutral. Time comes to us already framed within dominant discourses so that terms like time planning or laziness are more than just descriptors of individuals or characterisations of the self, they are deeply implicated in the policy framing of the ideal neo-liberal subject and the time orientation of the 'present future' (Clegg, 2010). Existing accounts of possible selves tend to see structural matters as constraints or enablements and treat social structural positioning in terms of 'race' and 'class', etc., as if they were variables. But this is to underestimate the ways mechanisms operate into the future and the increasingly morphogenetic character of global capitalism (Archer, 2012). While Archer may underestimate the continuing structuring power of privilege her argument for contextual incongruity and the difficulties of reading the future is a powerful one. In short, the following insight by Markus and Nurius is apposite but insufficient:

> An individual is free to create any variety of possible selves, yet the pool of possible selves derives from the categories made salient by the individual's particular sociocultural and historical context and from the models, images, and symbols provided by the media and by the individual's immediate social experiences. Possible selves thus have the potential to reveal the inventive and constructive nature of the self but they also reflect the extent to which the self is socially determined and constrained.
>
> (Markus and Nurius, 1986, p. 954)

As higher education researchers what we can take from the possible selves literature is a useful way of exploring the linkages between thinking and motivation, between imagining and becoming which preserves Archer's (2000) insight into the *sui generis* powers of human beings. It provides us with a way of designing studies which can interrogate the nature of connections between future self-conceptions and actions in the present through data-rich, close-up studies based on conceptualising possible selves as a theory of the middle range (Clegg, Stevenson and Burke, 2016). What extending the analytical scope of the possible selves literature does is to multiply the questions that can be asked about the self and the social, about the nature of the future and time, and about how policy and practice are discursively produced and constrained. Doing this extends the normative scope of theorising because it moves away from accounts of 'time', whether time management or social mobility narratives, which see students and others as lacking (Bennett and Burke, 2017). 'Possible selves' is fruitful to think with, and when combined with a critical approach and informed by theories of temporality and a sociological approach to the self, can be a powerful theoretical resource in helping us to conceptualise empirical research.

Note

1 I have made these arguments at greater length in Clegg, S. (2017) Critical and social realism as theoretical resources for thinking about professional development and equity. In B. Leibowitz, V. Bozalek and P. Kahn (eds) *Theorising learning to teach in higher education SRHE*, London: Routledge, pp. 141–156 and there is some repetition of this material in this section.

References

Adam, B. (1995) *Timewatch: The social analysis of time*, Cambridge: Polity Press.
Adam, B. (2004) *Time*, Cambridge: Polity Press.
Adam, B. and Groves, C. (2007) *Future matters: Action, knowledge, ethics*, Leiden: Brill.
Araújo, E. R. (2005) Understanding the PhD as a phase in time. *Time and Society*, 14, 2–3: 191–211.
Archer, M. S. (1995) *Realist social theory: The morphogenetic approach*, Cambridge: Cambridge University Press.
Archer, M. S. (2000) *Being human: The problem of agency*, Cambridge: Cambridge University Press.
Archer, M. S. (2007) *Making our way through the world*, Cambridge: Cambridge University Press.
Archer, M. S. (2012) *The reflexive imperative in late modernity*, Cambridge: Cambridge University Press.
Ashwin, P. (2009) *Analysing teaching-learning interactions in higher education: Accounting for structure and agency*, London: Continuum.
Ashwin, P. (2012) How often are theories developed through empirical research into higher education? *Studies in Higher Education*, 8, 35: 941–955.

Bennett, A. and Burke, P. J. (2017) Re/conceptualising time and temporality: An exploration of time in higher education. *Discourse: Studies in the Cultural Politics of Education*, http://tandfonline.com/doi/abs/10.1080/01596306.2017.1312285

Bernstein, B. (2000) *Pedagogy, symbolic control and identity: Theory, research, critique*, Oxford: Rowan & Littlefield.

Bhaskar, R. (2008) *A realist theory of science*, London: Verso.

Brown, P., Lauder, H. and Ashton, D. (2011) *The global auction: The broken promises of education, jobs and incomes*, Oxford: Oxford University Press.

Burke, P., Bennett, A., Bunn, M., Stevenson, J. and Clegg, S. (2017) It's about time: Working towards more equitable understandings of the impact of time for students in higher education. NCSEHE Report, University of Newcastle, NSW.

Clegg, S. (2004) Critical readings: Progress files and the production of the autonomous learner. *Teaching in Higher Education*, 9, 4: 287–298.

Clegg, S. (2010) Time future: The dominant discourse of higher education pedagogy. *Time and Society*, 19, 3: 345–364.

Clegg, S. (2012a) On the problem of theorising: An insider account of research practice. *Higher Education Research and Development*, 31, 3: 407–418.

Clegg, S. (2012b) Conceptualising higher education research and/or academic development as 'fields': A critical analysis. *Higher Education Research and Development*, 31, 5: 667–678.

Clegg, S. (2015) Adventures in meaning making: *Teaching in Higher Education* 2005–2013. *Teaching in Higher Education*, 20, 4: 373–387.

Clegg, S. and Bradley, S. (2006) Models of personal development planning: Practices and processes. *British Educational Research Journal*, 32, 1: 57–76.

Clegg, S. and Bufton, S. (2008) Student support through personal development planning: Retrospection and time. *Research Papers in Education*, 23, 4: 1–16.

Clegg, S. and Rowland, R. (2010) Kindness in pedagogical practice and academic life. *British Journal of Sociology of Education*, 31, 6: 703–719.

Clegg, S., Stevenson, J. and Burke, J. (2016) Translating close-up research into action: A critical reflection. *Reflective Practice*, 17, 3: 233–244.

Haggis, T. (2009) What have we been thinking of? A critical overview of 40 years of student learning research in higher education. *Studies in Higher Education*, 34, 4: 377–390.

Hey, V. (2006) The politics of performative resignification: Translating Judith Butler's theoretical discourse and its potential for a sociology of education. *British Journal of Sociology of Education*, 27, 4: 439–457.

Manathunga, C. (2014) *Intercultural postgraduate supervision: Reimaging time, place and knowledge*, London: Routledge.

Markus, H. and Nurius, P. (1986) Possible selves. *American Psychologist*, 41, 9: 954–969.

Merton, R. (1968) *Social theory and social structure*, New York: The Free Press, pp. 17–29.

Rossiter, M. (2003) Constructing the possible: A study of educational relationships and possible selves. In D. Flowers et al. (eds) *Proceedings of the 44th annual adult education research conference*, San Francisco: San Francisco State University, pp. 363–368.

Shahjahan, R. A. (2015) Being 'Lazy' and Slowing Down: Toward decolonizing time, out body and pedagogy. *Educational Philosophy and Theory*, 47, 5: 488–501.

Stevenson, J. and Clegg, S. (2013) 'My past is a double edge sword': The complex trajectories from further to higher education of adult learners in the UK. *Studies in Continuing Education*, 35, 1: 17–29.

Tight, M. (2004) Research into higher education: An a-theoretical community of practice? *Higher Education Research & Development*, 23, 4: 395–411.

Tight, M. (2008) Higher education research as tribe, territory and/or community: A co-citation analysis. *Higher Education*, 55, 5: 593–605.

Ylijoki, O. and Mäntylä, H. (2003) Conflicting time perspectives in academic work. *Time and Society*, 12, 1: 55–78.

Section 2

Using the possible selves concept empirically

Chapter 5

A discursive approach to understanding the role of educators' possible selves in widening students' participation in classroom interaction
Language teachers' sense making as 'acts of imagination'

Magdalena Kubanyiova

Introduction: the centrality of possible selves in the language learning–teaching relationship

The argument presented in this chapter is informed by my longstanding research agenda in educational linguistics located at a dynamic interface of additional language learning and teaching. At one side of this relationship, I have studied questions about what constitutes a meaningful language learning opportunity for those with diverse cultural, linguistic, and socioeconomic backgrounds and equally diverse needs to learn and use languages in their lives. The theoretical as well as empirical inquiry I have conducted with colleagues and doctoral researchers has led into research territories as wide-ranging as classroom climate, motivation, vision, group dynamics, willingness to communicate, intercultural communication, language ideologies, dialogic peer interaction, and teacher-led classroom discourse (e.g., Asker, 2012; Do, in progress; Kubanyiova, 2015; Nikoletou, 2017; Ogawa, 2018; Yue, 2014, 2016). At the other end of the language learning–teaching continuum, I have been intrigued by questions about how educators make sense of and transform such language learning opportunities into realities for their students in classrooms around the world and how they can be supported in doing so through teacher education and continuing professional development (Kubanyiova, 2014, 2016; Kubanyiova and Crookes, 2016). It is through probing into this interface and connecting the research concerns of two domains of educational linguistics – second language acquisition (SLA) and language teacher cognition – that my focus on language educators' possible selves has emerged.

Drawing on a socially oriented epistemological tradition represented by a participation metaphor (Sfard, 1998) and adopting a discursive orientation to studying cognition (Heritage, 2005), this chapter will discuss intellectual and ethical gains of re-interpreting teachers' possible selves as 'acts of imagination', a conceptualisation which highlights the prominent social, emotional, and moral dimensions of imagined selves in action and offers a productive link between how educators envision their futures and what difference this makes for students' participation in classroom life, especially for those from linguistically, socio-politically, and socioeconomically marginalised backgrounds.

Language learning opportunities as participation in teacher–student interaction

Research on whole-class teacher–student interaction has shown significant benefits of this type of classroom interaction for language learning opportunities and, by extension, for language learning (Hall, 2010), often exceeding those of peer interaction (Toth, 2008). It has been found, for instance, that one of the most ubiquitous, and traditionally dismissed as restrictive, patterns of teacher–student interaction, Initiation–Response–Feedback (IRF; Sinclair and Coulthard, 1975), in which the teacher initiates an exchange (I), the student responds (R), and the teacher gives feedback (F), can facilitate students' meaningful participation, public or private (Batstone and Philp, 2013; Ohta, 2001), in classroom discourse. Its effectiveness, however, depends on the purposes for which IRF is deployed and the way in which its three interactional moves are orchestrated by the teacher to encourage learner involvement in alignment with those purposes (Wells, 1993).

Expanding this argument, Walsh (2006) has proposed a context-sensitive framework for understanding classroom discourse, arguing that different microcontexts of teacher–student interaction (in his words, interactional *modes*) require different patterns of the teacher's use of language. To support this proposal, he has used classroom discourse data to demonstrate that a tightly controlled IRF pattern with the teacher's extensive use of display questions and evaluative feedback in the third move of the IRF exchange is highly effective in generating learning opportunities if the pedagogical aim is to enable students' language practice around a piece of material or to check and display correct answers. Such interactional microcontexts have been labelled by Walsh (2006) as *materials and skills mode* and *systems mode* respectively. In what he labels as *classroom context mode*, that is, teacher–student interaction with a pedagogical aim to encourage meaning-oriented communication, very different IRF strategies have been found effective. For instance, using the third move of the IRF exchange as an explicit positive evaluation (e.g., "very good") in a meaning-focused interaction has been found to function as conversation closure (Waring, 2008) and thus to hinder students' opportunities to participate in classroom discourse. In contrast, using the same part of IRF to invite students to expand, elaborate, or clarify their contributions, useful opportunities have been shown to arise for students' meaning-making even within the confines of IRF (Hall and Walsh, 2002). This and many other findings generated by a discursive approach to understanding students' language learning, conceptualised as participation in classroom interaction, have highlighted the need to adopt a context-sensitive approach to analysing classroom discourse in order to develop pedagogical principles for maximising students' participation in language learning.

Despite the critical insights that the previously mentioned strand of research has generated, studies from further afield within the broader domain of educational linguistics (Creese, Blackledge, and Takhi, 2014) and certainly within education research more generally (e.g., David, 2010) have shown that pedagogical goals are far from the sole concerns governing classroom interaction and that a range of social, political, linguistic, psychological, identity-relevant, and normative dynamics play a significant role in shaping students' access to participation in classroom life. Bringing together insights from across these disciplinary domains is therefore an important research pursuit to understand how widening participation is 'done on the ground' and this chapter addresses one of its multiple facets: the role of educators within these dynamics.

Language teacher cognition and possible selves: from cognitions to sense making

Language teacher cognition has been referred to in educational linguistics as an umbrella term to encompass research with the broad aim to understand language teachers and teaching (Borg, 2006). Most of its core empirical activity has centred around two primary objectives: first, to identify the range and types of cognitions, usually beliefs or knowledge, that language teachers have about different aspects of their work and about different domains of language curriculum and language educational process (e.g., Gatbonton, 1999); and second, to explain the relationship between language teachers' cognitions and practices (e.g., Basturkmen, 2012). Because in this tradition of inquiry teachers' "mental constructs" (Walberg, 1972) are assumed to be unavailable for direct observation (cf. Baker, 2014), they are typically accessed through various elicitation instruments, such as standardised questionnaires containing categorical belief/knowledge statements or carefully developed interview guides and stimulated recall protocols. The data gathered in this way are typically treated as reports of cognitions and often put in contrast with practice. This orientation to conceptualizing and researching cognition is akin to what Sfard (1998), discussing learning, has termed an acquisition metaphor, prompting an image of an educator's mind as a container to be filled with certain entities, that is, cognitions (such as beliefs, knowledge, or images of future selves) and of an educator as an acquirer and subsequently a possessor of those cognitions.

In contrast, the epistemological stance that I am taking in this chapter, and which has informed my theorising of both language teacher cognition in general and language educators' possible selves in particular, is broadly aligned with a participation-oriented perspective (Sfard, 1998), which shifts the focus from learning as acquisition of discrete units of knowledge to learning as participation in practice. Informed by a similar epistemological orientation, teacher cognition has been represented by conceptual metaphors such as cognition as gestalt (Korthagen, 2001), situational representations (Clarà, 2014), and patterns of participation (Skott, 2015). All of these, while distinctive in their conceptual rendering of cognition, emphasise teachers' situated, dynamic, and embodied knowing in action and, accordingly, place the study of teacher cognition in settings in which it finds expression: the contexts of teachers' participation in practice. Practices, which include a range of activities of teaching, such as discursive behaviours in teacher–student talk, but also the social practice of a research interview, are understood not as spaces in which educators' reified mental contructs, such as beliefs, knowledge, or possible selves, may or may not be applied. Rather, they are seen as "dynamic and evolving outcomes of individual and communal acts of meaning-making" (Skott, 2015, p. 24). This implies that the task of a researcher who intends to understand cognition as meaning making lies not in eliciting cognitions and separating them from practice, but rather in "disentangl[ing] patterns in the teacher's reengagement in other past and present practices in view of the ones that unfold at the instant" (Skott, 2015, p. 24).

In this chapter, I draw on data excerpts from my research with the aim to demonstrate the theoretical, methodological, and ethical promise of conceiving of *possible selves* in a similar vein – that is, through the lens of language teachers' "emergent sense making in action" (Kubanyiova and Feryok, 2015, p. 436). In other words, this chapter's key concern lies less in eliciting self-reported accounts of teachers' possible selves as propositions and more in studying how envisioned *future* selves may or may not be embodied in language educators' *present* practice and how, if at all, this may make a difference to students' access to learning opportunities in the classroom. There are two contexts of practice that I will pay attention to: the practice of teacher-led classroom discourse and the practice of the teacher's reflection on the classroom events, the latter being deliberately framed as practice rather than a report. In sum, the concept of educators' possible selves does not inform my analytical gaze from the outset, but is brought to the fore as my analytic inquiry into language learning opportunities in classroom discourse progresses.

The research participant: Iveta

The example I will use in this chapter comes from a larger project investigating the development of eight English as a Foreign Language (EFL) teachers in Slovakia who volunteered to participate in a year-long teacher development (TD) programme focused on the principles for creating engaging learning environments in their language classrooms (Kubanyiova, 2016). Here I focus on Iveta (pseudonym), a qualified university-educated EFL teacher at a state secondary school (11–18-year-old students) in Slovakia where EFL was one of the school subjects and was taught up to three times per week in 45-minute lessons. Iveta shared her mother tongue (Slovak) with her students, and data, collected over the period of one school year, include: (a) transcripts of audiorecordings and ethnographic field notes from *eight lesson observations*; (b) *five in-depth interviews* exploring Iveta's professional and personal history, her interpretations of the teacher development course material, and issues arising in lesson observations; (c) *ethnographic field notes from five visits to Iveta's school* containing additional informal interviews with colleagues and students and descriptive records documenting activities in this setting; and (d) *ethnographic field notes from the teacher development course sessions*, capturing what transpired in each session and documenting her and other participants' interactions, their contributions to the sessions, and their engagement with the teacher development course material.

A discursive approach within a grounded theory ethnographic study

Grounded theory ethnography (Charmaz, 2006; Charmaz and Mitchell, 2001) is a methodological and analytical approach guided by a flexible set of guidelines at the intersection of ethnography and grounded theory. Similar to ethnography, field notes of grounded theory ethnographers record individual and collective actions in situ, contain anecdotes and observations of people, settings, and actions, and pay attention to participants' perspectives and, particularly crucial for the purposes of this chapter, to their use of language. From the beginning of data collection, however, grounded theory ethnographers foreground the studied phenomenon or process and become progressively focused on significant analytical ideas which can offer a conceptual explanation of the 'thick descriptions'. According to Charmaz (2006), a grounded theory approach to ethnography can be summarised as "Seek data, describe observed events, answer fundamental questions about what is happening, then develop theoretical categories to understand it" (p. 25), and it is this blueprint that has informed my overarching methodological and analytical approach in the larger study. In addition to the extensive ethnographic field notes from visits to Iveta's school and from the professional development course in which she participated, the two types of data records that primarily inform the argument in this chapter come from two contexts of Iveta's practice: the practice of teacher–student interaction in her language classroom and the practice of her own reflection on both the classroom events and her professional and personal trajectories. The broad purpose of the analysis was to account for the nature of language learning opportunities that existed in Iveta's classroom interaction with her students and to develop a conceptual explanation for those accounts.

Although a substantial part of the grounded theory scholarship has argued for an approach to coding that treats empirical data as reports of phenomena and follows a prescribed set of analytical procedures, my approach is aligned with those such as Charmaz (2006), who see coding data in grounded theory as a way of "grappl[ing] with what it means" (p. 46), allowing for the adoption of a variable and flexible set of analytical frameworks to account conceptually for those meanings. To this end, and in line with the previously described concerns inherent in the participation metaphor to both language learning and language teacher cognition, I drew on discursive approaches that are well established in my home domain of educational linguistics.

As an initial coding stage, I adopted Walsh's (2006) framework for analysing classroom interaction, which acknowledges the situated nature of classroom discourse and assumes that different interactional patterns are appropriate in different instructional microcontexts. I examined a range of interactional features in Iveta's classroom discourse, such as the previously mentioned IRF patterns, display vs. referential questions, extended teacher turns, feedback, clarification requests, and confirmation checks, and sought to establish the extent to which these adhered to the pedagogic goals of a given interactional microcontext and thus, as is assumed by Walsh, contributed to the construction of learning opportunities. Going deeper in the analysis of teacher–student interaction to understand people's meaning making in action, I adopted some of the principles of conversation analysis which has the "capacity to examine in detail how opportunities for L2 learning arise in interactional activities" (Kasper, 2006, p. 83). Pursuing this discursive approach to analysing language learning opportunities, I was further interested in establishing how participants, and the teacher in particular, oriented to these interactional situations and what they themselves came to treat as learning opportunities (Kasper, 2004; Waring, 2008). This was achieved by examining how each turn was produced and received by all discourse participants and by paying attention to turn construction, word choice, or pause (ten Have, 2007).

To understand more fully the reasons behind Iveta's acting in particular ways in her classroom interaction with students, I departed from the typical approaches to researching teacher cognitions as participants' reports (cf. Borg, 2012) and examined instead the way in which Iveta's thoughts, interpretations of past experiences, emerging understandings, or future desires, were "displayed and responded to (or not) in talk and embodied conduct" (Potter, 2012, p. 576), including in her descriptions of everyday experiences and events (Heritage, 2005), such as her reflections on specific lessons, general language teaching methods, students, relevant educational policies, past personal and professional experiences, and perceived future challenges and desires. Equally, I was interested in understanding how the different settings and power dynamics (e.g., interviews with the researcher, conversations with colleagues, or informal interactions with students) may have shaped what, how, and why Iveta chose to engage with particular ideas, descriptions, and reflections, and what light these could shed on her "inherent theories-in-use" (ten Have, 2007, p. 31).

Through this complex but highly complementary set of discursive approaches to data analysis and a progressive focus on significant analytical ideas aided through extensive annotating, memoing, and conceptual borrowings across the fields of educational linguistics, teacher education, and psychology to generate theoretical explanations, the key theme discussed in this chapter was identified:

Iveta's sense making as emergent acts of imagination involving her *desired images of future selves* as central to this process. In the next section, I offer a snapshot of one interactional moment in Iveta's classroom with the aim to demonstrate both the nature of this type of analytical inquiry and the conceptual significance of the findings that ensued from it.

Iveta's practice of creating language learning opportunities in classroom interaction

Excerpt 1 depicts an interactional moment in Iveta's class of fifteen 17-year-old students with an intermediate level of English proficiency. Although the recording does not capture the fullness of Iveta's interactional exchanges with her students, and some of the private utterances made by students and responded to by Iveta in the public arena of teacher–student interaction remain inaccessible, this excerpt, nevertheless, represents a faithful account of the general participation patterns underlying classroom interaction in Iveta's lessons across her dataset. Excerpt 1 starts at the beginning of a lesson in which Iveta refers to and endeavours to recap a discussion that took place earlier in the week (not observed for the purposes of the project). Apart from the underlined utterances (which depict speech in the participants' mother tongue), the interaction was conducted in English, that is, the language the students were learning (see the Appendix for full transcription conventions). All names in the transcript are pseudonyms.

Excerpt I: sample teacher–student interaction in Iveta's class

(1) T: We talked about winning a lottery, winning a lot of money. What were we talking about?
(2) S1: About people who won a lot of money.
(3) T: Uhm? About the people who won a lot of money? And we were also talking about what we would do with the money. Right? For example, xxx, xxx, xxx, for example, Zuzana said, even if she's not here today ((T smiles)), she said she would give it to her parents. Do you remember? ((some noise, students comment, they seem to recall it)) You were so surprised, why would you give it to your parents? ((T laughs))
(4) xxx
(5) T: And also ehm Adrian said he would xxx and Pavol would buy a house. Uhm? But what else can you do with a lot of money. Can you think of anything else you can do with a lot of money? (1) You can buy a house? OK? But what else? What else can you do with a lot of money.
(6) S1: Charity.

(7) T: Charity. Adrian, ((laughs)) I didn't expect YOU to=
(8) S1: =xxx ((laughs))
(9) T: Perfect! This is what I wanted to hear. ((smiles)) I just didn't expect you to say that. ((laughs)) So I'm quite surprised that you are the one to think about it also. (1) OK. What is charity. What do you describe as charity. What is it.
(10) S1: Poor people.
(11) T: Uhm? Poor people. What else xxx?
(12) S1: Ehm xxx children.
(13) T: Eh?
(14) S1: xxx children.
(15) T: Children who are alone? Uhm?
(16) S1: Homeless.
(17) T: Homeless people. Uhm? What else. And not just Adrian, OK? ((laughs, others join. Adrian-S1 protests in L1, T laughs)) OK. What else comes to your mind? What do you understand by this word? (3) By charity. What can you understand? What comes to your mind. What picture do you have in mind when you hear charity?
(18) S2: xxx xxx xxx.
(19) T: An addiction. Uhm?
(20) S2: xxx.
(21) T: Uhm? xxx? (1) ((laughs)) xxx. So who can you help? With your money? (2) Let's give examples. Who can you fund? So poor people? Orphan children? (3)
(22) S1: xxx, xxx.
(23) T: Uhm, xxx.
(24) S1: xxx.
(25) T: So people who are needy? Uhm? So. (1) How can you help? To whom can you xxx and when. So the money can be used for what? (1) For medical care, for example. For people xxx of what?
(26) S1: xxx can buy clothes?
(27) T: Uhm, to buy clothes. Or the charity will buy them some clothes. Uhm? (3) What else? (2) Have you ever thought of being xxx in charity. Has it ever come to your mind? (2) Uhm? Who would you give the money. ((it's inaudible, but there probably was a private reply from a student which T overheard because she seems to build on that)) Orphan children, aha? (3) What do you think, let's say of xxx, an organisation for people with HIV (2). HIV AIDS. (1) What do

A discursive approach 67

you think about it? What is your opinion. (3) Hm? Is it good to help such people? Is it important to help them? Or we're not gonna do anything, because we're not going to help them. (1) I'm just asking about your opinion. It's OK if you think so. I just want to know
(28) S2: It's important to help them.
(29) T: Excuse me?
(30) S2: It's important to help them.
(31) T: Yes, it is important to help them. Why do you think so? What can we help them, what can we do for them?
(32) S2: Ehm, we can buy them some pills or xxx to cure them.
(33) T: Uhm? What else can we do. When talking about these illnesses, why is it important to give money? What else can be done? (1) Not just to help them, but also (2) to xxx. Isn't it, Veronika? ((a student who has not said anything so far))
(34) S2: xxx.
(35) T: Uhm? We know we can do this. xxx. What is important to do?
(36) S1: Many people around them. Many people who love them. Or. (1) Or (3)
(37) T: Yes, he's right. They don't need just our money.
(38) S1: xxx.
(39) T: But not only our money, but also our attention. (1) Uhm? (1) But how can we also help? That so many people are uneducated.
(40) S2: To teach some information.
(41) T: Information. So it is very important for the people to know what can be done for each other. Do you xxx. xxx. Are you informed (1) enough? Do you think you are informed enough? ((an exchange in Slovak between S1 and T follows, some laughter, some joking, mostly inaudible)) OK. So. Do you think that people in Slovakia are well informed about these things.
(42) Ss: No.
(43) T: No, you don't think so. And what about countries such as Ukraine? Are people well informed in Ukraine?
(44) S: No.
(45) T: What about the (1) medical ehm, is it sufficient? <u>What is sufficient</u>? (1) <u>Sufficient</u>. (3) Do you know that a lot of people suffer from HIV in Ukraine?

(46) S: No.
(47) T: We never think about it. There are a lot of
people who are infected because of the needle,
xxx. Because of xxx. So people really need to be
informed. People need to know, xxx, it's very important. (1) Uhm? Ehm, what do you think about (1) ehm,
what do you think is the most xxx of the other charities? Which one is the most important? (3)
(48) S2: Red Cross.
(49) T: Red Cross. Uhm? What does it do? (2) Everyone?
Do you know what Red Cross does? What does this
organisation do?
(50) S1: They are in war, in Africa, xxx, (1) They are
in many countries. They are everywhere. (1) If they
can.
(51) T: They are everywhere.
(52) S1: If they can, they are everywhere.

Although it is beyond the scope of this chapter to offer a close analysis of the lengthy transcript in Excerpt 1 or indeed to explain the larger sociocultural and sociohistorical context in which it is embedded, my aim is to highlight some of the key tendencies in Iveta's discursive practices which triggered my inquiry into her possible selves. To start with, the stretch of discourse shown here appears to resemble a previously mentioned *classroom discourse mode*, an interactional microcontext whose pedagogical aims include enabling learners to express their opinions or share experiences, activating their mental schemata, establishing a context, or promoting oral fluency practice (cf. Walsh, 2006). Iveta asks numer- ous and what appear to be genuine questions (e.g., turn 5, 21, 25), gives feedback on content rather than language forms (31), asks clarification questions (13, 29), and encourages further generation of students' ideas (13, 15, 17), all of which appear to match the pedagogic goals of classroom discourse mode and could therefore be treated as evidence of meaningful language learning opportunities.

However, a closer scrutiny of the unfolding moment-by-moment interaction in this segment reveals intriguing insights into Iveta's orientation to students' participation, not only suggesting that her goals for this exchange may differ from the meaning-oriented pedagogical goals, but also demonstrating rather different consequences for the nature of students' language learning opportunities. The first feature worth noticing concerns the frequency and distribution of students' contributions. It is clear that with the exception of a couple of longer than usual teacher turns (27, 47), student turns constitute a frequent feature of this stretch of discourse. The transcript makes it equally obvious, however, that most of them come from S1 (Adrian) who typically offers brief, one-word responses to Iveta's questions and sometimes engages in playful and at times off-topic exchanges with Iveta (7–9, 17), indicating a warm personal rapport. After Iveta's brief interven- tion in turn 17, the second participant, S2 (Pavol), makes a string of interactional contributions (18, 20, 28, 30, 34, 40, 48), most of which appear linguistically and topically more complex than those of S1. Although in addition to these two male students' participation in classroom talk, Iveta also addresses a third female student (Veronika, turn 33); this appears to be a token reference rather than genuine invitation, as it is not followed up any further, and, consequently, does not translate into Veronika's public participation in the interactional exchange. In sum, Iveta's interactional attention seems to be focused solely on these two students, also signalled in one of her opening turns (5): She explicitly, albeit not exclusively (see turn 3), draws on these two students' previous lesson's contributions as a way of creating an interactional context for this lesson's discussion.

The second feature worth noting is the topic, driven by the coursebook material, which suggests potential for students' deep intellectual and emotional engagement in meaning making, one of the core features of interaction in classroom discourse mode. A closer examination of Iveta's discursive treatment of students' contributions shows some engagement with the ideas they generated (25, 31, 37, 39, 41) and her frequent acknowledgement tactics ("Uhm?") sometimes work as a way of encouraging elaboration of students' ideas (15). Overall, however, the transcript gives an overwhelming sense that the primary focus of the exchange rests on the generation of alternative ideas in a list-like format, possibly with a purpose to arrive at a specific final idea. This hunch is corroborated by Iveta's deployment of "Uhm?", which effectively works as an evaluation strategy, especially when followed by repetition of the student utterance and a subsequent invitation (e.g., "What else?") to contribute yet another idea (11, 17, 27). Coupled with Iveta's minimal engagement with the content of what the students say (though some effort to the contrary is obvious in turns 36–39) and an occasionally unexpected turn in the flow of interaction triggered by Iveta's own suggestions (27, 39, 43), the teacher's frequent invitation turns do not appear to be initiated with the aim of enabling students to express their ideas but instead resemble opportunities to display knowledge and to arrive at some sort of a 'correct answer' ("Perfect! This is what I wanted to hear"; turn 9).

Without claiming to do justice to the richness of the interaction in Excerpt 1, this analysis suggests that the way in which Iveta deploys language in these interactional exchanges is not aimed at deepening and certainly not widening students' participation in meaning-making. It is true that some of the interactional features identified earlier may on the surface correspond with those inherent in meaning-focused interaction. However, these goals seem to be in tension with what Iveta is actually doing, pointing to potentially significant pedagogical consequences as well as ethical ramifications for what kinds of linguistic practices are available to whom in Iveta's classroom.

Iveta's practice of sense making in a research interview

Excerpt 2 portrays a segment from a longer interview conducted after the observed lesson, in which Iveta reflects on the lesson shown in Excerpt 1. It was by putting Iveta's classroom observation data in a relationship with her own reflections on it that I, as a researcher, began to sense that the tensions in Iveta's pedagogical goals in her classroom interactions might reflect a more pervasive and conceptually significant tendency in her overall dataset and require a full analytical attention if I were to understand wider consequences of Iveta's practice on language learning opportunities for her students.

Excerpt 2: Iveta's interview reflections on the observed lesson

> And another aim I had was that apart from getting them interested in what they were about to listen to, and, basically introduce the topic, I wanted to know their opinions, wanted to know what they thought about it, so to make them think about it. And you could see it for yourself, they would do this, they would do that, but it occurred to no one that someone might actually need the money. Maybe it will force them to think about it a bit at home too – because it's not just about teaching them English. It's about getting them to understand, in that lesson, something human, natural things, so who knows, maybe they will start to be interested, they weren't aware of a single charity. When you think about it – it's awful – they don't know a single charity; yes, Markiza [name of commercial tv channel with a charity attached to it], that's it. They don't know, but I think it's important. At least they have these articles in the coursebook, they can talk about it a little, maybe they become interested in it.

It is, once again, impossible to do full justice to the many layers of Iveta's practice of sense making in this interview excerpt, so I will restrict this discussion to the key insight for the purposes of this chapter. In juxtaposition with the transcript of the lesson (Excerpt 1) to which Iveta explicitly refers in this account, her reflection lays bare critical discrepancies between what objectively transpired and her own rationalisation of it in this research interview. How she positions students in her account ("but it occurred to no one that someone might actually need the money", "they don't know", "they couldn't name a single charity") is particularly intriguing in relation to what actually transpired in the observed lesson. As Excerpt 1 shows, the suggestion to give the winning money to a good cause ("<u>charity</u>" – turn 6) was offered by the student and those students with the chance to participate in the public classroom discourse not only demonstrated willingness to engage with the topic (even if, as discussed previously, such efforts may not have been fully followed up by Iveta), but there is evidence of their knowledge of at least one specific charity (the "Red Cross", 48; interestingly, the charity that Iveta mentions, Markiza, was not captured in the actual transcript, even though the possibility that the students indeed offered it as part of a private contribution remains) and general awareness of what charities do in different parts of the world (32, 36, 40, 48–52). These tensions suggest that Iveta's practice of sense making in this research interview may be done not from the perspective of actual classroom events, but rather from a vantage point of the imagined and desired; in other words, the two sets of data offer glimpses into how Iveta desires to be seen by the students, the researcher, and herself. It is here that the construct of possible selves (Markus and Nurius, 1986) as one's vision of their desired future selves, albeit not as separate from Iveta's present sense making but as embodied in it, began to emerge as conceptually relevant.

Iveta's desired future selves as 'emergent acts of imagination'

The insight from the examination of transcripts and field notes across the eight observed lessons and especially in conjunction with Iveta's reflections on them led to a deeper analytical appreciation of Iveta's practices which might have been puzzling when viewed in isolation, but which revealed previously hidden meanings when examined from the view of the emerging theme of desired future selves. For instance, almost all narrative accounts of her past experiences, including memorable episodes from her language learning history, language teaching episodes, or more general life experiences, foregrounded her position as someone who is "the best", "a star", "appreciated", someone who "made [people's] day" or who "changed [their] lives", as illustrated in the following two excerpts, one recounting her early language learning experience and the other referring to her university course.

Excerpt 3: Iveta's interview reflection on past language learning experience

> In year one in high school, they put me in the group of beginners, because I wanted it – but in fact, I wasn't of course a beginner, I was the best in the group. Oh, I was a star! I read the textbook ahead of lessons, so that I could be the best.

Excerpt 4: Iveta's interview reflection on her university course

> One of our classmates [in a university class] asked in the middle of the course, "Excuse me, what are those (inaudible; linguistic term)?" And you can imagine [the lecturer], she was absolutely horrified! And then she told him angrily, "Arrange private classes with Iveta!" So that was it. I have to thank her that I am good at English. That she . . . Maybe she doesn't even know how much she did for me.

While there is no doubt that these and similar accounts of past events capture Iveta's lived experiences, my field notes and research journal entries also document evidence of frequent tensions, contradictions, implausibility, and exaggeration that forced me to look beyond what Iveta was *saying* and try and understand what she was *doing* in her narratives (Holstein and Gubrium, 2008). Excerpt

5 illustrates this shift. It comes from the last interview in which I asked Iveta, sensing that teaching in her school was not something she had envisaged as her long-term career, what it was about her job that made her tick.

Excerpt 5: Iveta's interview reflection on what makes her tick

Iveta: It's this inner feeling that (2) I need to see it. The concrete outcome of my work.

Interviewer: And do you see it here, in teaching?

Iveta: Hmmm. (4) Difficult to say. Once I had that feeling when there was not much to do during the last classes of the school year with kids. And they said to me, "we're going to write what we think of you, would you like us to do that?" They said they'd done the same thing for their class teacher and they also wanted to do it for me. I said, "OK?" And they were like "but we're not gonna sign our names or anything" and I was like "OK?" Oh, can you imagine how I cried over those sheets of feedback! Like "Because of you I started to learn English." "Because of you I will study hard." And "I love you." Yes, you heard. "I love you."

I have no way of ascertaining whether the account she offers describes a past or as-yet-unrealised event and the shift in my analytical gaze does not ask of me to make this distinction. Instead, understanding that what Iveta is doing, be it in her classroom or in conversations with the researcher, is part of her engagement in *emerging acts of imagination* allows a significant conceptual, methodological, and ethical insight: These acts are not imaginary in the sense of fabricated, untrue, and therefore somehow unreliable; instead they give us glimpses into Iveta's imaginative accounts of her deeply desired future self as someone who is valued, appreciated, and loved. They may be as-yet-unrealised, but this does not mean they are separate from the here-and-now of Iveta's sense making; they are always embodied in it. And finally, and crucially, these acts of imagination have factual consequences for students' language learning opportunities. Iveta's data show that who gets to participate, when, and how may be linked more strongly to the teacher's goal to fulfil her deeply held desire to be appreciated than to the pedagogical goals of facilitating language learning opportunities in classroom discourse.

Conclusion: intellectual gains of studying possible selves as participation in practice

Locating the study of possible selves in practice through the participation metaphor offers a number of opportunities for studying HE contexts. First, taking an explicitly *discursive* approach helps us to reaffirm the power of the construct in aiding our understanding of people's actual investment in moment-to-moment practices in classrooms and communities. The empirical focus on one language educator's practice in this chapter has pointed to a significant role of educators' possible selves as emergent acts of imagination in shaping the patterns of students' participation in classroom interaction. Pursuing research on possible selves from this epistemological vantage point offers significant mileage for advancing broader educational agendas, such as widening participation, for it can shed light on how access to learning is enabled (or not) in the actual moment of educational action and what role educators' acts of imagination play in it.

Second, adopting an *ethnographic* lens to researching possible selves fosters a closer appreciation of connections between the psychological construct of possible selves and the sociological realities which place significant constraints on what individuals are able to envisage as possible. Iveta's desired image of herself as language educator did not appear in a vacuum, even if a full account of those realities was beyond the scope of this chapter (but see Kubanyiova, 2016). Indeed the models of practice in the wider educational and socio-political context that Iveta had been exposed to as a learner, a student teacher, and an educator offered limited alternatives to the images that fuelled her educational action. Acknowledging this is crucial. At the same time, however, the approach adopted in this study compels us to ponder ways in which Iveta's acts of imagination may have been constraining her own students' sense of what future images were available and to whom. Understanding the interface of psychological, sociological, and political dimensions of possible selves by adopting an ethnographic approach may therefore be a critical next step in advancing research on this construct.

And finally, pursuing the methodological and analytical principles of *grounded theory* has the capacity to open up the construct of possible selves to new theoretical insights. This study has shown that educators' possible selves may well have an inherent moral dimension; that is, they are likely to be inextricably linked with teachers' (and society's) broader values concerning the roles and tasks of language educators and education in general. A significant implication here is that if the desire to facilitate meaningful participation of students from marginalised backgrounds is not at the core of how educators envision themselves in their teaching worlds, they are unlikely to attune to and act upon such opportunities when they arise in the classroom and beyond. How teacher education programmes and wider cultural practices can foster educators' development of possible selves that are conducive to all students' learning remains central to ongoing research inquiry.

References

Asker, A. (2012) *Future Self-Guides and Language Learning Engagement of English-Major Secondary School Students in Libya: Understanding the Interplay between Possible Selves and the L2 Learning Situation.* Ph.D. thesis, University of Birmingham, Birmingham.

Baker, A. (2014) Exploring teachers' knowledge of second language pronunciation techniques: Teacher cognitions, observed classroom practices, and student perceptions. *TESOL Quarterly*, 48: 136–163.

Basturkmen, H. (2012) Review of research into the correspondence between language teachers' stated beliefs and practices. *System*, 40: 282–295.

Batstone, R. and Philp, J. (2013) Classroom interaction and learning opportunities across time and space. In K. McDonough and A. Mackey (eds) *Second language interaction in diverse educational contexts*, Philadelphia and Amsterdam: John Benjamins, pp. 109–125.

Borg, S. (2006) *Teacher cognition and language education: Research and practice*, London: Continuum.

Borg, S. (2012) Current approaches to language teacher cognition research: A methodological analysis. In R. Barnard and A. Burns (eds) *Researching language teacher cognition and practice: International case studies*, Bristol: Multilingual Matters, pp. 11–29.

Charmaz, K. (2006) *Constructing grounded theory: A practical guide through qualitative analysis*, London: Sage Publications.

Charmaz, K. and Mitchell, R. G. (2001) Grounded theory in ethnography. In P. Atkinson, A. Coffey, S. Delamont, J. Lofland and L. Lofland (eds) *Handbook of ethnography*, Los Angeles: Sage Publications, pp. 160–174.

Clarà, M. (2014) Understanding teacher knowledge from a cultural psychology approach. *Teaching and Teacher Education*, 43: 110–119.

Creese, A., Blackledge, A. and Takhi, J. K. (2014) The ideal 'native speaker' teacher: Negotiating authenticity and legitimacy in the language classroom. *The Modern Language Journal*, 98: 937–951.

David, M. (ed) (2010) *Improving learning by widening participation in higher education*, London and New York: Routledge.

Do, M. (in progress) *Imagining and Re-Imagining Oneself in a Study-Abroad Context: An Ethnography of Vision and Motivation in L2 Learning*. Ph.D. thesis, University of Birmingham, Birmingham.

Dörnyei, Z. and Kubanyiova, M. (2014) *Motivating learners, motivating teachers: Building vision in the language classroom*, Cambridge: Cambridge University Press.

Dörnyei, Z. and Ushioda, E. (eds) (2009) *Motivation, language identity and the L2 self*, Bristol: Multilingual Matters.

Gatbonton, E. (1999) Investigating experienced ESL teachers' pedagogical knowledge. *The Modern Language Journal*, 83: 35–50.

Hall, J. K. (2010) Interaction as method and result of language learning. *Language Teaching*, 43: 202–215.

Hall, J. K. and Walsh, M. (2002) Teacher-student interaction and language learning. *Annual Review of Applied Linguistics*, 22: 186–203.

Heritage, J. (2005) Cognition in discourse. In H. Te Molder and J. Potter (eds) *Conversation and cognition*, Cambridge: Cambridge University Press, pp. 184–202.

Holstein, J. A. and Gubrium, J. F. (2008) Constructionist impulses in ethnographic fieldwork. In J. A. Holstein and J. F. Gubrium (eds) *Handbook of constructionist research*, New York: Guilford Press, pp. 373–395.

Kasper, G. (2004) Participant orientations in German conversation-for-learning. *The Modern Language Journal*, 88: 551–567.

Kasper, G. (2006) Beyond repair: Conversation analysis as an approach to SLA. *AILA Review*, 19: 83–99.

Korthagen, F. A. (2001) *Linking practice and theory: The pedagogy of realistic teacher education*, Mahwah, NJ: Lawrence Erlbaum.

Kubanyiova, M. (2014) Motivating language teachers: Inspiring vision. In D. Lasagabaster, A. Doiz and J. M. Sierra (eds) *Motivation and Foreign language learning: From theory to practice*, Philadelphia and Amsterdam: John Benjamins, pp. 71–89.

Kubanyiova, M. (2015) The role of teachers' future self guides in creating L2 development opportunities in teacher-led classroom discourse: Reclaiming the relevance of language teacher cognition. *The Modern Language Journal*, 99: 565–584.

Kubanyiova, M. (2016) *Teacher development in action: Understanding language teachers' conceptual change*, Basingstoke, UK: Palgrave Macmillan.

Kubanyiova, M. and Crookes, G. (2016) Re-envisioning the roles, tasks, and contributions of language teachers in the multilingual era of language education research and practice. *The Modern Language Journal*, 100: 117–132.

Kubanyiova, M. and Feryok, A. (2015) Language teacher cognition in applied linguistics research: Revisiting the territory, redrawing the boundaries, reclaiming the relevance. *The Modern Language Journal*, 99: 435–449.

Markus, H. and Nurius, P. (1986) Possible selves. *American Psychologist*, 41: 954–969.

Nikoletou, P. (2017) *Understanding Students' Willingness to Communicate in L2 in the Higher Education Context in Greece: A Person-in-Context Relational Approach*. Ph.D. thesis, University of Birmingham, Birmingham.

Ogawa, H. (2017) A teacher's moral role in mobilizing students' motivation beyond L2 vision. *Apples: Journal of Applied Language Studies*, 11, 2: 5–23, http://apples.jyu.fi/article/abstract/519

Ogawa, H. (2018) *Investigating the Effect of Culture-Based Curriculum on Japanese College Students' L2 Vision as Intercultural Communicators*. Ph.D. thesis, University of Birmingham, Birmingham.

Ohta, A. S. (2001) *Second language acquisition processes in the classroom: Learning Japanese*, Mahwah, NJ: Lawrence Erlbaum.

Potter, J. (2012) How to study experience. *Discourse and Society*, 23: 576–588.

Sfard, A. (1998) On two metaphors for learning and the dangers of choosing just one. *Educational Researcher*, 27, 2: 4–13.

Sinclair, J. and Coulthard, M. (1975) *Towards an analysis of discourse*, Oxford: Oxford University Press.

Skott, J. (2015) The promises, problems, and prospects of research on teachers' beliefs. In H. Fives and M. Gregoire Gill (eds) *International handbook of research on teachers' beliefs*, New York: Routledge, pp. 13–30.

ten Have, P. (2007) *Doing conversation analysis: A practical guide* (2nd ed.), London: Sage Publications.

Toth, P. D. (2008) Teacher- and learner-led discourse in task-based grammar instruction: Providing procedural assistance for L2 morphosyntactic development. *Language Learning*, 58: 237–283.

Walberg, H. (1972) Decision and perception: New constructs in research on teaching effects. *Cambridge Journal of Education*, 7, 1: 12–20.

Walsh, S. (2006) *Investigating classroom discourse*, London: Routledge.

Waring, H. Z. (2008) Using explicit positive assessment in the language classroom: IRF, feedback, and learning opportunities. *The Modern Language Journal*, 92: 577–594.

Wells, G. (1993) Reevaluating the IRF sequence: A proposal for the articulation of theories of activity and discourse for the analysis of teaching and learning in the classroom. *Linguistics and Education*, 5: 1–37.

Yue, Z. (2014) Chinese university students' willingness to communicate in the L2 classroom: The complex and dynamic interplay of self-concept, future self-guides and the sociocultural context. In K. Csizér and M. Magid (eds) *The impact of self-concept on language learning*, Bristol, UK: Multilingual Matters, pp. 250–266.

Yue, Z. (2016) *Exploring Chinese University EFL Learners' L2 Willingness to Communicate in Action: Understanding the Interplay of Self-Concept, WTC and Sociocultural Context through the Lens of Complexity Theory*. Ph.D. thesis, University of Birmingham, Birmingham, UK.

Appendix

Transcription conventions

T	teacher
S1, S2	identified student
Ss	several students at once
xxx	unintelligible speech
<u>even if she's not here today</u>	utterance in Slovak (the teacher's and students' mother tongue)
.	falling intonation
?	rising intonation
!	exclamation
(.)	pause, less than a second
(3)	pause in seconds
(( ))	field notes, transcriber's comments
=	no gap between turns
YOU	especially loud and emphatic
Adrian, Pavol, Veronika	named students (pseudonyms)

Chapter 6

Shaping possible selves

The role of family in constructing higher education futures for students with dyslexia

Angela Murphy

Introduction

This chapter provides a new perspective on the shaping of possible selves, showing how they are highly influenced by familial contexts and temporalities. The research demonstrates the relationship between the past, present and future but also highlights that in order to make educational possible selves plausible, higher education providers should seek to understand the environmental complexities which enable or prevent educational possibilities. The study on which the chapter is based is a narrative inquiry of the possible selves of dyslexic healthcare students, and includes temporal reflections of experiences of growing up with dyslexia (a neurological condition affecting visual and auditory processing and influencing learning and the acquisition of literacy skills) from the perspectives of Master of Science (MSc) healthcare students in England.

MSc healthcare courses are specific post-graduate professional qualifications which provide students with relevant post-graduate degrees in order that they reach their possible selves of healthcare professionals (in this case) occupational therapists, physiotherapists and osteopaths. Access to these professions is also attainable from undergraduate courses in the United Kingdom but the students in this study have chosen to study at Master's level. Despite dyslexia making study harder (as well as other challenges discussed within the chapter), they have obtained all the relevant qualifications needed to obtain a place on these courses. The chapter explores the students' educational journeys from childhood to illuminate significant enabling factors and barriers in establishing their possible selves. By building upon the creativity allowed by narrative inquiry (Clandinin and Connelly, 2000), findings are presented using a form of performance ethnography, a way of communicating both the essence and spirit (Douglas and Carless, 2013) of the students' stories and of bringing the audience closer to the participants. This creates an interactive space and respects a pragmatic Deweyan ontology whereby experiences grow from experiences and everyday actions (Dewey and McDermott, 1973; Cutchin, 2004). The findings show that possible selves, previously understood as highly individualised, are in fact often shared or inherited within their initiation, perception and realisation (see Chapter 2 in this volume for a discussion of 'possible others').

The chapter first provides a brief explanation of the use of possible selves within this research, and it then explains what dyslexia is and some of the complexities of living with it, including the implications this may have on perceptions of possible selves and life trajectories. The chapter then presents data from the study using a performance ethnography approach in the form of a play script: Act 1, 'Shaping Possible Selves', which contains two scenes entitled: 'Well I don't Know Why You Can't Do It, 'cos You're My Daughter and You Can Do Anything' and 'Cheerleaders in the Background'. These are followed by a discursive analysis, which employs the conceptual lens of possible selves to provide a critical understanding of these students' experiences.

The concept of possible selves

Possible selves as a concept draws from representations of the self in the past and includes representations of the self in the future (Markus and Nurius, 1986). The concept builds upon and is a natural extension of the self-concept which is a system of affective-cognitive structures, referred to by Markus and Nurius (1986) as theories or schemas, of how one considers oneself. They are made salient by an individual's particular sociological, cultural and historical contexts, from images and representations provided by the media and immediate social experiences (Markus and Nurius, 1986). They have the potential to reveal the inventive and constructive nature of the self but also reflect the extent to which the self is socially determined and constrained (Markus and Nurius, 1986).

Possible selves play an important role in identity formation processes, with a strong relationship with identity exploration informed by social context, including past and anticipated experiences, influencing motivation and behaviour (Markus and Nurius, 1986; Oyserman, Destin and Novin, 2015). Often, they involve experimentation and employment of actions which elucidate and augment the likelihood of possible selves coming into fruition. An example of this lies within the combination of perceptions and actions involved in becoming anything a person aims to become (such as a health professional, a researcher or a student). It is through the elaboration of details related to the future possible self, such as engaging in the actions of research, that becoming the aimed-for self comes to be a meaningful and salient element of an individual's future identity and self (Dunkel and Anthis, 2001). The previous work of authors such as Daphna Oyserman and her colleagues show that the road map, path and context are as important as the destination if possible selves are to be realised (Oyserman et al., 2004; Oyserman, Johnson and James, 2010; Oyserman, Destin and Novin, 2015). This means that what people do on an everyday basis to become the possible selves they wish to become is fundamental.

In the study reported in this chapter, in order to become a health professional one has to engage in many behaviours and actions in order to gain a place on an appropriate course (for example, work hard and study). The motivation gained from the aspirational possible self is known to be important in that it influences the necessary everyday actions required to stay on and maintain the right path and avoid alternative routes which may lead to undesired possible selves. The research builds upon the assertion that the road map and path taken are vital but extends this beyond individual decision-making and effort, and demonstrates the importance, relevance and dependence on families and the instrumental influence they have on the ability to perceive and reach desirable educational possible selves.

Dyslexia, educational experience and studying in higher education

Dyslexia occurs in people of all races, backgrounds and abilities, and varies from person to person. It is independent of intelligence and can affect learning, the acquisition of literacy skills, processing of visual and auditory information and skills such as organisation and planning (British Dyslexia Association, nd; Stampoltzis et al., 2015). As a neurological medical condition it varies in its presentation and each individual will experience it differently as both weaknesses and strengths. It is said to be the most commonly declared disability internationally within higher education and it is known to present students with invisible difficulties which require different types of reasonable accommodations (Stampoltzis et al., 2015). Although people with dyslexia continue to be under-represented, there are growing numbers of students with dyslexia now studying in higher education in the United Kingdom (Beauchamp-Pryor, 2013) and many examples of people with dyslexia who achieve academically (Archer, 2003; McNulty, 2003; Collinson and Penkreth, 2010).

Certainty of prevalence of dyslexia is nebulous as routine screening does not take place and there are arguments surrounding it with quite distinct differences of opinion about the ways in which dyslexia should be categorised and therefore responded to. Research by advocates of a more holistic approach based on the social model of disability (MacDonald, 2006; Riddick, 2011; MacDonald, 2009a; MacDonald, 2009b) argue that restrictions experienced by people with dyslexia, however defined, are created by social environments which highly value literacy skills: "Hence dyslexia is both a social construct and a medical condition" (MacDonald, 2009b, p. 273).

Families can be significant influences on the development of possible selves for people with dyslexia. This may in part be due to shared dyslexic tendencies. Correlations are significantly higher between dyslexic parents and dyslexic children, indicating a strong inheritability which is seen to be even higher in children when both parents have dyslexia, with likelihood rising from 57% to 76% (Leavett, Nash and Snowling, 2014). In relation to parental self-report of dyslexia and links to children with it, the findings of Leavett, Nash and Snowling (2014) showed that parents who are less likely to recognise dyslexic tendencies within themselves are also less likely to identify the tendencies within their children. Given that dyslexia is inheritable, the inter-generational experience could (they claim) lead to cycles of educational disadvantage and inhibit social mobility. Furthermore, if parents have difficulties themselves with literacy skills, they may find it harder to support their child as problems and difficulties arise with school work (Bonifacci et al., 2013). Nevertheless, some researchers have identified a positive relationship between self-esteem and family relationships in people with dyslexia (Daderman, Nilvang and Levander, 2014; Stampoltzis and Polychronopoulou, 2009), suggesting that family rather than teachers and peers may play an important part in developing and maintaining self-esteem and positive self-image.

Despite arguments in favour of early screening and diagnosis (Department of Children Schools and Families, 2009a, 2009b), this does not routinely take place and many people reach adulthood and even higher education without diagnosis. Once in higher education, research has found that university tutors do not understand enough about how to teach students with dyslexia (Matthews, 2009), and there is a high rate of attrition amongst dyslexic students (Stampoltzis et al., 2015). It could therefore be argued that many people with dyslexia may find it difficult to perceive and reach future desired possible selves in higher education when opportunities, attitudes to assessment and pedagogical understanding are confused and present barriers.

More recently, there has been a reported increase in provision and support in accessing higher education with legislative changes to prevent discrimination and provide equality of access (Pino and Mortari, 2014) in some countries. In the United Kingdom, the Disability Discrimination Act (1995) and the Equality Act (2010) have imposed a legal obligation to reduce barriers and implement academic reasonable adjustments. However, without routine screening within school education, access to higher education remains problematic for those who disengage at school due to misunderstandings, confused pedagogical approaches and patchy provision. Furthermore, despite legislative changes, society positions people with dyslexia at the centre of conflicting discourses where they sink or swim depending upon the environment (Cameron and Billington, 2015; Riddell and Weeden, 2014). Cameron (2016) has suggested students in higher education may hide their dyslexia, or take pride in it, or feel ashamed of it (particularly if it implies they require help). Often this depends on how they judge dyslexia to be perceived in the setting and whether they consider discrimination is likely to take place (Dearnley et al., 2010).

The implications of not addressing diagnosis of dyslexia and having inconsistent non-inclusive approaches within education are many. There are potentially significant difficulties for people with dyslexia imposed by society which may act as barriers to perceiving and reaching potential possible selves. For possible selves can only include the selves which are possible to conceive of, and past academic experiences and psychological wellbeing affect views of what is possible (Stevenson and Clegg, 2011).

Methodology

As a research tool, the concept of possible selves, with its emphasis on temporality, provides a lens through which to view the experiences of growing up and studying in higher education with dyslexia. In the following sections possible selves is used to investigate the experience of students with dyslexia following a Master's programme at one university in England. Twenty-four semi-structured interviews were carried out over the course of one year with nine dyslexic healthcare students. The concept of possible selves informed the study design and analysis throughout. Interviews were transcribed and significant narrative plots were organised into acts and scenes of a play, drawing upon methods of performance narrative and performance ethnography (Denzin, 2003; Atkinson, 2004; Carless and Douglas, 2010; Douglas and Carless, 2013).

In the next section, data are presented in the form of one act from a play script. Readers are requested to imagine a performance whereby a light is shone on the participants, who are sitting in a row upon a stage. The font chosen has been used deliberately to emphasise the representation of the data in this way. The act is in two scenes, both of which highlight the importance of family. Scene 1, 'Well I Don't Know Why You Can't Do It, 'cos You're My Daughter and You Can Do Anything', focuses on parents, and Scene 2, 'Cheerleaders in the Background', focuses on siblings.

Act 1: shaping possible selves

Scene 1: 'Well I Don't Know Why You Can't Do It, 'cos You're My Daughter and You Can Do Anything'

Characters in order of appearance:

Narrator, Jessica, Maria and Abigail.

Narrator: Welcome to this Scene. Jessica, Maria and Abigail are going to reflect upon their experiences of growing up with dyslexia. We will begin with Jessica who was diagnosed in the final year of her undergraduate degree.

Jessica: They (parents) always said, "Oh you do have to push yourself harder than Gemma". So, I thought I just wasn't academically clever but they would always try to help and treat us equally but they would say, "You need to work harder than Gemma, she's naturally a little bit more, clever I suppose" (laughs). They never said it in that way, (laughing). They never told me what the teacher said until a few years ago.

In year 6 there was one teacher . . . who said something to my mum and dad. . . . They said, "Oh she's not going to get to university, she's not the cleverest child", things like that.

	Luckily my mum and dad, they never told me that, they kept it from me. My mum only told me that a year ago? Two years ago? Which was quite good. So, they kept that from me. But they had said that to her and yeah, my mum was quite upset, . . . I have got it. That happened.
Narrator:	It must have been confusing for Jessica's parents to know and understand what was possible for Jessica to achieve at school, particularly as she did not have a diagnosis. They carried on encouraging her to work hard and protected her from what the school teacher had said but I wonder if it influenced their shared perceptions of what was possible. Let's hear more from her.
Jessica:	It was just something that was almost expected. I wouldn't go on to those colleges that do 'A' levels . . . university was never in my . . . at that time I didn't want to go to university and didn't expect I'd ever go to university and thought, "I'll go straight in and do something I can get a job for" and do something I enjoyed. So, I never had the expectation myself. It just wasn't the expectation that I'd go to university. So, I always just thought because I was a much more hands on learner, I thought, "at college I'll go and do hairdressing, beauty or childcare", you know one of those. I got alright grades (GCSE's) and I think because I did that, I was sort of alright.

I don't know why just (pause) one day I just thought, "God I won't be able to write on a white board or a black board". You know . . . if we are doing literacy, what if I spell something wrong? If I get to a word like 'availability' I cannot spell it for the life of me I would have to check a dictionary, the teaching assistant might think I'm stupid. There's probably ways around it but for that profession I just felt like I wouldn't, it wasn't right for me then. |
| *Narrator:* | Jessica gained 10 GCSE's, yet she had no expectation to go to university or do A levels (often a pre-cursor to a university degree) and despite a possible self as a teacher she believed this was beyond reach. Let's hear from Maria, who gained a diagnosis of dyslexia age 11. |

Maria: My mum had always, she like, no one in our family had been to university and my mum . . . she was a single parent and she was a cleaner when I was younger so she was very much, "You are going to university! There is no other option". I always used to think, "Well I will go to university". There was no question of it. I guess it must have come from my mum really. . . . Well I could probably be a physicist (laughs) totally unrealistic expectations probably driven by my mum, saying I was going to work for NASA or something. She still says it to this day. I'm like, "Mum, you do realize I'm not going to work for NASA!" She says things like, "Well I don't know why you can't do it, 'cos you're my daughter and you can do anything". I think my mum thought I was some sort of genius. (Laughs). She had and still does have extremely high expectations of me that are just unrealistic.

Narrator: "You can do anything" is a strong thread in Maria's narrative which clearly came from her mother's positive attitude towards her abilities. Once Maria was diagnosed in first the year of high school she was moved to top sets for most subjects as she had good support from school to achieve her potential. Let's hear from Abigail who was diagnosed age 16.

Abigail: Both my parents were teachers, they really wanted me to be a teacher. I don't know if it was because of my skill set or because I always played teachers, but they really wanted me to be a teacher. Me and my mum had a really deep chat and she told me she felt really guilty that my sister Rachel was probably dyslexic but no one ever knew. She hated school and got in with the wrong crowd and had children very young.

She feels she failed a little bit with my sisters because she hasn't given them the confidence to go and do what they want. She says she's confident with me that what I want I'll just go and get it.

Scene 2: 'Cheerleaders in the Background'

Characters in order of appearance:

Anne, Narrator and Jo.

Anne: I don't know, me and my sisters used to joke 'cos like one of my sisters Hollie, she was really good at mathematics. . . . She wanted to be an accountant from day one whereas I was like, "Oomph, why do you want to be one of them?" (Laughs). They used to say, "You'll be the one in a council house, not in a proper job 'cos you don't want one and we'll be the ones earning the money".

If I had to do everything myself, I'd have given up but having such a good family gives you cheerleaders in the back sort of thing. So, when you've always got someone in the background behind you like my sisters, when I failed H.O.B. my sister said, "Send me it" and said, "Send me the marking criteria" and when she had a look at it she said, "Anne you've not mentioned that and what about that? Why haven't you mentioned that?" So constructively telling me what to do. "You've not done it right you know. We'll do it together. We'll sit down together and do it and I'll tell you if you are hitting the points on the marking criteria".

So, in some ways you know they give me that extra push of "Come on you can do this, we'll do it". Whereas if I didn't have that I'd have stopped ages ago. So, I think it is vital that you have people behind me. That's why I think I can carry on because they'll be like, "Oh have you not, well we're ready, what's wrong?" Even if they can't do it themselves I know they are with me and that's sometimes the main thing you need because without them you think 'cos when it's only yourself you don't have that much self-belief 'cos you question whether your self-belief is right or whether you're doing the right thing and they say "No, no, come on". It gives you a boost and that's where the boost comes from. I do want to carry on 'cos I think I would have stopped even undergraduate if I didn't have that push of people telling me "Oh go on, you can do it".

Narrator: Anne speaks interchangeably of the past and present interactions with her sisters. She received encouragement and practical support as an adult

Jo: but also teasing and suggestions that she would be poor and live in social housing when they were children. Jo's sisters were also influential. Let's hear what she experienced.

Jo: My middle sister is very academic and very logical. (Laughs) She's training to be a surgeon. So, she's one of those people who make a lot of sense. And then that was quite challenging because I always looked up to my sisters and she was the middle sister and I was like, well, I always compared myself to her and I wanted to be like her, but, but, I'm not like that. How do I get around that? 'Cos, I'm not that person.

Narrator: This brings us to the end of Act 1 Scene 2.

The role of family in shaping possible selves

That possible selves are not experienced in isolation by individuals is made clear in both scenes presented above. The familial roles involve protection, guidance, encouragement and support, helping the participants to negotiate and stay on the paths they hope to take in order to become who they wish to become. Inherent within the narratives are many types of strategies which are employed by parents to enable hopes and desires to be realised. Often ideas began with the parents' own perceptions of what may be possible.

Some participants and their families set their aspirations and expectations on roles the participants perceived to be beyond reach. Examples of this are in Jessica's desired possible self to become a teacher, perceived eventually to be beyond reach, and Maria's mother's aspirational possible self for Maria to work for NASA. In these examples, road maps (Oyserman et al., 2004) were put in place to so that perceived possible selves might one day come to fruition. These road maps were dependent upon familial implementation of agency, whereby some control was aimed for and often gained in relation to the aspirational possible selves parents envisioned for their children. However, there is ambiguity about some of the perceived destinations (Oyserman, Johnson and James, 2010) and the distance of the path to attain these possible selves could be judged too far and rejected by the individual (Wainwright, Nee and Vrij, 2016). This is particularly evident in the narratives of Jessica and Maria, who have both achieved possible selves as occupational therapists, rather than the proposed possible selves of teacher and scientist for NASA.

Parents are particularly motivated by hopes of avoiding negative consequences and of parental feared possible selves (Zhu et al., 2014). There are examples of parents withholding information from the participants while enacting agency to counteract negative events and consequences as well as maintaining a sense of hope and faith in the participants. Protection and efforts to guard their self-esteem and confidence with encouragement to persevere and maintain resilience is inherent. This is essential as confidence and self-esteem are often challenged during adolescence, having negative implications on perceptions of possible selves (Knox et al., 1998) but these constructs may be at greater risk due to dyslexia (Glazzard, 2010) and more so for those who experienced negative feedback or events at school (see Murphy, 2017).

Often, when there is confusion over which paths and destinations are perceived to be open and closed, many students see little point in persisting with academic work (Destin and Oyserman, 2009). This concept is challenged by all the participants in this research, particularly the students who assumed university was not for them. Confusion surrounding which paths are accessible is understandable when dealing with unknown difficulties. In the cases of those with no childhood diagnosis (Jessica, Jo, Anne) this is particularly complicated by the lack of understanding surrounding dyslexia. Dyslexia is often unrecognised and undiagnosed and families are relied upon to counteract the effects of learning environments which cater more to and highly value strong literacy skills. However, if a child has difficulty processing, retaining information, organising and planning tasks (also symptoms of dyslexia) these factors will also have an effect upon learning but may not be ascribed to dyslexic tendencies. Discrimination or learned helplessness (see Elliott, 2005) prevails whether diagnosis is in place or not as judgements relating to intelligence are made upon literacy and numeracy skills and most subjects rely on these to communicate knowledge. This has significant implications for developing perceptions for future possible selves, confusing the idiosyncrasies surrounding future possibilities and individual potential.

For the participants in this study an important point here is that they all remained engaged in school and this is largely due to familial intervention and shared employment of agency, although some prospective paths were mistakenly initially assumed closed. In the comparison made by Abigail's mother between her daughters' life paths it is apparent that in this case, Abigail's family began to realise dyslexia was possibly part of the wider family narrative once diagnosis took place for Abigail at age 16. Similarly, all the participants spoke of other family members with possible undiagnosed dyslexia; siblings, parents and grandparents (see Murphy, 2017). It is evident here confusion and lack of diagnosis have the potential to have a significant impact on life paths and destinations but also that Abigail's parents employed greater agency with Abigail's education than they were able to with her sister and their resultant life trajectories are very different.

The general lack of understanding surrounding dyslexia and its impact on life paths makes the nuanced approaches applied by some of the families all the more important. In some cases, it is apparent that this support continues into adulthood. Nalavany, Carawan and Bauber (2015) found family support into adulthood made a significant difference with self-esteem and confidence of people with dyslexia. Unfortunately, however, while most of the participants in this study could be considered to be fortunate to benefit from ongoing support, this also demonstrates a dependence upon their families beyond what would be expected as young and even mature adults.

It is already understood that families often have ideas of possible selves to be avoided which work to motivate and mobilise individuals and resources against unwanted futures such as parental divorce (Karagiannopoulou and Hallam, 2003) as well as general feared possible selves (Markus and Nurius, 1986). What is evident in these student narratives however is that tangible familial countervailing influences such as types of employment judged to be unsuitable, early parenthood or mental health problems work to motivate them and their families towards more desirable future selves. Although the family countervailing possible selves work successfully to motivate the participants, there is also evidence that in some cases they place pressure (Carroll, 2014) on them in their choice of life paths to succeed in areas found difficult or challenging as a result of their dyslexia. Knowing which destinations to aim for with parental aspirations is also shown to be a challenge.

For some participants, particularly Anne and Jo who are the youngest of three sisters, the narrative strongly communicates the protection and support they experience from their relationships with their siblings. The effect this has on possible selves (Markus and Nurius, 1986) is also clear and is epitomised by Anne's comment about giving up if she did not have their support. The narratives also highlight the importance of sibling relationships and emphasise that older siblings take on added caring and agentic responsibilities due to the dynamics of the relationship. This demonstrates how the sibling relationship is an important influence on the behavioural and social development of children (Fussell, Macias and Saylor, 2005) and therefore on the development of perceptions and the likelihood of reaching possible selves.

Within family contexts, some parents and siblings are role models, allowing the participants to experiment with provisional selves (Ibarra, 1999) often via vicarious learning (Wainwright, Nee and Vrij, 2016). The participants begin to experiment and learn skills and characteristics they aspire towards using in the future. They are able to mimic "trying on possible selves" (Burack et al., 1997, p. 534). This is a complex process which provides the participants with paradoxical situations of establishing which roles and identities to aspire towards but also which roles and paths are feasible when evaluated against internal and external feedback (Ibarra, 1999). Strategies not aligned with self and identity are rejected for those which are more congruent. This is epitomised within Jo's statement, "I'm not that person": having aspired to be like her sisters and in finding that neither of her sisters' identities fitted her own, she established a position for herself between two paradigms of medicine and the arts and according to her own skills, characteristics and abilities. Restrictions in identity can limit how someone perceives their sense of self and how they manage their social identity (Laliberte Rudman, 2002) and this is again shown by Jo whose academic aspirations grew following diagnosis (see Murphy, 2017).

Conclusion

The above narratives demonstrate an important development of the possible selves concept, to account for the role played by family in both the construction and the achievement of possible selves in higher education. For some participants, an imagined future in higher education was a shared familial narrative, experienced at times as pressure and impossibility, and negotiated over the course of their educational trajectories. For others, the narrative of a higher education future was heavily intertwined with the observed experiences and imagined futures of siblings. Each sibling's individual educational journey further positioned them in the shifting collective family narrative of participation in higher education. Using the possible selves concept to look at collective narratives of educational futures therefore acknowledges the complexities of family dynamics, as well as the powerful impact of familial belief and support on participation and success in higher education.

This use of possible selves also works to resist discourses of individualisation and deficit, particularly in the context of disability. As the above analysis shows, dyslexic students in higher education experience inequalities of access to and within higher education, caused by delays in diagnosis and ineffective teaching practices, amongst other factors. In the context of these inequalities, family narratives of possible selves become a crucial resource, often making up for or acting in response to structural barriers in higher education systems. While emphasising the role played by family in sustaining and supporting the possibility of higher education for some dyslexic students, this chapter also highlights family resource as a further educational inequality. For students without 'cheerleaders in the background', this chapter suggests, futures in higher education might be impossible.

References

Archer, M. (2003) *Structure, agency and the internal conversation*, Cambridge: Cambridge University Press.

Atkinson, P. (2004) Review essay. *British Journal of Sociology of Education*, 25, 1: 107–114. doi:10.1080/0142569032000155980

Beauchamp-Pryor, K. (2013) *Disabled students in Welsh higher education: A framework for equality and inclusion*, Rotterdam: Sense Publications.

Bonifacci, P., Montushi, M., Lami, L. and Snowling, M. (2013) Parents of children with dyslexia: Cognitive, emotional and behavioural profile. *Dyslexia*, 20: 175–190.

Burack, J., Irby, D., Carline, J., Ambrozy, D., Ellsbury, K. and Stritter, F. (1997) A study of medical students' speciality choice pathways: Trying on possible selves. *Academic Medicine*, 72, 6: 534–541.

Cameron, H. (2016) Beyond cognitive deficit: The everyday lived experience of dyslexic students at university. *Disability and Society*, 31, 2: 223–239.

Cameron, H. and Billington, T. (2015) 'Just deal with it': Neoliberalism in dyslexia students' talk about dyslexia and learning at university. *Studies in Higher Education*: 1–15.

Carless, D. and Douglas, K. (2010) Performance ethnography as an approach to health-related education. *Educational Action Research*, 18, 3: 373–388.

Carroll, P. (2014) Upward self-revision: Constructing possible selves. *Basic and Applied Social Psychology*, 36: 377–385.

Clandinin, J. and Connelly, M. (2000) *Narrative inquiry: Experience and story in qualitative research*, San Francisco: Jossey-Bass.

Collinson, C. and Penkreth, C. (2010) 'Sit in the corner and don't eat the crayons': Postgraduates with dyslexia and the dominant 'lexic' discourse. *Disability and Society*, 25, 1: 7–19.

Cutchin, M. (2004) Using Deweyan philosophy to rename and reframe adaptation-to-environment. *American Journal of Occupational Therapy*, 58: 303–312.

Daderman, A., Nilvang, K. and Levander, S. (2014) 'I dislike my body, but my parents are not disappointed in me': Self-esteem in young women with dyslexia. *Applied Psychological Research Journal*, 1: 50–58.

Dearnley, C., Elliott, J., Hargreaves, J., Morris, S., Walker, L., Walker, S. and Arnold, C. (2010) Disabled people effective practitioners: Enabling a healthcare work force which reflects society. *The International Journal of Inter-Disciplinary Social Sciences*, 5, 8: 259–274.

Denzin, N. (2003) *Performance ethnography, critical pedagogy and the politics of culture*, London: Sage Publications.

Department of Children Schools and Families (2009a) Identifying and teaching children and young people with dyslexia and literacy difficulties: An independent report from sir Jim Rose to the Secretary of State for Children, Schools and Families. *Crown Copyright*, www.interventionsforliteracy.org.uk/assets/Uploads/The-Rose-Report-June-2009.pdf

Department of Children Schools and Families (2009b) Lamb inquiry: Special educational needs and parental confidence. *Crown Copyright*, www.dcsf.gov.uk/Lambinquiry

Destin, M. and Oyserman, D. (2009) From assets to school outcomes: How finances shape children's perceived possibilities and intentions. *Psychological Science*, 20, 4: 414–419.

Dewey, J. and McDermott, J. (1973) *The philosophy of John Dewey: Two volumes in one*, Chicago: University of Chicago Press.

Douglas, K. and Carless, D. (2013) An invitation to performative research. *Methodological Innovations Online*, 8, 1: 53–64.

Dunkel, C. and Anthis, K. (2001) The role of possible selves in identity formation: A short term longitudinal study. *Journal of Adolescence*, 24: 765–776.

Elliott, J. (2005) The dyslexia debate continues: Response. *The Psychologist*, 18, 12: 728–729.

Fussell, M., Macias, M. and Saylor, C. (2005) Social skills and behaviour problems in children with disabilities with and without siblings. *Child Psychiatry and Human Development*, 36, 2: 227–241.

Glazzard, J. (2010) The impact of dyslexia on pupil's self-esteem. *Support for Learning*, 25, 2: 63–69.

Ibarra, H. (1999) Provisional selves: Experimenting with image and identity in professional adaptation. *Administrative Science Quarterly*, 44: 64–791.

Karagiannopoulou, E. and Hallam, S. (2003) Young adults from divorced and intact families: Possible selves relating to future family life. *International Journal of Adolescence and Youth*, 11: 91–111.

Knox, M., Funk, J., Elliott, R. and Greene Bush, E. (1998) Adolescents' possible selves and their relationship to global self-esteem. *Sex Roles*, 39, 112: 61–80.

Laliberte Rudman, D. (2002) Linking occupation and identity: Lessons learned through qualitative exploration. *Journal of Occupational Science*, 9, 1: 12–19.

Leavett, R., Nash, N. and Snowling, M. (2014) Am I dyslexic? Parental self-report of literacy difficulties. *Dyslexia*, 20: 297–304.

MacDonald, S. (2006) *Hidden Biographies: Dyslexia, Disability and Social Class*. A thesis, Submitted for the Degree of Doctor of Philosophy in the School of Geography, Politics and Sociology University of Newcastle upon Tyne.

MacDonald, S. (2009a) Windows of reflection from adults with dyslexia: Conceptualising dyslexia using the social model of disability. *Dyslexia: An International Journal of Research and Practice*, 15, 4: 347–362.

MacDonald, S. (2009b) Towards a social reality of dyslexia. *British Journal of Learning Disabilities*, 38: 271–279.

Markus, H. and Nurius, P. (1986) Possible selves. *American Psychologist*, 41, 9: 954–969.

Matthews, N. (2009) Teaching the invisible disabled students in the classroom: Disclosure, inclusion and the social model of disability. *Teaching in Higher Education*, 14, 3: 229–239.

McNulty, M. (2003) Dyslexia and the life course. *Journal of Learning Disabilities*, 36, 4: 363–381.

Murphy, A. (2017) *Possible Selves and Occupational Potential of Healthcare Students with Dyslexia*. Unpublished thesis, Leeds Beckett University.

Nalavany, B., Carawan, L. and Bauber, S. (2015) Adults with dyslexia, an invisible disability: The mediational role of concealment on perceived family support and self esteem. *British Journal of Social Work*, 45: 68–586.

Oyserman, D., Bybee, D., Terry, K. and Hart Johnson, T. (2004) Possible selves as road maps. *Journal of Research in Personality*, 38: 130–149.

Oyserman, D., Destin, M. and Novin, S. (2015) The context sensitive future self: Possible selves motivate in context, not otherwise. *Self and Identity*, 14, 2: 173–188.

Oyserman, D., Johnson, E. and James, L. (2010) Seeing the destination but not the path: Effects of socioeconomic disadvantage on school focused possible self-content and linked behavioural strategies. *Self and Identity*. 1–19.

Pino, M. and Mortari, L. (2014) The inclusion of students with dyslexia in higher education: A systematic review using narrative synthesis. *Dyslexia*, 20: 346–369.

Riddell, S. and Weeden, E. (2014) Disabled students in higher education: Discourses of disability and the negotiation of identity. *International Journal of Educational Research*, 63: 38–46.

Riddick, B. (2011) Dyslexia and Inclusion: Time for a social model of disability perspective? *International Studies in Sociology of Education*, 11, 3: 223–236.

Stampoltzis, A. and Polychronopoulou, S. (2009) Greek University students with dyslexia: An interview study. *European Journal of Special Needs Education*, 24, 3: 307–321.

Stampoltzis, A., Tsitsou, E., Plesti, H. and Kalouri, R. (2015) The learning experience of students with dyslexia in a Greek higher education Institution. *International Journal of Special Education*, 30, 2: 157–170.

Stevenson, J. and Clegg, S. (2011) Possible selves: Students orientating themselves towards the future through extracurricular activity. *British Educational Research Journal*, 37, 2: 231–246.

Wainwright, L., Nee, C. and Vrij, A. (2016) 'I don't know how, but I'll figure it out somehow': Future possible selves and aspirations in 'at risk' early adolescents. *International Journal of Offender Therapy and Comparative Criminology.* 1–20.

Zhu, S., Tse, S., Cheung, S. and Oyserman, D. (2014) Will I get there? Effects of parental support on children's possible selves. *British Journal of Educational Psychology.* 1–19.

Chapter 7

Unintended imaginings
The difficult dimensions of possible selves

Matt Lumb

Introduction

Drawing from diverse theoretical perspectives and traversing two methodologically different stages of a study, this chapter seeks to contribute a 'cautionary tale' to the field of equity and widening participation (WP). Specifically, the chapter explores the unintended consequences of a university outreach programme of mentoring and associated research activity informed by, among other theoretical foundations, the concept of *possible selves*. Positioned as a practitioner-researcher, I present this work as 'close up' (Clegg, Stevenson, and Burke, 2016) to an ongoing investigation that is developing new modes of personal practice via increasingly complex understandings of – and sensitivities to – the layers of inequality operating within the field.

A purpose of this chapter is to share the different understandings of practice that developed across two methodologically dissimilar stages of a research-informed practice project. In the first stage of investigation, the psychological possible selves model was synthesised with a sociological framework to analyse the future-orientated narratives of high school students who were part of the mentoring programme. In the second stage, these analyses were revisited via a participatory methodology to deconstruct some of the difficult dimensions of the programme, and of the conceptual framework deployed. A second and related purpose of this chapter is to raise the ever-present spectre of symbolic violence that pervades the ethically fraught (Stevenson and Leconte, 2009; Burke and Hayton, 2011) field of equity and WP. In fact, it is my contention that elements of the programme of research-informed practice from which this study draws have unwittingly wreaked symbolic forms of violence on stakeholders of my practices, which is a primary motivation for my own advocacy on the importance of 'close-up' praxis-based forms of practice (Freire, 1972).

Crick (2016) uses Picasso's 1937 painting *Guernica*[1] as a think piece in a recent book review.[2] In Crick's eyes, the painting reflects Arnett's interpretation of Arendt's concept of 'dark times' in its complication of the simplistic historical binary of darkness as equated with 'evil' and lightness equated with 'good'. This complication is a theorisation of the difference between 'artificial light' from modernity (which floods the environment with the cheerful optimism of progress to conceal the human condition and inhibit authentic communication) and 'genuine light' from 'lamp holders' (who realise that humanity can only shine against the backdrop of darkness, and understand the importance of human frailty and limitation).

This analogy connects with my own sense of conflict in terms of the moral dimensions of a research-informed practice project investigated in this chapter. For a time, I uncritically steered a project that hurled the imaginations of young people into an uncertain future against an unacknowledged backdrop of a neoliberal 'war waged by the financial and political elite against youth, low-income groups, the elderly, poor minorities of colour, the unemployed, immigrants and others now considered disposable' (Giroux, 2014). Having developed more optimistically critical perspectives, I now advocate for a critical praxis (Freire, 1972) that attempts to bring 'genuine light' to critical reflection and critical action *with* stakeholders of my practices rather than simply imposing programme logics or 'theories of change' *on* fellow community members. The chapter therefore sets out the multiple contexts from which this criticality emerged, before explaining the different theoretical foundations, methodologies, and methods that comprised the two stages of the study. Following this, theoretical and methodological commitments from stage two of the study help to unpick some of the problematic assumptions of the conceptual basis of the investigation, identifying in particular how students were interpreting the programme and research interventions as demands for performances of *valuation*. A section on the 'wickedness' of the future, and the difficult dimensions of projected selves and futures, highlights the ethical dilemmas of the field. I conclude by theorising the possibility of a 'dark hope' generated in times of despair and nurtured when 'genuine light' guides approaches to research and to practice, which builds on an observation made by Virginia Woolf:

> The future is dark, which is the best thing the future can be, I think.
> Virginia Woolf, 18 January 1915 (Solnit, 2014)

Multiple contexts of the chapter

A key purpose of this chapter is to explore how contextual forces shape sensibilities of the possible. It is therefore important to contextualise the emergence of this chapter, and to locate myself so that the reader gains some access to my perspectives on the research-informed practice foundations of the work. Discussed in this section of the chapter are the policy, the personal, and the programmatic contexts of the work – the last of which leads to a contextualisation of the psychological and sociological theories guiding practice and research over the two stages of the study.

The policy context relates to my positioning within the structures of an Australian university, and specifically in connection with a programme of practice funded by national policy focused on the in/equity of access to higher education in Australia. WP has emerged as a policy concern in numerous national contexts (Burke, 2017) and, while the Australian higher education sector has a long history of equity-oriented policies (Gale and Parker, 2013), a significant and ongoing federal government investment commenced following the Bradley Review[3] in 2008 via the establishment in 2010 of HEPPP, the Higher Education Participation and Partnerships Program. A growing demand for evidence of the 'effectiveness' of this policy has driven much debate around the local, regional, and national efforts to research and evaluate the practices taken up by universities across the country. Comprehensive and rigorous reviews of initiatives across the student lifecycle have been conducted including the *Equity Initiatives Framework* (Bennett et al., 2015) that presents an appraisal of the evidence of impact. In addition, a recent evaluation of the HEPPP conducted by Acil Allen Consulting (2017) simultaneously praised the programme while calling for a more coherent national framework for the production of evidence of efficacy. The importance and difficulty of evaluating WP policy and funding structures cannot be underestimated. Harrison and Waller (2017) have identified increasing research and policy interest in higher education participation across parts of the globe, with a particular focus on determining the effectiveness of initiatives, often by measuring the easily measurable. Harrison (2012) argues that statistics (admissions data) used to evaluate the success of Aimhigher, a well-funded UK outreach initiative, were something over which Aimhigher had no control. Harrison claims that this slippage undermined political support for the initiative and contributed to its demise. Clearly, the consequences of poorly conceived evaluation of policy and practice can be serious.

Sociologists of education have demonstrated the ways in which those who occupy privileged social positions are able to leverage their capitals and networks to 'game' schooling and higher education systems, thereby perpetuating privilege (Whitty, Hayton, and Tang, 2016; see also Chapter 8 in this volume). WP establishes a moral minefield, where the broader 'game' outlined above goes largely unacknowledged, and where practitioners are positioned to *target* fellow community members using notions of *low*-ness (usually *low* socioeconomic status). The aspiration for, access to, and participation and success in and beyond higher education for different groups is a matter of growing research (Whitty, Hayton, and Tang, 2015), and Burke (2012) has critiqued the largely *atheoretical* nature of much WP practice, research, and evaluation. This study emerged from this WP minefield, as the author and a group of university students conducted a mentoring programme with local school communities. In doing so, the group identified the possible selves concept (Markus and Nurius, 1986) as a tool as they navigated what became a complex journey of research-informed practice.

Markus and Nurius (1986) developed the idea of possible selves in the field of cognitive psychology to connect the imagined future self with present behaviours. In their view, possible selves are manifestations of enduring goals, aspirations, motives, fears, and threats and include not only desired possible selves (selves we hope we can become) but also feared possible selves (selves we are afraid we will become). Largely, the model has been used in the US context with broad applications including in education, often attempting to explain and predict educational motivation. Closer to the field of this investigation, Stevenson and Clegg (2011) have explored more socially constructed university student orientations towards the futures through extracurricular activity using the possible selves construct. Stevenson and Clegg identify three different orientations towards the future in their investigations: time future, time present, and the past and future in the present.

The mentoring programme in question here emerged from conversations with educators in five public high schools in Newcastle and the Hunter Valley region which *can* be described as having 'low socioeconomic status', where perceived issues of 'engagement' in the middle years of high schooling were a concern in terms of ongoing educational participation. It was in discussion with these educators that the programme developed and it was in concert with structural pressures to evaluate programmes in particular ways that the first stage of the study arose.

A dimension of this programmatic context relates to being a WP outreach practitioner, first finding the possible selves construct and then using it to guide tentative steps into programmatic and evaluative research methodology. Outlining the development of this theoretical foundation through the course of the programme is important to contextualise the study further. This next section explains how the first methodology emerged.

Aspiration, narrative, and possible selves

The mentoring programme borrowed heavily from story-sharing approaches. This literature is discussed here alongside my experience of negotiating both the problematic discourse of 'aspiration' in the WP field, and the complexity of notions of self and selfhood.

The strong narrative turn in the social sciences, and educational studies in particular, has at least in part been influenced by Jerome Bruner's work presenting narrative as a specific 'mode of knowing' (Bruner, 1991). As a cognitive psychologist, and constructivist, believing that the principal function of mind was 'world making' (Bruner, 2004), he explored the ancient narrative of the self as a form of storytelling we use not only to construct our realities but to find our place in these worlds. Bruner encourages us to think about our mind's incontrovertible 'precommitment' to our lives as stories, however incoherent they may at times seem since 'any story one may tell about anything is better understood by considering other possible ways in which it can be told' (Bruner, 2004, p. 709).

A troubling and ongoing discourse of the WP field is the supposed 'poverty of aspiration' that conflates the idea of material poverty with that of assumed aspirational poverty. In this way, groups and individuals are constructed as 'lacking aspiration' for participation in higher education and, therefore, in need of having their aspirations 'raised'. Despite extensive critique in the UK and Australia, the discourse continues (for example, see Regional Universities Network, 2017).

As a means of locating myself, I reject this deficit construction of persons 'lacking aspiration'. It does not represent my experiences working in strong and rich local communities underrepresented in higher education. Policy and programme language underpinning this agenda consistently deploys the term *aspiration* in disrespectful ways, misrecognising and misrepresenting individuals and communities. As an outreach practitioner, the young people I was working with certainly had aspirations. Often these aspirations explicitly involved further and higher education. Without a 'legitimate' framework to understand patterns of difference between and among groups of young people, and perhaps to share appropriately the richness of these aspirations, it is easy to fall into a trap.

The literature I was engaging with at the time on the notion of aspiration helped establish the first stage of this study and included explorations of 'navigational capacities' Appadurai (2004), 'determinants of aspiration' (Gutman and Akerman, 2008), and varying 'capacities to aspire' (Gale, 2010). I was reading Copestake and Camfield (2010) as they warned against treating aspiration as a single rather than a multidimensional concept and instead focused on the subjective qualities of poverty and well-being. I read Nathan's (2005) argument that aspirations are modified through conscious interventions in the shape of education, communication, and exposure to the world. And in the UK context I read Baker et al.'s (2014) findings that 'we have good reason to think that aspirations may play at least some role in the educational attainment process' (p. 527) which often led to ongoing participation in education.

A critical understanding of the ways aspirations are 'tied in with complex structural, cultural and discursive relations, identities and practices' (Burke, 2012, p. 119) challenges the way that aspirations are often held up as concrete 'things' that could be revealed. Similarly, Frye's (2012) argument that educational aspirations should be interpreted less as rational calculations but more as assertions of identity suggests that, 'rather than using what they know about the present to sharpen their view of the future, youth use visions of a brighter future to refine their narratives about themselves and transcend their present reality' (p. 2). It is important, therefore, to consider aspirations alongside understandings of selfhood and identities.

The concept of the self is complex, contested, and problematic. Sociologists since Erving Goffman have promoted notions of the performed self with no stable, coherent core. Skeggs reminds us that the notion of the 'good' and 'proper' self '(the governmental normative subject, be it a reflexive, enterprising, individualising rational, prosthetic, or possessive self) or even the self produced in conditions not of its own making, such as Bourdieu's habitus, all rely on ideas about self-interest, investment and/or "playing the game"' (2011, p. 496). Skeggs also details how 'personhood is produced through public performances that enable public recognition and delineation between proper and improper selves' (p. 501). This is a powerful reminder that any work with or on 'selves' is engaging in a complex and contested field, and there is a real need to consider the histories, the politics, and the attendant discourses when 'selves' are the focus of attention.

Importantly for this study, Skeggs (2011) investigates the processes of how persons who are excluded from the possibilities of attaching value to themselves do so. In this, Skeggs advocates for moving beyond personalism to 'personhood'. If aspirations are conceptualised as 'assertions of identity', then it became important for my WP programme to explore how the young people we were engaging with understood what was constructed as desirable, as well as what was possible, for their imagined future selves.

Having laid down the theoretical foundation for the research-informed practice context, I move now to explain how this study evolved over two distinct stages; the first being directly influenced by the literature above, the second implementing a more nuanced methodology that folds the research study back onto itself.

Two stages, two methodologies

The programme of research-informed practice evolved over two distinct stages, each involving very different methodologies and methods. The development of the programme is explored here in part as a call for suspicion of approaches in the field of WP that measure, count, technologise, and ultimately de-humanise. I will now introduce the two different stages that have come to shape the study.

Stage one – high volume 'micro-narrative' interviews

The stage one methodology arose directly from structural pressure to 'capture' and categorise 'changes in aspiration' as young people participated in a mentoring programme. The mixed method approach was grounded in an unrecognised and implicit positivist research paradigm, although it did include some interpretative elements. The quantitative data (psychological survey instruments deployed pre and post the mentoring programme) have been discarded for the purposes of this analysis. The qualitative data (large-volume, relatively short interviews pre and post the mentoring programme with students both inside and outside the programme) are retained for this study, for interpretation in the first stage, and for co-interrogation in the second stage. The methodology in phase one sought to identify change in aspiration using a synthesis of: possible selves theory, an endorsement of Bruner's narrative construction of self and reality, and Mische's (2009) notion of 'projectivity' (narrative dimensions of projected futures – *reach, breadth, clarity, contingency, expandability, volition, sociality, connectivity, and genre*).

In preparation for outreach practice, the university student mentors were introduced to Markus and Nurius' possible selves concept and to Mische's narrative dimensions of projectivity prior to the mentoring programme across multiple training sessions. Four mentoring programmes were conducted in 2015 with ten university student mentors and between twenty and thirty school student mentees participating in each programme. Each programme ran for six weeks, with a two-hour mentoring session per week, predominantly located in school. Mentors were paid university students from a range of degrees who were trained in a coaching approach to mentoring. The programme took a story-sharing approach with sessions commencing by eating together while the programme 'content' included exploring character strengths, recognising resilience, building awareness of career influences, developing a vision of a valued future, and mapping the journey (hope maps).

Across the four school sites, ninety-six micro-narrative interviews with high school students were conducted. This involved pre and post mentoring programme interviews 10–12 weeks apart, with forty-eight different students in years eight, nine, and ten of high school (approximately aged 14–16 years).

Interview questions were related to the young person's sense of their future possibilities. They were encouraged to interpret this in any way they thought appropriate, i.e. they were welcome to talk about education, family, work, play, hopes, fears, etc. Each interview lasted approximately five minutes. Recordings were transcribed and analysed using the chosen methodology, i.e. attempting to identify 'hoped for' and 'feared for' possible selves using Mische's (2009) dimensions of projectivity: reach, breadth, clarity, contingency, expandability, volition, sociality, connectivity, and genre of these aspirations.

Given that partner high schools are public schools administered by the NSW Department of Education and Communities, a SERAP (State Education Research Approval Process) approval was obtained in addition to University of Newcastle human ethics approval. Importantly for the second stage of the study, students (with parental consent) had the option to give permission to be re-contacted later in their public school journeys.

Stage one – findings

Programmes of practice and research interviews are 'interventions' in the lives of young people. It is my position that the mentoring programme and the research interviews, both borrowing heavily from the possible selves construct, provoked the students to perform a 'valuable-ness': a re/presentation of possible *value-able* selves. In making this case, I am drawing here also on Muniesa (2012) who presents value as a practical action – as 'valuation', an activity that considers reality while provoking it. This seems related to the student performances of possible selves and imagined futures in this study. The students in my study were largely from less privileged backgrounds. It was common for them to relate possibilities and imagined futures that spoke to the idea of the respectable governed self via themes of helping, saving, and protecting.

> My uncle was in the army so that's why I want to join the army. It's just what I've wanted to do since I was little, so, just wanting to help people.
>
> Yeah my Dad's a nurse, he works with mentally disabled people and he likes working with people like that and he gets a lot out of it. I considered it a while ago to be a nurse, and my Dad was really supportive . . .

> I think it would be tough but good as well, like with being a lawyer to defend families as well as with DOCS that would be good as well because I could help out kids and stuff. Well, if kids were in danger in their home you could take them away and put them somewhere safe. And if you're a lawyer, if there's bad people you could lock them up and stuff and make the world a safer place.

The possible selves construct is generative in that it allows for plurality and multiplicity, yet, when it comes to using this conceptual tool to understand aspirations, I am reminded that an emphasis on individual aspirations can be problematic and:

> misses out the significant interconnections between a subject's aspirations and their classed, racialized (hetero)sexualized and gendered identities, ignoring the social, spatial and cultural contexts in which certain subjects are constructed.
>
> (Burke, 2012, p. 105)

The forces Burke highlights here can certainly be identified as an influence on the students in their interview and workshop sharing, and in a particular way. The student narratives of possibility can be read as attempts to 'attach value to themselves to defend against misrecognition and devaluation, through the performance of respectability' (Skeggs, 2011, p. 503). To do this, in the context of the intervention of the programme and interviews, students were drawing on what was of value to them, their experiences of requiring 'help', of being 'saved', of knowing the importance of 'protection'. They were also accepting or rejecting dominant discursive forces of valuation, to narrate *valuable* possible selves, i.e. selves that could be valued by the social realities they felt were likely. I do not here want to judge the presentation of a future 'self' that helps, saves, or protects. The socialised nature of the narrated future selves could be seen as encouraging. I am however concerned about the way that young people might have experienced a mentoring programme and interview structure where they were pressured to *valuate* their future selves against the backdrop of a shifting social canvass where they are increasingly being told that they will need to entrepreneur themselves a career.

Stage two – collective praxis

The stage two methodology took a praxis-based approach to exploring the unintended consequences of WP activity, acknowledging the increasingly dominant neoliberal agendas for globalisation, privatisation, and decentralisation of education (Naidoo and Whitty, 2014), and seeking to navigate this treacherous terrain with a pedagogy of ethics and of care. This stage borrows methodological inspiration from critical traditions, feminist perspectives, and post/structural understandings of power, values, and knowledge. Conducting this second stage involved reconnecting with a small group of research participants from the first stage, eighteen months further along their schooling journey. The reconnection was an attempt to deconstruct assumptions and analyses from the first stage, and to understand how students were continuing to engage with ideas of self, possibility, and the future.

To facilitate this effort I chose a Pedagogical Methodology (Burke, Crozier, and Misiaszek, 2017) to guide the research design, the methods of data production, and the iterations of analysis. Pedagogical Methodology (PM) aims to 'cultivate spaces of praxis and critical reflexivity for "research that makes a difference"' (Burke et al., 2017, p. 49). While Burke and colleagues accept and explore the ways difference-making is a fraught concept, I was enticed by PM because I understood it to provide the possibility of 'opening up collaborative, collective, dialogical and participatory . . . spaces which, through the research processes, engage participants in pedagogical relations' (p. 52).

My methods reflect the nature of the methodology outlined above. A number of research participants had moved on to study in the final years of their high schooling (aged 16–17 years) at a local 'senior campus'. An invitation was made to those participants who had consented to be re-contacted, to re-join the study via a series of workshops over a single school term (ten weeks). Each week, for forty-five minutes, I facilitated a themed dialogic encounter and reflection process. Themes chosen were an attempt to provide appropriate access to some of the conceptual/theoretical tools I have found powerful in my ongoing research apprenticeship. We conversed about safe spaces, notions of power, conceptions of time, and debates on agency and structure. Ten students have regularly attended the workshops, providing a small community of praxis to deconstruct their experiences of being in mentoring programmes (or not, as the case might have been), of being interviewed, and of continuing their education and life journeys. Workshops have borrowed from the Freirean problem-posing style (Freire, 1972). They have also been audio recorded and transcribed. Each student had a journal for recording reflections they might have had during each of the workshops. As part of the workshop series, the students were given access to the transcripts of the micro-narrative interviews from stage one.

Freire (1972) understands dialogue as a relational process between equals, one that requires mutual trust and respect, care and commitment. The dialogic method of enquiry then requires each participant to question what they know and to accept that the dialogic process will make it possible for existing thoughts to shift and for new knowledge to be created (Freire, 1972). In creating a dialogic space, I consciously attempted to reflect and express the methodological elements embedded in PM – for example, recognising power relations, remaining as aware as possible of the difficulties and importance of holding together the dimensions of representation, redistribution and recognition (Fraser, 1997) and thinking about my own and the students' embodied experiences (McNay, 2008; Burke, 2012).

The transcriptions of the workshop dialogue were read multiple times to draw out emergent themes for further analysis and interpretation. The school students kept in-workshop journals, which I read after each session, trying to learn *with* and from the students as they engaged with unfamiliar concepts. A key aim has been to create a generative space for the imagination. I have hoped to acknowledge with students the discourses of deficit and the politics of misrecognition that can so easily and unwittingly shape WP encounters; discourses that construct underrepresented groups in particular ways, preventing the possibility of more socially just educational realities.

Having now introduced the multiple purposes and multiple contexts of the study, and having provided a treatment of the different approaches to investigation across the two stages of the study, I move now to consider whether a narrative perspective on Mische's dimensions of projectivity provides insight into the possible selves construct as young people are asked to consider the future.

Possible 'value-able' selves

Mische (2009) is interested in bringing the future into sociological research. To do so she builds on the phenomenology of Heidegger and Schutz, adopting the notion of 'projectivity'. Mische details wanting to bring into conversation psychological and sociological conceptualisations of *hope*, to appreciate the reasons people act (or do not act) in particular ways. In the first stage of the study I drew on the high volume micro-narrative interviews from stage one of the study to explore whether Mische's narrative dimensions of projected futures – *reach, breadth, clarity, contingency, expandability, volition, sociality, connectivity, and genre* – were a productive analytical framework for understanding narrated possible selves.

By re-engaging with research participants in stage two of the study, using PM, it has been illuminating to understand in a deeper way the performance at play in both programmatic and interview contexts – a performance of *respectability*. There was certainly interview data that could be interpreted to align with Burke's (2012) study, which found that young men and women sharing imagined selves and futures were guided directly by hegemonic discourses of gender, and which highlighted *respectability* as one common type of aspiration. There was however a broader pattern in play in the data I had collected. This pattern appears linked with not just values but also *valuation* – and the pressure to be *value-able* in the future, given the present neoliberal realities – and helps understand difficulties with the possible selves construct when broadening our perspectives from the purely psychological (see also Chapters 3 and 4 in this volume).

Abigail, a relatively more privileged young person in the context of the school she attended, reflects in her journal immediately after reading the transcript of the micro-narrative interviews about possible selves and imagined futures from eighteen months prior:

> I believe that I answered the questions based on what I thought you wanted to hear.

The section of transcript upon which Abigail was reflecting includes the following quote, which links to the notion of respectability being important to processes of recognition and subjective construction:

> Like, I want something, I want a job that other people can look up to and stuff and think, 'Wow, she went through all that to get . . .'

Abigail's family are well educated and she speaks of the future with a calm control. While acknowledging the interview was a performance of a particular form of aspiration, she does not seem injured by the process. But what are the implications if a student does not feel it is possible to be of value given their experiences of the discursive fields of, for example, their education? What are the consequences for the production of possible selves and imagined futures? How do they *valuate* themselves?

> I'm a dog, chasing cars.
>
> (Adam)

Adam's note is confronting. Written during a workshop in stage two of the study, in the margins of a transcript of an interview we had completed together more than eighteen months prior, the metaphorical comment is scribbled next to a passage where he details a fraught relationship with his Mum when they discuss the future.

> My mother is always like, 'What do you want to be when you grow up?' and I always respond with, 'Do I look like a guy with a plan?'

In a workshop conversation on how the interview processes made people feel, Adam shares the following:

> Nothing but the feeling of vomit, surging through my body.

Adam's nauseated response to an interview about possible selves and imagined futures in the context of a school is telling. His background is, at least in part, one of inter-generational educational disruption and fragmented family history of employment. The interview transcript tells a story of an unwilling performer of the *valuation* I have theorised. It would be easy from the interview stage to construct him as a 'shy', awkward young person. Yet here is further cause for methodological caution, for when you read Adam's journal from the second stage of the study and spend some time in discussion with him, it is clear that he is a deep thinker and a willing participant in discussion when a safe space is constructed. And, returning to Adam's scribbled note shared earlier, I am tempted to re-interpret this not as a tragic and derogatory metaphor of the self, but as an apt evaluation of the field of education; that the noisy array of 'choice' is actually a tricky and loaded arena where 'catching' something comes with increasing risk and potential injury.

Having considered the possibility that students, when confronted with the challenge to narrate possible selves and imagined futures, are performing a complex temporal *valuation* of themselves and their realities, I move now to explore this temporal dimension in more detail. Specifically, I acknowledge the difficulty, the 'wickedness' of the possible selves construct when used to challenge students regarding imagined futures in programmatic and research settings.

Possible selves and the 'wicked' future

The mentoring programme and associated research process challenged young people to perform a 'proper personhood' as outlined in the previous section but with an additional dimension thrown in, that of the shifting future where this performance must build a coherent narrative from an individualised platform.

In proposing a conceptual language in which to do the sociology of the future, Tutton (2016) approaches the field differently to Mische, drawing inspiration from Rittel and Webber's (1973) notion of the 'wicked problem' (social system problems that present as confusing, conflicting, value-laden, and where ramifications are difficult to assess). To do so, he discusses the onto-epistemological status of the future as explored in sociology, tracing histories of thinking and theorising about how difficult and pernicious the future is, before promoting the future's wickedness as a product of its 'entanglement of matter and meaning'. The particular type of 'wickedness' Tutton selects to work with is an obscure meaning that has to do with something being 'difficult to do something with' (2016, p. 3). This *difficulty* is at the heart of the purpose of the chapter in that the possible *valuable* selves I was coercing students to perform in programmatic and research contexts were utterly impossible acts that produced confusion and value-laden conflict.

My study identified an interesting inter-generational effect related to 'time management' as a technology of control (Burke et al., 2017). Commonly, students in the interviews and then again in the more intimate workshop environment would present their possibilities (and sense of selves) in the light of the time they *invested* and in neutral biological and clock-time terms, i.e. accepting the discourse of equally available time, regardless of backgrounds and circumstance.

> It's possible, it just depends on how much time and effort I put it.
> (Nikita)

> My mum went to University once, she did Nursing, studying on the computer and stuff, and she, um, quit out of that a couple of times because it got too difficult with everything else that was happening at the time.
> (Jenny)

> It helped me to talk to my Mum because she has been to University and she told me 'Don't just go too quick into University and give yourself some time or you might make too much work for yourself'.
> (Cassie)

> My mum and dad always drill into me that rugby should come second. . . . I have long hours at training and being a Physio you have to get a high ATAR and do well at school and it's hard to fit it in because you want to practice and get better but you also have to study and get smarter. It's a time management thing.
>
> (Teo)

In the stage two workshops we discussed access to time in their education (for example, in the contexts of assessment deadlines and/or family responsibilities). Students were asked to reflect on their transcripts and whether access to time impacted on their sense of the possible.

Edna was a student who in the workshops spoke with anger about being medicated for many years due to being misrecognised as 'disengaged' and 'unable to concentrate'. She shared that she will be repeating Year 11 next year, and spoke briefly in the workshop on time about how she cooks dinner for the family each evening. She admitted to finding it difficult to meet assessment deadlines but seemed to refuse to link the two, in defence of her 'caring for the family'. In her workshop journal, she recorded the following:

> I have a history of being isolated because I have a tendency to be childish. It takes time for people to change. But sometimes people and things don't change. I still want to be a teacher but I also want to go into the army and be a journalist but I have no idea how to put all these together.

In this same workshop, Abigail (a competitive swimmer with Vet surgeon parents) recorded the following reflection in her journal at the end of the same session:

> I do really enjoy sport, nutrition, and earth and environmental science. I also enjoy helping and caring for others. I think that the amount of choices and possibilities that are available are making it hard in finding something that I will love as a career. I don't really know what I want to do as a career yet. I still have time.

These two students, from very different circumstances, are both finding the future a 'wicked' place (Tutton, 2016) given the prevailing forces in their lives, yet Abigail seems secure in the knowledge that she 'has time'. It is revealing that Abigail also mentions 'enjoying' caring for others, yet not in the context of the day-to-day sustenance of a family, as with Edna. In Abigail's case, it is the more charitable model of using 'spare' time and resources to care when it is convenient, or in the context of a career trajectory.

A related time practice operating in both the interview and workshop data of this study is an assessment of the time risk associated with certain education and career trajectories.

> Civil Engineering or something like that or anything to do with IT and computing, they interest me, but then again that whole scary part of that I

don't know what I want to do and they take a long time to get so you can't go 'I'll do this and I'll do that'.

(Jarrod)

Jarrod assesses the risk of investing his time in particular (difficult) further study while knowing that he is unsure of the pathway. He went on to confide in the interview that a more likely option is the police force or military where this perceived risk is less of a concern. The assessments young people are making here are difficult with 'complete' information. Yet they are even more difficult when the young person's background and circumstance might mean they are relying more on presentations and websites than on knowledge through relational networks.

Anxiety about the future was a strong theme in both the interviews and the workshops and could be understood as a product of the impossibility of the performance demanded via programmes and interview structures. Students tended not to describe (as the possible selves construct might predict) feared-for selves that they were looking to avoid becoming; instead they tended to share generalised anxiety, as in the following quotes from different students across the interview process in stage one of the study.

> "I'm really *queasy*" . . . "I'm kind of *nervous* for my future, I don't really know what's going to happen" . . . "In my future just want success, that's all that I want but I'm *scared* that something *bad* might happen and I won't be able to reach it" . . . "That's what I was *worried* about because if I did music *I don't know* what I would do jobwise. If I became a music teacher *I don't think* I could teach kids like in my class. *I don't have* much patience" . . . "Well, I think I'm just going to have to *get over it*, figure out a way to move past it and get over it" . . . "I *fear* what will happen is that I'll go to University and I'll study something that *won't help me* get where I want to be".

(emphasis added)

As outreach practitioners, we need to sensitise ourselves to these forces. Working in *care-less* ways, we run the risk of perpetuating 'The myth of equal conditions for the exchange . . . an essential illusion of capitalism, a legitimation provided by classical political economy *and* liberalism' (Skeggs, 2011, p. 499). Young people from underrepresented backgrounds, through targeting via measures such as 'low SES' and via WP programme development based on deficit framings, are surviving a version of this social contract predicated on a meritocratic sleight of hand and lubricated by the discourses of opportunity and success. The situation is however far from hopeless. In workshops, the students and I created spaces together that held promise; spaces sustained by respectful dialogue where performances of *respectable aspirations* were not coerced into production, and where critical hope was welcomed (Bozalek et al., 2014).

Concluding thoughts

'The triumph of dark times will thus occur when every individual is separated from another yet acts with the cheerful and banal confidence that he or she is serving the ends of history' (Crick, 2016, p. 152). Returning to Picasso's *Guernica*, the painting depicts an artificial light hanging from the ceiling, objectively bathing even the horror of war in a neutral light, cloaking genuine human suffering under the guise of 'progress'. In contrast, a warm and genuine light from a hand-held lamp acknowledges the suffering and the darkness, courageously illuminating the care and humanity of the face-to-face encounter. For me, this analogy speaks to the chapter in two ways. Firstly, it warns of the tragedy of 'individualisation' in education processes (the bureaucratic procedure that uniquely identifies individuals for the purpose of social administration), a process of personalisation nourished by the first stage of my study where engagement with, and investigations of, aspirations were approached as discrete 'things' to be developed and measured. Secondly, it speaks to the need for methodological consideration and care in fields of practice and investigation when embodied subjectivities (Burke, 2012) are at stake, and where the objective 'artificial light' of neoliberal 'evidence' construction compels the practitioner-researcher imaginations away from human encounter.

The PM used to guide re-connection with mentoring programme participants and research participants draws on, at least in part, Freirean perspectives and approaches to education processes. Freire's *Pedagogy of Hope* (2014) describes how the emotive, passionate dimensions of silence-shattering dialogue can call into possibility a 'lovelier world', an anticipation of valued change. It was during this second stage of the study – in a series of workshops that developed over time, where power relations and embodied identity formations were considered, where issues of redistribution, representation, and recognition were reflected upon, and where an openness led to acceptances of vulnerability – that young people in this study spoke most often about *hope*.

Students in the second stage of the study talked about hope in a way that was different to the performance of *valuable* 'hoped for' possible selves. The PM was opening up space for the development of sociological imaginations, and for the slow interrogation of power and of discourse circulating in the young people's lives. In the workshops, students spoke of hope in critical terms (Bozalek et al., 2014), in relation to rebellion and resistance. They spoke of hope in terms that resemble the *ontological need* that Freire (2014) explains. They spoke of a hope manufactured in times of relative despair yet as a resource that facilitates action toward valued futures. They spoke of hope as a resource that does not accept the present, and believes change is possible.

Berlant's (2011) notion of 'cruel optimism' is one conceptual tool available to help reveal and unpick difficult dimensions of the WP moral minefield, yet I worry about the way it embraces a pessimism that undermines the emancipatory potential of critical academia and the possibility of applied sociology. In this chapter, I have advocated for approaches that do not simply acknowledge the sociological forces 'in play' but also fold them into the co-production of programmes of practice as a resource. University outreach programmes funded to engage with marginalised groups in local communities both intentionally and unintentionally challenge young people to perform particular forms of aspiration from what can be a deeply uncertain present. In this example, it was the performance of possible *valuable* selves divorced from an authentic recognition of the circulating social forces. Perhaps in tension with 'cruel optimism' is a 'dark hope' – a social dynamic that resists the hegemonic 'artificial light' of modern technologies, and makes possible cooperative movement from critical reflection-action to critical action-reflection and back again; a social dynamic that knows, acknowledges, and has experienced *suffering*, yet holds the possibility of resourcing collective efforts to reduce it.

Notes

1 Picasso's *Guernica* depicts a town's destruction during the Spanish civil war.
2 In his review of Arnett's book that explores Hannah Arendt's body of work – *Communication Ethics in Dark Times: Hannah Arendt's Rhetoric of Warning and Hope*.
3 The Australian Government initiated the Bradley Review of Higher Education in March 2008 to examine the sector and seek recommendations for reform and improvement. Emeritus Professor Denise Bradley AC led the review.

References

Acil Allen Consulting (2017) *Evaluation of the Higher Education Participation and Partnerships Program*, https://docs.education.gov.au/system/files/doc/other/final_heppp_evaluation_report_2017.03.16_0.pdf (Accessed 29 September 2017).
Appadurai, A. (2004) *The capacity to aspire: Culture and the terms of recognition*, Redwood City, CA: Stanford University Press.
Baker, W., Sammons, P., Siraj-Blatchford, I., Sylva, K., Melhuish, E. C. and Taggart, B. (2014) Aspirations, education and inequality in England: Insights from the effective provision of pre-school, primary and secondary education project. *Oxford Review of Education*, 40, 5: 525–542. doi:10.1080/03054985.2014.953921
Bennett, A., Naylor, R., Mellor, K., Brett, M., Gore, J., Harvey, A., James, R., Munn, B., Smith, S. and Whitty, G. (2015) *Equity initiatives in Australian higher education: A review of evidence of impact*, CEEHE, NSW: Centre of Excellence for Equity in Higher Education, University of Newcastle.
Berlant, L. (2011) *Cruel optimism*, Durham, NC: Duke University Press.
Bozalek, B., Leibowitz, B., Carolissen, R. and Boler, M. (2014) *Discerning critical hope in educational practices*, London: Routledge.
Bruner, J. (1991) Narrative construction of reality. *Critical Inquiry*, 18, 1: 1–21.
Bruner, J. (2004) Life as narrative. *Social Research*, 71, 3: 691–710.
Burke, P. J. (2012) *The right to higher education: Beyond widening participation*, London and New York: Routledge.

Burke, P. J. (2017) Access to and widening participation in higher education. In J. C. Shin and P. Teixeira (eds) *Encyclopaedia of International Higher Education Systems and Institutions*. Amsterdam: Springer. doi:10.1007/978-94-017-9553-1_47-1

Burke, P. J., Bennett, A., Bunn, M., Stevenson, J. and Clegg, S. (2017) *It's about Time: Working towards More Equitable Understandings of the Impact of Time for Students in Higher Education*, www.newcastle.edu.au/__data/assets/pdf_file/0008/350864/TIME_ONLINE.pdf

Burke, P. J., Crozier, G. and Misiaszek, L. (2017) *Changing pedagogical spaces in higher education: Diversity, inequalities and misrecognition*, Abingdon, UK: Routledge.

Burke, P. J. and Hayton, A. (2011) Is widening participation still ethical? *Widening Participation and Lifelong Learning*, 13, 1: 8–26.

Clegg, S., Stevenson, J. and Burke, P. J. (2016) Translating close-up research into action: A critical reflection. *Reflective Practice*, 17, 3: 233–244. http://dx.doi.org/10.1080/14623943.2016.1145580

Copestake, J. and Camfield, L. (2010) Measuring multidimensional aspiration gaps: A means to understanding cultural aspects of poverty. *Development Policy Review*, 28, 5: 617–633.

Crick, N. (2016) Book reviews. *Rhetoric and Public Affairs*, 19, 1: 150–153. doi:10.14321/rhetpublaffa.19.1.0150

Fraser, N. (1997) *Justice interruptus: Critical reflections on the 'post socialist' condition*, New York: Routledge.

Freire, P. (1972) *Pedagogy of the oppressed*, Harmondsworth: Penguin Books.

Freire, P. (2014) *Pedagogy of hope*, London and New York: Bloomsbury Academic

Frye, M. (2012) Bright futures in Malawi's new dawn: Educational aspirations as assertions of identity. *American Journal of Sociology*, 117, 6: 1565–1624. doi:10.1086/664542

Gale, T. (2010) Rethinking higher education: Implications of the Australian Government's expansion and equity agenda. Paper presented at the Teaching & Learning Annual Symposium, Centre for Regional Engagement (CRE), University of South Australia.

Gale, T. and Parker, S. (2013) *Widening Participation in Australian Higher Education*, www.researchgate.net/publication/312496550_Widening_Participation_in_Australian_Higher_Education (Accessed 1 October 2017).

Giroux, H. (2014) Truthout interviews Henry A. Giroux on neoliberalism. *Truthout*, www.truth-out.org/news/item/24367-truthout-interviews-henry-a-giroux-on-neoliberalism (Accessed 1 October 2017).

Gutman, L. M. and Akerman, R. (2008) *Determinants of Aspiration, Centre for Research on the Wider Benefits of Learning*, http://eprints.ioe.ac.uk/2052/1/Gutman2008Determinants.pdf (Accessed 1 October 2017).

Harrison, N. (2012) The mismeasure of participation: How choosing the 'wrong' statistic helped seal the fate of Aimhigher. *Higher Education Review*, 45, 1: 30–60. http://eprints.uwe.ac.uk/17900/

Harrison, N. and Waller, R. (2017) Success and impact in widening participation policy: What works and how do we know? *Higher Education Policy*, 30, 2: 141–160. https://link.springer.com/article/10.1057/s41307-016-0020-x

Markus, H. and Nurius, P. (1986) Possible selves. *American Psychologist*, 41, 9: 954–969.

McNay, L. (2008) *Against recognition*, Cambridge: Polity Press.

Mische, A. (2009) Projects and possibilities: Researching futures in action. *Sociological Forum*, 24: 694–704. doi:10.1111/j.1573-7861.2009.01127.x

Muniesa, F. (2011) A flank movement in the understanding of valuation. *The Sociological Review*, 59: 24–38. doi:10.1111/j.1467-954X.2012.02056.x

Naidoo, R. and Whitty, G. (2014) Students as consumers: Commodifying or democratising learning? *International Journal of Chinese Education*, 2, 2: 212–240. https://doi.org/10.1163/22125868-12340022

Nathan, D. (2005) Capabilities and aspirations. *Economic and Political Weekly*, 40, 1: 36–40.

Regional Universities Network (2017) *Higher Education Reforms Must Work to Support Regional Universities and Students*, www.run.edu.au/cb_pages/news/Budget_changes_Birmingham.php (Accessed 1 October 2017).

Rittel, H. and Webber, M. (1973) Dilemmas in a general theory of planning. *Policy Sciences*, 4: 155–169

Skeggs, B. (2011) Imagining personhood differently: Person value and autonomist working-class value practices. *The Sociological Review*, 59, 3: 496–513. doi:10.1111/j.1467-954X.2011.02018.x

Solnit, R. (2014) Woolf's darkness: Embracing the inexplicable. *The New Yorker*, www.newyorker.com/books/page-turner/woolfs-darkness-embracing-the-inexplicable (Accessed 5 August 2017).

Stevenson, J. and Clegg, S. (2011) Possible selves: Students orientating themselves towards the future through extracurricular activity. *British Educational Research Journal*, 37, 2: 231–246. doi:10.1080/01411920903540672

Stevenson, J. and Leconte, M.-O. (2009) 'Whose ethical university is it anyway?': Widening participation, student diversity and the 'ethical' higher education institution. *International Journal of Diversity in Organisations, Communities and Nations*, 9, 3: 103–114.

Tutton, R. (2016) Wicked futures: Meaning, matter and the sociology of the future. *The Sociological Review*, 65, 3: 478–492, https://doi.org/10.1111/1467-954X.12443

Whitty, G., Hayton, A. and Tang, S. (2015) Who you know, what you know and knowing the ropes: A review of evidence about access to higher education institutions in England. *Review of Education*, 3, 1: 27–67. doi:10.1002/rev3.3038

Whitty, G., Hayton, A. and Tang, S. (2016) The growth of participation in higher education in England. In P. J. Burke (ed) *Widening participation in higher education: International perspectives*, Centre of Excellence for Equity in Higher Education Occasional Paper (1). Newcastle, NSW: Centre of Excellence for Equity in Higher Education, University of Newcastle, pp. 20–31, www.newcastle.edu.au/__data/assets/pdf_file/0010/253882/ONLINE-SINGLE-PG.pdf

Chapter 8

Transitions from higher education to employment among recent graduates in England
Unequal chances of achieving desired possible selves

Vanda Papafilippou and Ann-Marie Bathmaker

Introduction

This chapter uses the concept of possible selves to examine processes of making the transition from undergraduate study to the world of work in England, focusing specifically on career futures in the accountancy sector. Inequalities in access to high status professional careers in sectors such as finance and accountancy have been identified as a significant policy concern in the UK (Panel on Fair Access to the Professions, 2009; Milburn, 2012), with research by Ashley et al. (2015) providing evidence of the sort of practices in firms that contribute to unequal access to these professions. In this chapter, we examine the issue from the perspective of graduates themselves, and consider how they experience transitions through undergraduate study and into these professions. We focus on the negotiation and construction of possible selves, and provide insights into how structures and social practices interact with subjectivities and the dispositions of individuals, in ways that enable or inhibit the realisation of desired possible selves, paying particular attention to the role of gender, ethnicity and social class.

The chapter is based on data from the Paired Peers project (2010–2017), a longitudinal study of young people who studied at the two universities of Bristol in England, which followed their progress through university and into the world of work following graduation, and which had an explicit focus on social class, gender and mobility. Our analysis focuses on three participants in our study, all of whom wished to progress into employment in a Big Four Accounting Firm.[1] The lens of possible selves allows us to draw out both the affective and material dimensions involved in the construction of possible career selves over time. Our analysis highlights how an imagined future in an elite accounting career is made possible or impossible through a combination of the ways in which individuals are able to mobilise and cultivate suitable capitals as a result of structures and opportunities at university, their capacity to 'package' personal capital in order to succeed in graduate recruitment processes, and their sense of fit with practices in the workplace, all of which interact with longer term, more subjective processes of constructing possible career selves. The chapter therefore aims to provide a different narrative on 'the mobility experience' (Friedman, 2014, p. 360) to that presented through analysis of statistical data, and offer insights into how individuals experience mobility and how they make sense of social trajectories, 'not just through "objective" markers of economic or occupational success, but also through symbols and artifacts of class [and in our study gender and ethnicity]-inflected cultural identity' (Friedman, 2014, p. 352).

The next section of the chapter outlines our use of possible selves as a framework for examining the construction of graduate careers. In the following section we discuss recent literature on graduate careers in the professions. We then outline our methodology before presenting an analysis that focuses on the experience of three participants in our study who hoped to progress to careers in Big Four Accounting Firms. In the final sections we discuss how we have put 'possible selves' to work within a framework of analysis that takes account of structuring features of social spaces, therefore using possible selves to consider psycho-social and subjective processes of mobility, without losing sight of the important dynamic between structure and agency.

Possible selves and the construction of graduate career futures

The concept of 'possible selves', first introduced by Markus and Nurius (1986), originates in social psychology. The concept encapsulates ideas of what a person would like to become in the future (the ideal self), what they fear becoming (the feared self), as well as what they in reality could become (possible self) (Markus and Nurius, 1986). As a lens for analysis, possible selves places an emphasis on the temporal, proposing that a person's aspirations, motives and goals involve a complex interplay between representations of the self in the past, present and imagined future (Henry and Cliffordson, 2013; Markus and Nurius, 1986). In the field of psychology, researchers have argued that constructions of possible selves can influence self-esteem and academic achievement, playing a cognitive and affective role in motivation, leading to a strong impact on how an individual initiates and structures their actions, not only in realising ideal possible selves but also in preventing feared ones (Markus and Nurius, 1986; Markus and Ruvolo, 1989; Oyserman and Fryberg, 2006; Ruvolo and Markus, 1992). It is argued that the more developed a possible self is, the more this motivates a person and encourages goal-directed behaviour towards desired results (Oyserman, Terry and Bybee, 2002; Oyserman et al., 2004). So, for example, in the context of our study which focuses on graduate careers, a targeted approach towards job applications has been identified as a key determinant of a positive employment outcome, enabling a smooth, linear trajectory to a graduate career (Shury et al., 2017).

A sociological reading of possible selves looks to how the structures of a particular social space frame and constrain the selves that are perceived as possible to imagine and become (Stevenson and Clegg, 2011). We draw on Bourdieu's work in our analysis, whose concept of habitus (Bourdieu, 1977) is a helpful reminder that external 'objective' structures are not simply the context in which individuals seek to construct possible selves, but become embodied in individuals' dispositions, in their subjectively experienced horizons for action, and their sense of what is both possible and impossible for them to be and become. This sense of what is possible is linked to knowing the rules of the game, and having a 'feel for the game' (Bourdieu, 1998, p. 83), which helps to maximise chances of success (see Chapter 7 in this volume). In the context of graduate career pathways, locating the concept of possible selves in an analysis that takes account of the structures of the social space enables us to highlight on the one hand how a 'successful' trajectory to a high status career is enabled by a strongly developed possible career self, which encourages purposeful, goal-directed activity towards that career. On the other hand, having a focused approach with a clear career plan requires knowing the rules of the game and having the resources to play the game effectively. For those without such resources, it is much more difficult to follow a smooth and linear career trajectory. Our data suggest that a strong possible career self constitutes a valuable form of capital in its own right; it enables individuals to envisage and plan for a career future, and can be packaged as a desirable attribute in a context of intense competition for graduate jobs (see Tomlinson, 2008).

In order to locate our use of possible selves in relation to the focus of our study, in the next section we discuss recent literature that demonstrates the unequal picture of access to the professions for graduates in the UK, before moving on to present the experiences of the three participants in the Paired Peers project, who hoped to progress to high level careers in the accountancy profession.

The context for possible career selves in the finance and accountancy professions

In the UK there is now extensive evidence that careers in key professions including finance and accountancy, and particularly high status careers in these professions, are not equally open to all. There are continuing patterns of inequalities based on class, gender and race in the occupational destinations of students (HEFCE, 2015), and in earnings associated with high status professional careers (Britton et al., 2016). Analysis of quantitative data from students who graduated between 1999 and 2009 (Crawford et al., 2016; Macmillan, Tyler and Vignoles, 2015; Macmillan and Vignoles, 2013[2]) finds that three years after graduation, more socio-economically advantaged graduates (those whose parents have higher status occupations themselves or those who come from areas with higher levels of higher education participation[3]) are more likely to be in the highest status occupations. Furthermore male graduates are around 2.3 percentage points more likely to enter the highest status occupations three years after graduation compared to females, and black graduates are 2.7 percentage points *less* likely to enter the highest status occupations than their white peers

(Macmillan and Vignoles, 2013, p. 9). The researchers conclude that: 'These findings provide powerful evidence that degree attainment is not enough to equalize socio-economic differences in early career entry into elite occupations' (Crawford et al., 2016, p. 564).

With regard to the accountancy profession specifically, Ashley et al. (2015) report that while leading accountancy firms do not publish social mobility data, the information gathered from firms in their study suggests very marked inequalities based on type of school attended, one of the markers of socio-economic status used in England. They found that up to seventy percent of job offers were made to graduates educated at a selective state or fee-paying school in a single cohort, compared to four percent and seven percent of the population as a whole attending such schools. The same pattern applied to university attended, with typically forty to fifty percent of applicants at leading accountancy firms educated at a Russell Group university.[4] These Russell Group applicants received between sixty and seventy percent of all job offers. The high proportion of applicants from these universities was a direct result of elite firms' recruitment and attraction strategies, which comprised campus visits and targeted advertising specifically aimed at these students. The advantages of coming from a more privileged social background for gaining employment in a top firm were therefore enhanced further by attending a high ranking university. Moreover, Crawford et al. (2016) find that even among those attending the same (high status) university, attaining the same degree class in the same subject, those from more privileged backgrounds were more likely to access the top professions.

A number of ways in which these patterns of privilege are sustained has been identified in recent research studies. Opportunities for internships during undergraduate study now form an increasingly important form of capital to list on a graduate CV. While the availability of internships with top graduate employers has increased, the Sutton Trust (2014) reports that thirty-one percent of these roles continue to be unpaid, making them out of reach for those without the resources to support themselves while doing unpaid work. Moreover, research into educational elites in France and England has found that students at elite universities mobilise existing and new networks and connections to arrange *exclusive* internships, which position them favourably for entry to the labour market (Tholen et al., 2013). Notions of top talent in recruitment processes compound these advantages. Duff (2017, p. 1082) reports that the Big Four Accounting Firms employ a discourse of hiring 'the brightest and the best' to satisfy perceived client demand, and look for elite credentials to demonstrate the prestige and specialisation of their workforce. Ashley et al. (2015) find that at interview, companies look for non-educational skills and attributes, such as the capacity to present a 'polished' appearance, display strong communication and debating skills and act in a confident manner. Employers interviewed for their research admitted that their practices of associating talent with attributes that align with middle-class norms and behaviours may disadvantage talented students who have not benefited from similar educational advantages or been socialised in a middle-class context, no matter how great their aptitude for a professional career in all other respects (Ashley et al., 2015, p. 11).

Recent research therefore suggests that for graduates who are not from highly advantaged backgrounds, and who have not been able to mobilise resources to their advantage during their undergraduate study in order to position themselves advantageously for a future career, imagining a possible self in professions such as accountancy and finance is not encouraged by the practices and cultures of these sectors. Graduates who are female and/or from black African and black Caribbean backgrounds are additionally disadvantaged (see Davidson, 1997; Morrison and Von Glinow 1990). In the next section, following an outline of our methodology, we present an analysis of three participants' experience of seeking to construct future career selves in the accountancy profession.

Methods

The data presented in this chapter are from two phases of a longitudinal qualitative study (the Paired Peers project, funded by the Leverhulme Trust), which followed the progress of a cohort of students through their undergraduate study in England and into the labour market. Phase one (PP1) (2010–2013) tracked an initial cohort of ninety middle-class and working-class students from eleven academic disciplines studying at the two universities in Bristol: the 'elite' University of Bristol (UoB) and the 'post-1992' University of the West of England (UWE). Phase two (PP2) (2014–2017) followed fifty-five of the original cohort over their first four years of life post-graduation.[5]

The main method of data collection involved in-depth biographical interviews of one to one and a half hours, using a semi-structured interview schedule. Interviews were face-to-face in phase 1, and were either face-to-face or conducted via Skype in phase 2, as participants were spread geographically across the UK and other parts of the world. All interviews were recorded and transcribed. The data were analysed using NVivo software, based on a content analysis approach, using thematic codes which were agreed through discussion in the research team. These codes were identified from a combination of reading the data, our reading of existing research literature and the use of a conceptual frame that drew on the work of Bourdieu, which made us alert to issues of habitus, capitals and social fields. In order to code, classify and analyse data we followed an abductive approach, by systematically employing the thematic codes that were identified prior to analysis while also being alert to subsequent themes that could arise from the data. Codes that were used for the analysis in this chapter comprised: Career Development, Employment (Hours, Job experience, Recruitment, Salary), Future, Identity (Self-identity, Social identity, and Work identity) and Transition from University to Work.

Fourteen of the participants in the project progressed to employment in the finance or accountancy sectors. Of these fourteen, seven were categorised as coming from middle-class backgrounds and seven from working-class backgrounds; nine graduated from the University of Bristol and five from UWE; ten were male and four female. Two were from black and minority ethnic backgrounds, one working-class male participant and one middle-class female participant. Here we present the experience of three of these students, who have been selected because they all aspired to work for a Big Four Accounting Firm while at university: Nathan (UoB, Law, middle-class, white), Leo (UWE, Economics/Finance, working-class, white) and Carly (UoB, Economics/Finance, middle-class, black African).

Nathan: successfully realising an ideal career self

Nathan came from an established, middle-class background, with parents who worked as doctors running their own general practice. He attended a provincial grammar school and chose the University of Bristol to study Law because it is a 'well respected course' (interview 4) and the degree would enable him to achieve his career aspiration of working in the city, while leaving options open if his career plan did not work out.

From the very first interview with Nathan, he spoke of his determined and careful career planning, and of his aspirations for an ideal career self, running his own business. This strongly developed sense of possible career manifested itself in determined planning to work hard and independently throughout his degree in order to achieve the highest grades possible:

> There's another lawyer in our accommodation who I get on quite well with and we just go to the library and just do work sort of like 9 to 5 kind of thing, eat lunch, go to lectures and then prepare for tutorials and then come home at night and just sort of chill out.
>
> (Interview 1)

Nathan described himself as 'competitive' (interview 1), 'incredibly career-focused' and 'driven' (interview 4), and he was well aware that a degree was not enough to succeed in the graduate recruitment game:

> By the time you get to the stage of applying for things academics are taken as a given, like 2:1 is the minimum expectation. Everyone has a 2:1 at least. Everyone has As at GCSEs, you've just got to try and differentiate yourself by doing something extra like Investment Society, or an internship, or I do mooting in my spare time.
>
> (Interview 4)

He explained how he invested in cultivating his chances for success while at university:

> Obviously applying for internships, because that's the main way in that industry that you get a job. Like learning in my spare time, I'm studying at the minute for a Certificate in Corporate Finance, which has slightly fallen

by the wayside because the volume of work at the minute is very intense. Also Investment Society, so helping other students get into the industry or get interested about it as well, so looking through CVs and things like that. What else? Like mooting, things like that, just things that build up your CV really, all the things that I'm doing at the moment.

(Interview 4)

This capacity to mobilise and cultivate suitable capitals, all geared towards an ideal future self, was demonstrated further in the way he described the process of securing a graduate job in a highly prestigious investment bank. His comments suggest that he is already a 'fish in water', and can take for granted that his confidence as a middle-class male will work to his advantage:

So through like Investment Society and talking to people on the stands, I got chatting to him [senior member of investment bank 1]. And then chatted to him at an event as well, got his card. Then I was in London so I thought 'well I've got an hour before my interview with [investment bank 2]'. . . . So I went to his office and phoned him up and asked him if he would come for coffee. And he did, so we went for coffee, had a chat – about football actually. . . . And after that conversation I got an e-mail about 3 days later . . ., asking me to attend the final round interview.

(Interview 3)

Nathan graduated with a first class honours degree, and moved into employment with a top investment bank. In his first year, he was top ranked and got 80–90 percent of his salary as a bonus, reaching an annual salary of nearly £100,000. He said he was headhunted daily by private equity firms and hedge funds, but chose to remain in his existing post for a little longer, while at the same time starting to get involved in the start-up scene in order to begin his own business as he had originally planned, and materialise his ideal self (interview 7). After two years at the bank, Nathan changed company and became a Hedge Fund Asset Manager, partly for promotion and better pay (£60,000 plus 100 percent bonus), but mostly so that he could work shorter hours than the twelve-hour days he had been putting in. He saw this new job only as a temporary one: 'I still don't think I will be here in my new job for ever because my longer term game plan had always been to go and try and do something entrepreneurial' (interview 9). After less than a year he left the company on very good terms in order to set up his own company with a friend. When he was asked how he imagined his future self, he said:

Hopefully I will still be doing something I love, whether that is because I'm still running the company and it's grown and we're in the US or we're in Asia and I'm working with great people that I enjoy working with. Or it's not that and I've managed to find my way back to another finance job.

(Interview 10)

This process of following a smooth and carefully planned path to success and the realisation of his ideal self was considerably different to the unfolding of Leo's career, to which we turn next.

Leo: impossible ideal self and the construction of a realisable alternative

Leo came from a working-class family. His father was a train driver and his mother was not employed outside the home, and he grew up in an economically deprived area of South Wales. In his first interview, Leo described his ideal future self as an aeronautical engineer. However, he was unable to pursue this goal, because he needed a maths A-level to get a place on an engineering degree and he had dropped maths at the age of 16. No-one had advised him of this at the time, and subsequently he could not envisage postponing university for two years in order to study for a maths A-level.

He progressed to UWE to study economics and finance, but was ambivalent about a career in this area, not least after working in an accountant's office during a gap year before university, which he described as 'dull'. Even though he recognised that this work experience was very useful in terms of his CV, he struggled from the very beginning to see a future work self in accounting:

I: Have you got a career in mind?
Leo: Not really no, it's quite daunting. But I didn't enjoy accounting all that much so I don't really want to go back to that route.

(Interview 1)

Throughout his studies Leo achieved high grades (first class honours). However, he did not invest in building his professional profile and cultivating additional capital. He did not participate in any societies (he joined only the climbing society towards the end of his second year), and he had little time to take on an internship as he worked in bars and supermarkets during term-time and during his summer vacation.

He did not appear to have any exposure to accountancy-related jobs, which may well have contributed to the difficulty in imagining a future work self in the sector (Hardgrove, Rootham and McDowell, 2015). His family did not have social networks that could help him with gaining access to future employment in this area, as he explains here:

I: And in terms of your parents and stuff, you know with their sort of jobs and things, are there any links that they could . . . I know your dad works on the railways.
Leo: I'm not sure how their recruitment system works. I don't think, yeah, I don't think, it's all done from like central offices so it's not . . .
I: So it's not like 'Here's my lad, he wants a job'.
Leo: Yeah, it used to be like that, but no.

(Interview 7)

He did not have a sense of how he might use opportunities such as the Milk Round (where employers visit universities as part of their attraction and recruitment process):

I: Did you go to Careers Fairs or the Milk Round?
Leo: Milk Round? No. I went to the one Careers Fair when it was in the ECC [University Exhibition and Conference Centre] but I didn't stay there very long, I didn't think I got much from it.
(Interview 4)

Even towards the end of his studies, Leo told us that he did not think he was investing enough effort into applying for a graduate scheme:

Another thing that I was meant to do is apply for grad jobs. I've only applied for two, and got turned down for one, still waiting on the other one, but yeah I haven't really put as much effort into finding a graduate scheme as I should have.
(Interview 6)

Despite graduating with a first class degree, Leo's progression to graduate employment did not follow a linear and smooth trajectory. Over the summer after graduation he was offered the opportunity to attend the assessment centre for one of the Big Four Accounting Firms. However, he was unsuccessful and 'out of desperation' (interview 7) he turned to casual unskilled work (first as a delivery driver for six months and then in a post room for another six months). He was not in a position to take time out to think through an ideal future career, with no-one who could support him to do this, and he struggled with searching for jobs that related to a graduate career self:

I: So this sounds quite clinical now, but have you got a strategy for where you want to go next or . . . ?
Leo: No, not at all.

He eventually quit his job in the post room, and started applying for jobs in accounting, but after 'a few dozen' unsuccessful applications, he was under pressure to find a job as he had spent all his savings. He managed to get a fixed-term contract in a university research grants office. This invigorated Leo's interest in the sector and gave him a career pathway to follow. He began to envisage a future work self in a finance department of a university – it appeared viable and offered a structured career route:

Somewhere like where I'm working now would be good, . . . because you could like work up, there's like loads of opportunities in the university. In the Finance department alone there's like 160 people or something.
(Interview 8)

A priority for Leo was financial stability; he wanted to 'get somewhere permanent and settled', as he felt that only then would he 'be able to look forward' (interview 8). At the end of his fixed-term contract, Leo was offered a permanent post and he started applying internally for higher positions in the finance department of the university. This was not, however, a story of finally working towards an ideal self. Leo did not feel 'particularly driven' towards his career, and he still felt that career planning 'always seems like something for further in the future' (interview 10). Nevertheless, while Leo's narrative was not a story of imagining and working towards an ideal career self, the secure post that he eventually achieved, with structured opportunities for progression, provided the conditions which enabled him to look towards a realisable career future. For Carly, the final participant considered in this chapter, both the process of transition through university, as well as the move into employment, were much more difficult and uneven.

Carly: future imperfect – finding a way to a viable possible self

Carly was from a middle-class black African background. Her parents moved to England from Nigeria when her two brothers were very young, and Carly was born and raised in England. Carly defined herself as British – 'I'd say pretty much the only thing Nigerian about me is probably just my parents and my skin tone' (interview 9), and she closed down any further discussion of her ethnicity. There was a silence about her Nigerian family background until several years after graduation, when she expressed an interest in knowing more about the family's Nigerian origins.

She attended a local comprehensive school, and in her first interview, she explained how she had imagined a possible future self, studying English and creative writing. However, her family appear to have dissuaded her from a route that did not offer an obvious career future. Since she was also good at maths, her elder brother encouraged her to consider accountancy. In Year 11 at school he helped her to secure work experience in a Big Four Accounting Firm, and when we first met her, it appeared that her ideal future self now was to follow in her brother's footsteps:

I: So what made you think of doing Accounting and Finance?
Carly: Well I just thought . . . like Maths has always been my strongest subject so I just thought 'OK what's the first thing I can think of' and yeah I thought it was quite a good choice for like a degree, maybe a career as well if I fancied it.
I: Did you talk to your brother about it?
Carly: Yeah a little bit. Yeah he seemed to get through the course like pretty well, and it's just nice knowing that if I get stuck or something there's always someone who's like been through the same stuff, so that's good.
(Interview 1)

She was successful in getting a place to study Accounting and Finance at the elite University of Bristol, but despite this apparently beneficial first step, she expressed considerable uncertainty and fear about her future career self. During her first year of undergraduate study she said, 'I just can't imagine myself having a career at the moment' (interview 2), and in year 2, although she aspired to get onto a graduate scheme with a Big Four Accounting Firm, she was unsure whether it was what she wanted or 'just because it's kind of the norm' (interview 4). Reflecting back on her university experience after she had left, she explained how the competitive mind-set of her peers affected her; she found it 'daunting that these like 18-to-19-year-olds were already thinking about career progression' (interview 8).

Carly knew what was needed to successfully play the game, and was aware that to build her stocks of capital to enhance her chances of getting onto a graduate scheme with a top accountancy firm she needed to apply for an internship. However, although she firmly defined herself as British and silenced her Nigerian background until some years after she graduated, she found it difficult to fit into the taken-for-granted and 'normative whiteness' (Mirza, 2006, p. 106) of the university setting: 'At home I'm perceived as quite an outgoing person. . . . But it took me two months to just not be awkward' (interview 1). She appeared to invest her time in leisure activities that would make her fit in, rather than engage in the concerted cultivation (Lareau, 2011) of desirable capitals through extra-curricular activities described by Nathan earlier.

Moreover, she was not achieving high grades and feared that employers would not offer her an internship (interview 4). This feared self, associated with not becoming an accountant, appeared to have a detrimental effect on Carly's academic achievement. While she continued to hope for a high final grade in her degree, instead of improving, her grades deteriorated significantly: 'It's kind of like I know for a fact that I can do better. So yeah last year I wasn't very motivated for some reason, which is odd' (interview 5). Having a taken-for-granted successful academic self proved unhelpful when faced with difficulties, and she was unable to work out strategies to get back on track. She explained:

> I just hated asking for help, which is weird because that's why my tutors are there, but yeah, so if I got stuck on something I'd either try to force myself to understand it, or I'd just kind of bury myself away from it.
> (Interview 5)

Carly graduated with a third class honours degree (the lowest grade for an honours degree), a grade which 'pretty much just wiped out the graduate route' (interview 7). She returned to the family home in the north of England and set about trying to gather as much work experience as she could in the accounting industry, through a variety of precarious, low status and badly paid contracts. None of these posts offered room for development and progression, unlike the graduate schemes that she had imagined pursuing:

> There are a lot of like, say, graduate schemes where you go in and after a year you get this position and things like that, but in this one it's kind of . . . yeah

you can't really see a progression ladder, so it's more just like trying to add value, and when you think you've added enough value then you'd go and ask for a pay rise.

(Interview 9)

After two years, Carly found herself struggling with the 'ruthless' working culture and corporate mentality of her company (interview 9). The longer she worked in the sector, the more she distanced herself from her aspirations of a future work self in accountancy, yet felt trapped into a place where her horizons for action were limited to her immediate situation:

> Just from the environment, I think I'd lost a lot of confidence anyway and I'd kind of put myself in a mindset where I was thinking I'm not really qualified to do anything else. So I had a lot of self-doubt, I was like 'where do I go, who else will take me on?' if that makes sense.
>
> (Interview 10)

Carly took time off for stress and health reasons, and then returned to work part-time. She then found the strength to change jobs. Her new post did not necessarily require a degree, but she felt much happier, which she associated with two factors. The first was her female manager, who gave her structure and support:

> In my previous job there wasn't like a clear measure of how you were doing, it never really got assessed. Whereas here, like within my first month, I had a meeting and it was like 'so how do you think you've been doing, how's it been going, is there anything we can improve on', so like it was just a lot more structured.
>
> (Interview 10)

The second factor was the friendly, non-competitive workplace culture:

> It's quite laid back and there isn't anyone who I don't feel as though I couldn't go to for help. So like I feel more relaxed in myself and I'm asking a lot more questions, and just everyone's quite open with each other as well which is really nice.
>
> (Interview 10)

As she began to regain her confidence with the support of her new female manager, Carly started to build a renewed sense of a possible self in the accountancy sector, no longer aspiring to a top job in a Big Four company, but instead to a career that she saw as viable and realisable.

Discussion

Our three narratives provide insights into the interaction of cultural, structural and social processes that contributed to the development of the career identity and future work selves of these young graduates. Nathan's case study highlights the virtuous circle of access to suitable resources, such as networks, that offer 'glimpses of the future' and support the development of strongly focused motivation (Hardgrove, Rootham and McDowell, 2015; Henry and Cliffordson, 2013). His established middle-class background meant that he was a fish in water from an early age with regard to constructing a desired possible career self, and as a result knew the steps he needed to follow in order to achieve it. Furthermore, any expression of a 'feared self' was more an articulation of 'plan B', involving strategies to get back on track, and to revise overall goals based on experience. His smooth and linear trajectory meant that only four years after graduation, he was already starting to materialise his ideal self, very different to the experience of Leo and Carly.

Leo provides a strong contrast to Nathan. His apparent ambivalence and wavering motivation towards a future career could easily be read as a deficit in young people from working-class backgrounds to envisage a possible future self. But, as recent research on aspirations emphasises, it is not *having* aspirations that are the problem, it is being able to realise them (Thornton et al., 2014). We would argue that Leo's narrative demonstrates the importance of the sorts of resources, starting in the family, that are taken-for-granted by Nathan, in the construction and realisation of possible and ideal future selves. Throughout Leo's narrative there are examples of how easily aspirations can be disrupted by events in a person's educational and subsequent employment career, which turn a possible future self into an impossible dream. Despite Leo's interest in engineering during upper secondary education, he was not advised that he needed a maths qualification and was effectively excluded from following this path. Once at university, he was expected to make his own luck, and while an undergraduate, there appeared to be a vicious rather than virtuous circle of lack of exposure to his proposed future occupation including opportunities for internships, that produced faltering motivation. On graduation, he did not progress smoothly to a graduate career, but spent a year in precarious, low-skilled jobs. However, once he did obtain a graduate job, he then began looking for ways to progress his career, benefiting from the structured pathways of progression within his workplace.

Carly's narrative points to the hidden injuries of race, despite her middle-class background. Her experience suggests that middle-class resources are not an automatic answer to achieving an elite graduate career, highlighting the psycho-social aspects of the development of career identities, and pointing towards the ways in which these have material effects on an individual's progress. Her silence concerning her ethnicity is not surprising, as she attempted to fit into what we have described elsewhere as the 'whiteworld' of university life in Bristol (Bathmaker et al., 2016, chapter 7), and this silence was possibly part of her struggle to fit in with her career-driven peers. Trying to reproduce her brother's successful career path did not enable her to maintain her motivation, and her academic progress faltered significantly. Like Nathan she moved into precarious employment with limited career prospects, which had a detrimental effect not only on the construction of a possible self in the accountancy sector, but also on her mental health. Like Nathan, she also benefitted from more enabling structures and cultures in her subsequent workplace, which eventually opened up the possibility of constructing a viable future self.

Concluding comments: putting 'possible selves' to work

In this chapter we have sought to put the concept of possible selves to work within a framework of analysis that draws on the work of Bourdieu, and takes account of the structuring features of social spaces that create inequalities in the positions and practices that are possible for different agents within those spaces. What our analysis suggests is that in Bourdieu's (1997) terms a strong possible career self could be viewed as a form of capital in its own right, which brings advantages in particular social fields, and which is unequally accessible to all. The concept of 'possible selves', on the other hand, has enabled us to articulate the psycho-social and the subjective in processes of mobility. In combining these conceptual resources, we have sought to engage with the important dynamic between structure and agency in the development and progress of graduate careers.

Acknowledgements

This research was funded by the Leverhulme Trust [grant number F/100 182/CC]. We acknowledge the work of the PP1 and PP2 research teams which forms the basis for the paper: Harriet Bradley (PI), Jessica Abrahams, Ann-Marie Bathmaker, Phoebe Beedell, Laura Bentley, Tony Hoare, Nicola Ingram, Vanda Papafilippou and Richard Waller.

Notes

1 The Big Four Accounting Firms are the four largest accounting firms that dominate the industry (PwC, Deloitte, EY and KPMG).
2 The research study by these authors uses data from the UK Higher Education Statistics Agency *Longitudinal Destination of Leavers from Higher Education*, for students who graduated in 2006/7.
3 Socio-economic disadvantage here and in HEFCE (2015) is based on HEFCE's measure of participation in higher education in local areas (POLAR3). Quintile 1 is an area of lowest participation, and therefore most disadvantage; quintile 5 is an area of highest participation, and therefore most advantage.
4 The Russell Group describes itself as a group of 'world-class, research-intensive universities', and consists of twenty-four UK universities, www.russellgroup.ac.uk/about/our-universities/ (Accessed November 2017).
5 For details of participant recruitment, the status and reputation of both universities, as well as the operationalization of social class, see Bathmaker et al. (2016).

References

Ashley, L., Duberley, J., Sommerlad, H. and Scholarios, D. (2015) *A qualitative evaluation of non-educational barriers to the elite professions*, London: Social Mobility and Child Poverty Commission, www.gov.uk/smcpc (Accessed March 2017).

Bathmaker, A. M., Ingram, I., Abrahams, J., Hoare, T., Waller, R. and Bradley, H. (2016) *Higher education, social class and social mobility: The degree generation*, London: Palgrave Macmillan.

Bourdieu, P. (1977) *Outline of a theory of practice*, Cambridge: Cambridge University Press.

Bourdieu, P. (1997) The forms of capital. In A. H. Halsey, H. Lauder, P. Brown and A. Stuart Wells (eds) *Education: Culture, economy and society*, Oxford: Oxford University Press, pp. 46–58.

Bourdieu, P. (1998 [1994]) *Practical reason*, Cambridge: Polity Press.

Britton, J., Deardon, L., Shephard, N. and Vignoles, A. (2016) How English domiciled graduate earnings vary with gender, institution attended, subject and socio-economic background. IFS Working Paper W16/06, London: Institute for Fiscal Studies.

Crawford, C., Gregg, P., Macmillan, L., Vignoles, A. and Wyness, G. (2016) Higher education, career opportunities, and intergenerational inequality. *Oxford Review of Economic Policy*, 32, 4: 553–575. ISSN 0266-903X

Davidson, M. J. (1997) *The black and ethnic minority woman manager: Breaking the concrete ceiling*, London: Paul Chapman Publishing.

Duff, A. (2017) Social mobility and Fair Access to the accountancy profession in the UK: Evidence from Big Four and mid-tier firms. *Accounting, Auditing & Accountability Journal*, 30, 5: 1082–1110.

Friedman, S. (2014) The price of the ticket: Rethinking the experience of social mobility. *Sociology*, 48, 2: 352–368.

Hardgrove, A., Rootham, E. and McDowell, L. (2015) Possible selves in a precarious labour market: Youth, imagined futures, and transitions to work in the UK. *Geoforum*, 60: 163–171.

Henry, A. and Cliffordson, C. (2013) Motivation, gender, and possible selves. *Language Learning*, 63, 2: 271–295.

Higher Education Funding Council for England (2015) Differences in employment outcomes: Equality and diversity characteristics. Issues paper (2015/23). Bristol: HEFCE.

Lareau, A. (2011 [2003]) *Unequal childhoods: Class, race, and family life* (2nd ed.), London: University of California Press.

Macmillan, L., Tyler, C. and Vignoles, A. (2015) 'Who gets the top jobs? The role of family background and networks in recent graduates' access to high-status professions. *Journal of Social Policy*, 44, 3: 487–515.

Macmillan, L. and Vignoles, A. (2013) *Mapping the occupational destinations of new graduates*, Research Report, London: Social Mobility and Child Poverty Commission, www.gov.uk/smcpc (Accessed September 2016).

Markus, H. and Nurius, P. (1986) Possible selves. *American Psychologist*, 14, 9: 954–969.

Markus, H. and Ruvolo, A. (1989) Possible selves: Personalised representations of goals. In L. A. Pervin (ed) *Goal concepts in personality and social psychology*, Hillside, NJ: Erlbaum.

Milburn, A. (2012) *Fair access to professional careers: A progress report by the independent reviewer on social mobility and child poverty*, London: The Cabinet Office, www.gov.uk/government/uploads/system/uploads/attachment_data/file/61090/IR_FairAccess_acc2.pdf (Accessed November 2017).

Mirza, H. S. (2006) Transcendence over diversity: Black women in the academy. *Policy Futures in Education*, 4, 2: 101–113.

Morrison, A. M. and Von Glinow, M. A. (1990) Women and minorities in management. *American Psychologist*, 45, 2: 200–208.

Oyserman, D., Bybee, D., Terry, K. and Hart-Johnson. T. (2004) Possible selves as roadmaps. *Journal of Research in Personality*, 38: 130–149.

Oyserman, D. and Fryberg, S. (2006) The possible selves of diverse adolescents: Content and function across gender, race and national origin. In C. Dunkel and J. Kerpelman (eds) *Possible selves: Theory, research and applications*, New York: Nova Science Publishers, pp. 17–40.

Oyserman, D., Terry, K. and Bybee, D. (2002) A possible selves intervention in order to enhance school involvement. *Journal of Adolescence*, 25: 313–326.

Panel on Fair Access to the Professions (2009) Unleashing aspiration: The final report of the panel on fair access to the professions. London: Cabinet Office.

Ruvolo, A. and Markus, H. (1992) Possible selves and performance: The power of self-relevant imagery. *Social Cognition*, 10: 95–124.

Shury, J., Vivian, D., Turner, C. and Downing, C. (2017) Planning for success: Graduates' career planning and its effect on graduate outcomes. Research Report (DFE-RR668), www.gov.uk/government/publications (Accessed June 2017).

Stevenson, J. and Clegg, S. (2011) Possible selves: Students orientating themselves towards the future through extracurricular activity. *British Educational Research Journal*, 37, 2: 231–246.

Sutton Trust (2014) Internship or Indenture, Research Brief, Edition 2, www.suttontrust.com/research-paper/internships-unpaid-graduates/ (Accessed October 2017).

Tholen, G., Brown, P., Power, S. and Allouch, A. (2013) The role of networks and connections in educational elites' labour market entrance. *Research in Social Stratification and Mobility*, 34: 142–154.

Thornton, A., Pickering, E., Peters, M., Leathwood, C., Hollingworth, S. and Mansaray, A. (2014) School and college-level strategies to raise aspirations of high-achieving disadvantaged pupils to pursue higher education investigation. Research Report for Department for Education, www.gov.uk/government/publications/school-level-strategies-to-raise-aspirations-to-higher-education (Accessed November 2017).

Tomlinson, M. (2008) 'The degree is not enough': Students' perceptions of the role of higher education credentials for graduate work and employability. *British Journal of Sociology of Education*, 29, 1: 49–61.

Chapter 9

Imagining a future
Refugee women, possible selves and higher education

Jacqueline Stevenson

Introduction

Possible selves, both feared and desired, are greatly affected by transitional life periods (Rossiter, 2007). The processes and exigencies of migration as a period of transition, in particular, have been shown to have significant impact on the development and actualisation of possible selves including those of immigrant women (Crocker, 2010), immigrant undergraduate students (Wambua and Robinson, 2012) and undocumented immigrants (Gonzalez et al., 2015). There is, however, a dearth of research on the impact of migration on the possible selves of refugees where previous selves have been rendered impossible through processes of *forced* displacement.

For refugees the extreme temporality experienced as a consequence of fleeing their home countries and claiming asylum, as well as the asylum and resettlement processes themselves, may shape the ways in which they are able to think about their futures. At the same time many refugees are highly aspirational (Morrice, 2013; Stevenson and Willott, 2007) and may seek to access further and higher education in order to regain previously held wealth, status or professional employment (Willott and Stevenson, 2013; Morrice, 2011, 2013). Despite such aspirations, however, little is known about the salience of refugees' education or employment aspirations, how these aspirations connect to either desired, or feared, possible selves, or, crucially, how structural barriers such as poverty or ill health may affect refugees' ability to either think about their futures or put strategies in place to attain desired futures selves.

This lack of evidence is problematic since, without a clear understanding of how hoped-for possibilities are being shaped, elaborated and threatened both by, and within, the exigencies of being a refugee, those working to enable them to become established within their new social milieu may not be able to effectively support the development of specific plans for action or give clear direction in the pursuit of those goals. This includes formal and informal mentors, as well as education and employment advisors who operate both as sources of possible selves and also as a context for their elaboration (Fletcher, 2007).

To correct this omission, in this chapter I first outline the social, housing, health and employment experiences of those seeking asylum in the UK before drawing on interviews with eighteen refugee women participating in educational programmes to evidence how their previous possible selves (both planned and attained) had been lost or fractured through the process of seeking asylum in the UK. I then show how, based on calculations about external conditions not of their own making (Archer, 2000, 2007), including poverty and the need to support their children, the women make decisions about whether to pursue desired possible selves or settle for what is termed here as their 'survival selves'. In presenting their accounts I challenge much of the prevailing thinking about possible selves, including that individuals are able to build on their pasts to think into the future, that possibilities for attaining a desired self are largely available and that all individuals are able to equally marshal the resources needed to attain, or avoid, particular futures. In doing so I also evidence, again contrary to much of the prevailing possible selves literature, how past possible selves can be much more powerful than current or future possible selves, and that avoiding feared selves can be more important than attempting to attain desired ones.

In making these claims I therefore seek to evidence how and why the possible selves construct needs to be augmented with sociological analysis so that the structural conditions faced by refugees, or other impoverished or disadvantaged groups, are both recognised and accounted for when seeking to understand why they make the decisions they do.

Refugees in the UK

The most recent figures from the United Nations High Commissioner for Refugees (UNHCR, 2017) indicate that 65.6 million people had been uprooted from their homes by conflict and persecution at the end of 2016 with 22.5 million people fleeing across international borders as refugees. The definition of a refugee comes from the 1951 Convention relating to the Status of Refugees. Under the Convention a refugee is a person who,

> owing to a well-founded fear of being persecuted for reasons of race, religion, nationality, membership of a particular social group, or political opinion, is outside the country of his nationality, and is unable to or, owing to such fear, is unwilling to avail himself of the protection of that country.
> (United Nations General Assembly, 1951, p. 153)

The term 'asylum seeker' is used to describe someone who has lodged an application for protection but whose claim has not yet been finally decided. When all appeals have been exhausted they may be referred to as a 'refused' or 'failed' asylum seeker (UNHCR, 2006; Refugee Council, 2017).

Although all these terms have international legislative definitions they are often ill-used – particularly the term 'illegal asylum seeker'. In addition, whilst developing countries bear by far the greatest burden, hosting over 86% of the world's refugees, the UK takes in very few asylum seekers, receiving only 30,603 new applications in 2016 with only around half of all applications for permanent asylum being successful (House of Commons, 2017). This equates to just over 5% of all migrants arriving in the UK annually.

In contrast the term 'migrant' is used to describe those who move countries purely for economic reasons, the term 'immigrant' to describe a person who comes to live permanently in a foreign country, and the term 'illegal migrant/immigrant' someone who has no legal rights to take up such permanent residence but is attempting to do so. As the UNHCR (2016) notes, however, using the generic term 'forced migrant' to cover all those 'who have been displaced by environmental disasters, conflict, famine, or large-scale development projects . . . shifts attention away from the specific needs of refugees and from the legal obligations the international community has agreed upon to address them' (n.p.). Keeping these distinctions is important, therefore, as the legal status accorded to each of these directly affects the forms of support they are entitled to. For this reason, throughout this chapter, the terms 'refugee', 'asylum seeker' and migrant have been accorded to each of these groups directly. The term 'forced displacement' is, however, used to refer to the process of involuntary displacement for some or all of these same people.

The granting of refugee status has huge significance in relation to entitlements to benefits, housing and employment. In the UK asylum seekers are not allowed to claim benefits or work and must live in National Asylum Support Service (NASS) mandated housing. In contrast refugees are entitled to claim benefits and to work. However, as a group, they invariably remain impoverished (Allsopp, Sigona and Phillimore, 2014) as a result of being underemployed or unemployed despite their qualification levels.

There are no officially collated statistics on refugee unemployment; however, evidence suggests that it is far above the national average (Platts-Fowler and Robinson, 2011; Evans and Murray, 2009; Bloch, 2002), Moreover, men are over four times as likely as women to be in paid employment. Across both genders, where refugees are employed they are also more likely to be on temporary contracts and/or being paid at minimum wage level (UNHCR, 2013; Evans and Murray, 2009; Bloch, 2008). In short 'there remains a "refugee gap" where refugees perform poorer than both citizens and other immigrant groups'[1] in relation to gaining work commensurate with their skills and experience (UNHCR, 2013, p. 11). This is despite the fact that, contrary to how both refugees and asylum seekers are positioned in the media as 'unskilled' or 'unemployable' (ECRI, 2010; The Migration Observatory, 2013), approximately half of refugees hold a qualification on arrival in the UK (Bloch, 2002; Daniel et al., 2010), many have worked in professional roles prior to fleeing their countries of origin (Willott and Stevenson, 2013) and up to a quarter had gained an undergraduate or postgraduate degree in their country of origin (Ipsos MORI, 2010; Crawley and Crimes, 2009).

Being unemployed, or working in low-paid, low-skilled jobs when they have previously engaged in professional or skilled careers, can have profound consequences for refugees' mental health (Willott and Stevenson, 2013). In addition refugees are frequently isolated (in part because they will have had to leave their NASS accommodation once their claim for asylum has been granted), which can be exacerbated by the isolation of unemployment, and they may be suffering from the on-going trauma of the asylum process (Robjant, Hassan and Katona, 2009; Papadopoulos et al., 2004). Experiences of detention, insecurity in relation to their status and, for asylum seekers, the threat of removal following an unsuccessful claim for asylum (Filges, Montgomery and Kastrup, 2016), can all have negative and detrimental effects on mental and physical health (The Forum, 2014). However, whilst many refugees experience poor mental and physical health (Jayaweera, 2010; Warfa et al., 2006), it can be worse for refugee women who are more affected by violence than any other women's population in the world (Freedman, 2016; Nobel Women's Initiative, 2016). The Refugee Council, for example, found that more than 70% of the women involved in their Powerful Women's Project had experienced violence either in their country of origin or in the UK; 57% had experienced gender-based violence in their country of origin with 44% having been raped; and just under 30% had been tortured. Moreover, half had mental health needs and over 20% had acute mental health problems (The Refugee Council, 2012).

Refugees and asylum seekers are, therefore, often having to learn new languages and linguistic practices, may be living apart from their families or no longer have close family alive, and are usually trying to re-establish their lives and develop new future possible selves, in a social milieu which may feel alien, isolating and lonely, whilst dealing with poor mental health (The Forum, 2014).

Refugees, employment and the place of higher education

For many refugees employment difficulties can act as a specific driver for participation in those forms of education which can be a route to better employment. Refugees choose to engage with education and training for multiple reasons, of course, including learning to speak English, for pleasure, for social interaction and/or to increase self-esteem (Phillimore et al., 2003). Morrice's (2011) research found, however, that the prime motivation to learn came from the realisation that their existing qualifications counted for little in the UK. Although there is limited research evidencing female refugees' specific participation in the labour market, the research that has been conducted (Bloch, 2002; Willott and Stevenson, 2013) indicates that not only are refugee women less likely to be in employment than men but that for those in employment their work also fails to reflect the skills that they have brought with them and, for the most part, they face occupational down-grading greater than that experienced by men (Bloch, 2002, 2004).

For many refugees[2] gaining or regaining educational qualifications also offers a route to re-establishing professional occupations, or re-securing employment commensurate with their skills (Willott and Stevenson, 2013). Higher education in particular can also be regarded as a place wherein they may regain a sense of identity, self-esteem and self-worth lost through the trauma of bereavement, persecution and relocation (Stevenson and Willott, 2007; Willott and Stevenson, 2013). Indeed the growth in institutional support being offered to refugees evidences the increasing recognition of the place of higher education in enabling refugees to re-establish themselves in their new social environment. This includes those institutions which have become part of the Scholars at Risk network,[3] those working with Amnesty or Article 26[4] to provide support to students and those offering their own institutional bursaries and scholarships.

Migration, refugees and possible selves

Refugees are, invariably, part way through a journey, suspended between the 'here' and the 'there' (Bagnoli, 2007) with their experiences, unsurprisingly, often described through spatial or geographic journey metaphors, such as resettlement being a process of 'remooring' (Deaux, 2000), or metaphors of flight or flow, often portrayed pejoratively by the media (Shariatmadari, 2015), for example as a swarm, torrent or flood. Griffiths, Rogers and Anderson (2013) have more recently offered five temporal considerations of migration: as flows and moments; rhythms and cycles; tempos; synchronicity and disjuncture; and the future (noting that the past has been given much greater attention in studies of migration). Migration can thus simultaneously be regarded as a process of movement through time – with the future as the 'not yet' (Adam and Groves, 2007) – as well as through space and place, and is thus a phenomenon bound up with issues of context.

This can in turn have a profound effect on an individual's present self (Geller, 2015; Jaspal, 2015) as well as how they conceptualise themselves as being or becoming in the future, namely their future possible self (Crocker, 2010), defined as

> an individual's cognitively-based, future-oriented aspect of one's self-concept, developed within specific socio-cultural contexts. They are 'the ideal selves that we would very much like to become . . . the selves we could become, and the selves we are afraid of becoming'.
> (Markus and Nurius, 1986, p. 954)

Possible selves evolve over time, depending on context (Geller, 2015). Indeed, as Frazier and Hooker note, adults' possible selves continue to change because, 'despite the stability and enduring nature of the adult self-concept in adulthood, the adult self-concept continues to be "contextually sensitive and dynamic"' (2006, p. 44) – dealing as it does with uncertainty and the imaginary (Hermans, 2001) as much as the real and the material. Thus many possible selves can be temporary, provisional or makeshift ways of being (Ibarra, 1999). Indeed Markus and Nurius argued that 'individuals can reflect on their possible selves and that these selves are not identical with their current or now selves' (1986, p. 958). Possible selves can therefore be conceptualised as a cognitive bridge to the future since they indicate how 'individuals may change from how they are now to what they will become' (Markus and Nurius, 1986, p. 961). Thus possible selves can, arguably, help people chose new ways to behave, including on a provisional basis (Ibarra, 1999).

For this reason possible selves can play a powerful role in motivating and regulating goal-directed behaviour, operating as they do as a conceptual link between cognition and motivation. That is because they are perceived to contain the strategies needed to attain goals through self-schema which enable the effective processing of the information, procedural knowledge, skills and strategies required to achieve a desired future-oriented state (Meara et al., 1995). In her research with adult learners Rossiter (2007, pp. 6–7), for example, suggests that

> a positive possible self for a student who aspires to earn a degree will include vivid images of herself having achieved the goal. Perhaps she will envision herself at graduation, framing her diploma, or accepting a promotion at work. Through this imaging and elaboration positive possible self-constructions serve to bridge the distance between the current state and a desired end state.

Possible selves therefore play both a cognitive and an affective role in motivation (Markus and Ruvolo, 1989) as they influence expectations by facilitating a belief about what is possible, or not (see Chapter 2 in this volume).

As empirical work has evidenced, however, simply imagining a possible self is not sufficient to motivate unless the future possible self is linked to concrete action in the present, through agentic journey-metaphors such as the 'roadmap' (Oyserman et al., 2004) or the goal-as-journey metaphor (Landau et al., 2014). In other words it is only through the undertaking of particular actions, in pursuit of certain goals, that possible selves act as 'catalysts and legitimators of not just reasoning but planning and behaviours' (Geller, 2015, p. 5). Thus the present self acts as an orienting point of 'being in the world' (Grønseth, 2006) whilst possible future selves act as 'barometers' of negotiations between sociocultural and structural influences and aspects of agency (Geller, 2015).

Using the possible selves concept in undertaking research with refugees therefore allows fears, hopes and expectations to be foregrounded, as well as how these are or are not linked to building 'roadmaps' into the future. It also allows for refugees' actual and metaphorical journeys to be explicated, as well as illuminate how their imaginings of the future are informed by their pasts, and how these pasts affect their experiences of the present.

Teaching and researching with refugees

The research on which this chapter draws took place in the Yorkshire and Humber regions. Until the early 1990s, most asylum seekers and refugees settled in

London and the South East (Allsopp, Sigona and Phillimore, 2014) leading to sustained pressure on local authorities in the South. As a consequence the then government introduced a dispersal policy in 2000, sending refugees and asylum seekers to parts of the country where social housing was available. Under the dispersal programme, around 20% of asylum applicants in the UK were dispersed to the Yorkshire and Humber region between 2002 and 2008 (Lewis et al., 2008). Since then, whilst the number of asylum dispersal cities has increased, the region remains a key dispersal area and, consequently, an area where many refugees choose to settle once their claims for asylum have been accepted. In addition the region is a hub for the resettlement of Syrian refugees as part of the government's national resettlement programme. Both statutory and voluntary agencies across the region have responded to the challenges posed by the numbers of dispersed asylum seekers and settled refugees by funding and delivering a large number of projects designed to support access to further and higher education and/or employment, including projects focussed specifically on meeting the needs of refugee women.

Over the last decade I have both researched with and taught many refugees involved in such education projects across the Yorkshire and Humber regions – three of which are drawn on in this chapter. The first project was a ten-week course funded by a small refugee support organisation[5] comprising practical sessions focussed on helping refugee women develop their CVs, write personal statements, craft both job and course applications and gain better awareness about UK higher education. I both taught the course and undertook a series of interviews with refugees designed to better understand their individual aspirations and frame the taught elements of the course. The second project was a voluntary project run by a national refugee support organisation located in Leeds. The project supported refugee and asylum-seeking women, particularly those with children, hoping to access further or higher education or employment. I was involved as a volunteer mentor, which involved interviewing women about their aspirations in order to facilitate their access to practical support to help them attain their goals. The final project was an access to higher education course for migrant women (including refugees) in Leeds funded by the European Social Fund. I taught the course, which centred primarily on the development of portfolios of evidence and reflective accounts of experience to underpin submission of accreditation of prior learning, as well as help develop the knowledge, skills and confidence needed to progress on to full degree courses.[6] As part of the portfolio-building activities I conducted individual interviews with all the participants.

In this chapter the experiences of eighteen women are presented, approximately half of all those who I interviewed across the three projects. All the women came from different backgrounds but had all been in the UK for more than one year (and less than five) and all had refugee status with indefinite leave to remain in the UK[7] (see Table 9.1 at the end of this chapter for demographic information). They had also all previously worked in professional or managerial roles but were currently unemployed or working in low-skilled or low-paid jobs. In addition, through participation in the three different projects they were (initially) seeking to reframe their career possible selves and establish 'roadmaps' (Oyserman et al., 2004) that might help them to attain desired possible future selves or avoid feared ones.

The research interviews

Whilst possible selves have largely been explored through the use of questionnaires, the construct lends itself well to narrative,[8] since 'the possible self consists of a story we tell about ourselves in a hypothetical future situation' (Erikson, 2007, p. 355;[9] see also Chapters 3, 6 and 7 in this volume). In effect narrative *is* (or is at least to some extent) the recounting of the imagined possible self, whilst both narrative and the imagined future self can be understood as a 'personal myth', that is 'an act of imagination that is a patterned integration of our remembered past, perceived present, and anticipated future' (McAdams, 1993, p. 12). Moreover narrative can help researchers understand individuals' lives from their (emic) perspective rather than from the viewpoint of the external observer (Goodson and Sikes, 2001) and is concerned with understanding 'the individual's unique and changing perspective as it is mediated by context' (Miller, 2000, p. 12). In addition, as Erel (2007) notes in her research with migrant women, narrative research allows researchers to foreground the agency and subjectivity of their research participants. Thus narrative allows researchers to

> elicit not only what happened, but also how people experienced events, and how they make sense of them. Individual stories are, therefore, an important vantage point for exploring the links between subjectivity and social structures.
>
> (Erel, 2007, para 3.3)

A further layer of methodological usefulness is that narrative identity can (or at least has the potential to)

> reconstruct(s) the autobiographical past and imagines the future in such a way as to provide a person's life with some degree of unity, purpose, and meaning. Thus, a person's life story synthesizes episodic memories with envisioned goals, creating a coherent account of identity in time.
>
> (McAdams and McLean, 2013, p. 232)

All the participants were therefore interviewed about their reasons for participating in the projects, what hopes and expectations they had for their futures, the barriers and opportunities they had encountered in attempting to regain lost lives and how these expectations had been shaped (if at all) as a result of their experiences of both seeking asylum and resettlement.

All the interviews were fully transcribed and the analysis presented in this chapter took the form of repeated reading of individual transcripts, paying close attention to the refugees' temporal orientations, the different possible selves they articulated and how elaborated and salient these were, the levels of agency and the link between agentic possibilities and the effect on agency of structural conditions. The selves described were not always distinct: a particular self (e.g. to retrain as a doctor) could simultaneously be articulated as a desired future career self as well as an ought-to parental self (as retraining would bring in money and improve familial outcomes). These selves might be integrated, for example the doctor as role model, or at conflict with each other, for example the tensions envisaged as a full-time working mother. In addition the described selves were not always stable, rather they would shift and blur during a single interview.

However, although there was marked variation across the women's accounts three key themes emerged: stories of fractured and lost possible selves, accounts of desired and feared possible selves and the tensions between true and ought-to possible selves.

Possible selves: fractured and lost

Fractured selves

Whilst both hoped-for and feared possible selves remain stable over time, where change does happen it is largely assumed to be emergent in nature (Frazier et al., 2000). However, such assumptions do not take account of those individuals for whom change is massive, unexpected and sudden, such as asylum seekers (or others such as those who are bereaved, made redundant or terminally ill, for example). For all the women interviewed, their previously realised selves (e.g. to have become a doctor or a teacher) as well as the future possible selves they envisaged (e.g. to run their own clinic) had been fundamentally fractured, first by the processes which led to their forced displacement, and second through the extreme temporality experienced as a consequence of the asylum process:

> It was such a shock; one day I was a doctor and next day I was not.
>
> (Farah)

> It happened so fast. The soldiers came in the night and we all just had to flee and we never went back; so I had to leave the clinic behind and all that I had built up.
>
> (Lina)

> It all just ended, everything I had, had done, wanted to be, my future all just ended; I don't know what will happen to me now; I have lost my friends, my home, my job
>
> (Habiba)

And, finally, possible selves had been fractured by the on-going dislocation arising from the asylum process, as well as efforts to resettle in the UK:

> I came here on a plane but I didn't know where I was until I was here. Then I was sent to a detention centre for a few months which frightened me, I found it really frightening and then I was moved to Bradford in the November and . . . I didn't dare go out for most of the year.
>
> (Khadija)

> One day I was out in the fields and the soldiers came and I just ran. My children were with my grandmother and we were separated . . . for a long time I thought they were all dead and I was on my own. Then I found them; but they were not the same children . . . and I was not the same mother.
>
> (Grace)

The loss of formerly realised selves was a recurrent theme across the interviews, described in ways that evidenced an on-going sense of profound sadness, in relation to lost family, lost homes, lost jobs and lost status:

> I was a professional person with status and a good job, looked up to, respected; now I am nothing and have nothing and have to start again from nothing.
>
> (Shakiya)

> The soldiers came in the night and took my husband. He was a lawyer . . . [and] had become very outspoken against the government. They came in to the house where I was sleeping with my children and they dragged him out . . . we never saw him again. We knew that we would be next and so we packed up and left the next day. The children were crying, I was crying. . . . We went to the next town. We sent people out to try and find what had happened to my husband and they came back and said that he had been killed. . . . We managed to get a bus over the border and then we got a plane here because my sister is here.
>
> (Dema)

As with many other refugee women (The Refugee Council, 2012; Phillimore et al., 2007) most of those I interviewed remained traumatised to some extent by their experiences, and the shockwaves that rippled out from such events had on-going implications for the women's ability to think about their futures:

> I can't stop remembering back to who I was and what I was and I can't think how that will be again.
>
> (Habiba)

Unlike the immigrant women in Crocker's (2010) research who had become resigned to such losses, however, many of those I interviewed were still coming to terms with their changed circumstances. In part this was because this dislocation had been so profoundly shocking but also because the women had moved from lives of (relative) wealth, status and privilege (for example many had been privately educated) to ones of poverty, unemployment and poor housing. The fact that the women were participating in the education projects outlined above indicates that they had not (yet) given up hope that they could regain previous selves: 'I will become a teacher again. I will not give up' (Zahra); 'I know that I will have my shop again one day' (Joyce). However, such hopes were being framed against the backdrop of living in significant and on-going poverty and disadvantage.

Lost selves, poverty and ill health

Refugees have often been dispersed (as asylum seekers) to areas of high deprivation, low employment and low educational attainment (Allsopp, Sigona and Phillimore, 2014). They may be living in sub-standard housing, unemployed and isolated (Allsopp, Sigona and Phillimore, 2014; Bloch, 2008). It is unsurprising therefore that refugees are amongst the poorest of all social groups in the UK (Allsopp, Sigona and Phillimore, 2014), with women in particular more likely to be living in poverty (Bloch, 2004). In addition incidents of violence, racism and other forms of prejudice or discrimination are (relatively) high amongst forced migrants (Hirsch, 2017). The powerful loss of past possible selves is therefore compounded by the conditions in which refugees find themselves:

> I need to work. Living in this flat[10] is not good for me and my family. It is a very bad area, lots of bad people, lots of crime. . . . I want a house in a place where we can feel safe. I cannot imagine being here in another year. It would be terrible.
>
> (Parvin)

> There is damp all over the walls . . . grey fur growing, all up the walls and black mould . . . the landlord he doesn't care . . . we want to move but it is difficult for people like us to get a house.
>
> (Mariam)

Material disadvantage as well as the on-going trauma of the asylum process results in many refugees having both poor mental and physical health (The Refugee Council, 2012; Jayaweera, 2010; Warfa et al. 2006). This, again, was reflected in the data, making the gulf between their present circumstances and what they had lost even more poignant:

> First we were in detention centre and then we were given a flat which was frightening because I didn't know anyone and I was always afraid and it was cold and dirty and everything was broken. We had no money, I struggled to feed my children . . . and I cried and cried for my husband and all the things

> I had left behind – my house, my job, my friends. . . . It was unbearable. I just wanted to go home.
>
> (Dema)

> Sometimes I just cry. I feel sad and I just cry . . . I am frightened. All of the time, in case bad things happen again.
>
> (Khadija)

> I do not like the people here. I miss my family, my friends . . . I do not want to stay like this . . . it makes me too sad.
>
> (Noor)

The women described having to decide between participating in those activities which might help to regain a lost past or attain a new future and dealing with more pressing issues in the present. This was particularly the case in relation to concerns over schooling for their children – many of whom also had poor mental or physical health:

> My daughter, she is struggling. She is finding the school so difficult and she has many problems with her health. I worry about her. She is ill many times. I worry . . . I have to spent a lot of time at the school, at the doctors, at the hospital
>
> (Dema)

These concerns affected their participation in the education projects where I encountered them. On multiple occasions the women were either absent, arrived late or left early because they had appointments with various bodies connected to the welfare system – benefits, housing or health.

The prevailing possible selves literature suggests that people are able to build on their pasts in thinking about their futures and that people construct possible future selves in ways that parallel how they remember their past selves (Strahan and Wilson, 2006). For these women, however, the loss of their past possible selves, and the deep sadness this engendered in them, as well as the material circumstances they now found themselves in, had a profound impact on both how they thought about their future selves as well as the extent to which they were able to realise them.

Possible selves: hoped-for, unclear future, feared and survival selves

Hoped-for selves

The two salient desired or hoped-for selves that the women described were the professionally employed woman, and that of role model in the community and/or family:

> I was a doctor and that is what I want to be again because it is important to me and my family and now there is only me responsible for them. But now I do nothing and it is bad for me, for my family, I have always worked, made them proud. And I do not want to have to be given money, I want to earn it. I am ashamed to take money from the government but they will not recognise my qualification here.
>
> (Farah)

> I will be a dentist again. I will qualify, have a job, rebuild my life, have my own clinic.
>
> (Lina)

> I have to make my children proud of me. I am shamed to be like this so I will do anything I can to work, you can give me any job, pay me anything and I will do it because that is what a mother should do, provide for her children.
>
> (Noor)

These two desires, either singularly or together, were articulated by all the women whose experiences are presented here. However, only a small number of these desired possible selves seemed in anyway realisable. Whilst much of the existing literature on possible selves suggests that those with highly developed career possible selves are more goal-oriented and more likely, when encountering threats to the viability or attainment of their desired self, to persist or construct alternative possible selves (Meara et al., 1995; Pizzolato, 2007), the women's on-going personal and educational concerns continually threatened their attempts to rebuild their lives. The challenges of poor housing, inadequate financial support and ill health – either theirs or their children's – took up time and emotional resources and made persisting with attempts to attain future goals a daily struggle.

In addition, although their possible selves had saliency (for example to become a doctor again having already been a doctor) the women faced a lack of recognition of their existing qualifications, a common experience for refugees (Bloch, 2004, 2008; Willott and Stevenson, 2013). Thus those qualified as lawyers, dentists, doctors or teachers would have to retrain or requalify to re-become the selves they once were:

> I don't have the right qualifications to teach in this country. I trained as a teacher in Pakistan but here they say I am not trained as a teacher. I have argued and pleaded but they just say 'no; you are not a teacher!'
>
> (Shakiya)

The tangible barriers they faced in accessing higher education, combined with the material disadvantages they were facing, meant that remaining goal-oriented was frequently a struggle. Moreover the massive time and financial implications of retraining led many of the women to try and rethink new possibilities but these were often vague and uncertain.

The unclear future self

For many of the women their future, and the self they might become in that future, was unclear. This lack of clarity was not, however, because they necessarily lacked any personal capacity to imagine a future. Rather they either lacked knowledge about how to attain a particular outcome or their unclear future self was linked to barriers that the women knew they faced. For example, the women knew little about the context of UK further or higher education and had often been given unclear, confusing or contradictory advice from support staff in universities (Stevenson and Willott, 2010; Willott and Stevenson, 2013). They were often wrongly advised as to their fee status and regarded as international students even though refugees are treated as home students for fee purposes. They were also confused about the value of different courses in enabling them to attain postgraduate employment, or the extent to which they could use their existing qualifications (if recognised) to retrain. Nonetheless the perception that gaining a degree would allow them to escape from poverty remained a firmly held belief:

Laila: I want to do a degree, go to university, get a degree. I need to do everything I can to get a degree.
Interviewer: Why do you want to get a degree?
Laila: I need to have a degree so I can get a job; it is important to have a degree to get a job.
Interviewer: What do you want to do once you have a degree?
Laila: It doesn't matter; I just want to get a degree. When I have a degree I can get any job, maybe a lawyer or a teacher, then I will have a job.

Even if status was correctly assigned, however, the women's possibilities for taking up a university place were uncertain since refugees face restrictions on accessing student loans whilst they only have limited leave to remain.

On finding out such new barriers many of the women eventually abandoned one hoped-for future self and started to rethink a new one:

Interviewer: What job are you hoping to do?
Laila: I want to be a teacher. . . . I was a teacher in Pakistan.
Interviewer: Can you use your Pakistani teaching qualification to teach in the UK?
Laila: If I can't then maybe I will become a dentist. Or work in a hospital. . . . I want to do a degree, go to university, get a degree. I need to do everything I can to get a degree.

The lack of clarity of such possible selves is problematic, however, since the possible self is unlikely to lead to concrete actions in the present. That is because, as Oyserman and James (2009, p. 737) note,

Vague, general possible selves lacking behavioral strategies cannot function to guide self-regulation because they provide neither a specific picture of one's goals nor a road map of how to reduce discrepancies between the present and one's future.

Feared selves: poverty and loneliness

Across the narratives all the women (whether they had salient desired future selves or not) described three feared futures selves. The first was the impoverished self (remaining unemployed, in low-paid employment and/or living on benefits):

> It is bad, bad, being on benefits, I need to find a job. If I have work we can start to rebuild our lives. I have always worked, always provided for my family and it is shameful to be poor.
>
> (Grace)

> I was respected woman before. I had a career, a profession. Now I am unemployed and that is a terrible feeling. . . . I have to find a job, get my life back. Being unemployed is terrible for me.
>
> (Dema)

The second was the insecure self (in relation to work, housing, income, health or family):

> I need to get a flat we can stay in and make a home. We have moved a lot and it is not good for the children. They have to go to new schools, make new friends. It is very bad for all of us.
>
> (Uzma)

And the third was the lonely self. All three of these feared selves might be experienced simultaneously.

> I am very scared. I would like to get a job so I can make friends and be happy. But I cannot get a job so . . .
>
> (Jasminder)

For the women these feared selves appeared plausible (Oyserman, Ager and Gant, 1995) as they were based on a known (and experienced) reality, whilst their hoped-for selves lacked saliency because they did not have a concrete sense of what was possible within their new social milieus.

Survival selves

Possible selves include an experience of being an agent in this future situation (Erikson, 2007); in other words possible selves are framed in relation to whether an individual can perceive themselves as being agentic in the creation or attainment of desired (or feared) change. Moreover possible selves are engendered through a belief that the self is able to assimilate to future circumstances which in turn promotes optimism and trust in the ability to make changes (Markus and Wurf, 1987). The women involved in these projects, however, were keenly aware that despite their aspirations and desires they ultimately lacked the power to change their lives. In consequence many of them eventually put aside any hope of becoming their desired future career or role model self and focussed instead on simply surviving – adopting instead what is referred to here as a 'survival self'.

It was not that the women lacked agency *per se* – indeed they exhibited high levels of agency in trying to get decent education for their children or in improving their English language skills. Rather what affected their power to make a difference were the seemingly insurmountable structural barriers they faced during the process of seeking and gaining asylum and resettlement. This in turn constrained what possibilities they believed (or perceived) were available to them and affected their sense of hope:

> What can I do? I cannot teach in this country. I cannot teach despite being a teacher for many years. . . . I cannot change things so that I can teach.
>
> (Shakiya)

> I just cannot seem to get things sorted . . . every day there is a new problem to deal with; it is never ending. I cannot see it getting better. I do not know how to make things change.
>
> (Uzma)

> I cannot make this possible. I am too tired. I am tired of fighting.
>
> (Farah)

It is perhaps unsurprising therefore that a strong theme across the interviews was the conflict between whether they should continue to try and become their true (desired) possible selves or become selves shaped by the need to simply survive.

Possible selves emerge at a particular moment in time 'e.g. through an epiphany experience, after deep self-reflection, as a circumstance of a planned or unplanned life change, or in anticipation of a life change' (Frazier and Hooker, 2006, p. 50). In consequence, as Hitlin and Elder note (2007, p. 171), 'temporal orientations are shaped by situational exigencies, with some situations calling for extensive focus on the present and others requiring an extended temporal orientation'. For these women their hoped-for selves (to become the professionally employed woman, or the community and/or familial role model, or both) were competing with their 'survival selves': that is to undertake any job that will bring in income and to not take money from the state.

> I just need to work; get a job, earn money, pay my bills and support my family. Perhaps one day I will be able to live my dreams but for now . . .
>
> (Jasminder)

This was particularly the case for those women who had children and who articulated the necessity of making personal sacrifices for the benefit of their family and in the hope their children would benefit from this in the future:

> All my dreams are now gone and the future I thought I would have – gone and so now I will just work hard and make what money I can and then my children, they will have a future.
>
> (Farah)

In short, the structural constraints of the women's present lives were profoundly shaping what possibilities they believed were open to them, and shaping decisions about what selves they should instead become. For many of the women, therefore, the need to survive meant that they ended up tearing up or completely revising their old 'roadmaps', creating new ones which would allow them to attain a new 'survival self'.

Possible selves, refugees and reclaiming the sociological

Throughout the analysis in this chapter, the concept of possible selves has been used to explore narratives of the self in different temporalities, to show how selves that have become impossible continue to be imagined alongside present and imagined future selves, as well as survival selves. At the same time, sociological concerns particularly with the social and material conditions facing refugees have been interwoven with the more psychologically oriented lens of possible selves. This has enabled a foregrounding of the social and material exigencies and structural barriers that refugees encounter, as well as the struggles they face in seeking to understand what possibilities are available to them or to exercise agency over conditions both not of their own choosing (Archer, 2000, 2007) and not of their own making (Marx, 1852). The analysis therefore evidences how individual experience is located within the context of the structural opportunities and constraints that make possible or impossible the attainment of an imagined 'possible self'. In doing so, the analysis draws attention to the limitations of a decontextualized notion of possible selves.

The women's stories also challenge the assumption in much of the possible selves literature that trajectories into the future (including into higher education) are linear and that individuals are able to build on their pasts to think in to the future. Rather their stories elucidate how complex pasts can, at times, threaten to disrupt both present and future trajectories, particularly when past selves have been lost or fractured through the process of, for example, forced migration.

Much of the possible selves literature also assumes that possibilities for attaining a desired self are present, and that individuals are able to develop and implement strategies to attain particular futures. Indeed, in their seminal work, Markus and Nurius (1986) suggested that the outcome for a desired (or feared) future self is ultimately dependent upon the individual, rather than the circumstances that they have encountered. In reality, as this research evidences, those who are impoverished or disenfranchised, such as refugees, do not have the same access to material or emotional resources, or share the same possibilities of marshalling these to become desired future selves as do other more privileged groups (see also Chapter 8 in this volume).

Finally, and fundamentally, as Archer notes (2003, 2007) the capacity to imagine the self into the future involves a recognition of the personal powers of individuals to form a view about their fundamental concerns, whether these are future orientated or not. Power and agency shape what futures people believe are possible and realisable: those who have neither, and who also have concerns about (and realities of) poverty, loneliness or instability, may hold desired possible selves that are largely unrealisable. In addition, it may be their feared selves that are more strongly driving actions in the present than their desired ones; in the case of the women described here a lack of power over one's life may force the abandonment of a desired future self and the adoption instead of a 'survival' one. For those who face structural disadvantage, therefore, the exigencies of their present circumstances fundamentally shape and limit what possibilities are open to them. Through augmenting the possible selves construct with sociological analysis, this chapter allows for structural inequalities to be made clearer and shows that not all selves are possible to all people.

Table 9.1 Participant demographics

Project	Pseudonym	Nationality	Age	Previous occupation
Project One	1. Habiba	Pakistani	39	Teacher
	2. Khadija	Guinean	47	Hospital care worker
	3. Farah	Iranian	61	Doctor
	4. Joyce	Sudanese	54	Optometrist
	5. Zahra	Iranian	51	Teacher
	6. Noor	Iranian	53	Educational administrator
	7. Parvin	Iranian	43	Teacher
Project Two	8. Grace	Ghanaian	45	Dental technician
	9. Tabina	Pakistani	37	Hospital administrator
	10. Dema	Pakistani	32	Lecturer
	11. Shakiya	Pakistani	37	Teacher
	12. Mina	Iranian	44	Healthcare assistant
Project Three	13. Mariam	Egyptian	49	Business woman
	14. Inderjeet	India	32	Teaching assistant
	15. Jasminder	India	31	Home maker
	16. Lina	Iraqi	43	Dentist
	17. Uzma	Pakistani	28	Home maker
	18. Laila	Pakistani	39	Administrator

Notes

1 This is not just a UK phenomenon but a global one.
2 Asylum seekers are treated as international students for fee purposes; this largely excludes them from making applications as they are also not entitled to a student loan. Refugees are treated as home students for fee purposes but there are limitations on accessing student loans whilst they only have limited leave to remain.
3 Scholars at Risk arranges temporary research and teaching positions for scholars in danger www.scholarsatrisk.org.
4 Article 26 is working with an increasing number of universities to support students who have sought sanctuary in the UK to access and succeed in higher education, http://article26.hkf.org.uk.
5 Now defunct.
6 Projects One and Three took place whilst I was employed at Leeds Beckett University.
7 Indefinite leave to remain (ILR) is also called 'permanent residence' or 'settled status' as it gives permission to stay in the UK on a permanent basis (Refugee Council, 2017).
8 Here the term 'narrative' is used to cover both the recounting of the story as well as the 're-storying' of the story. These terms are sometimes referred to separately as 'story' and 'narrative' respectively.
9 Of note, Erikson doesn't use interviews in his research.
10 Some of the interviews took place in the women's homes.

References

Adam, B. and Groves, C. (2007) *Future matters: Action, knowledge, ethics*, Leiden: Brill.
Allsopp, J., Sigona, N. and Phillimore, J. (2014) *Poverty among refugees and asylum seekers in the UK: An evidence and policy review*, IRiS Working Paper Series, No. 1/2014, Birmingham: Institute for Research into Superdiversity.
Archer, M. S. (2000) *Being human: The problem of agency*, Cambridge: Cambridge University Press.
Archer, M. (2003) *Structure, agency and the internal conversation*, Cambridge: Cambridge University Press.
Archer, M. S. (2007) *Making our way through the world*, Cambridge: Cambridge University Press.
Bagnoli, A. (2007) Between outcast and outsider: Constructing the identity of the foreigner. *European Societies*, 9, 1: 23–44.
Bloch, A. (2002) *Refugees opportunities and barriers in employment and training*, Research Report 179, London: Department for Work and Pensions.
Bloch, A. (2004), Making it work: Refugee employment in the UK. Asylum and migration working paper 2. London: Institute for Public Policy Research.
Bloch, A. (2008) Refugees in the UK labour market: The conflict between economic integration and policy-led labour market restriction. *Journal of Social Policy*, 37: 21–36.
Crawley, H. and Crimes, T. (2009) *Refugees living in Wales: A survey of skills, experiences and barriers to inclusion*, Swansea: Centre for Migration Policy Research.
Crocker, J. R. (2010) *The Influence of Adult Upgrading on the Possible Selves of Foreign-Trained Professional Women*. ProQuest Diss. and theses, University of Alberta, Canada, https://era.library.ualberta.ca/files/g445cf81n/Crocker%20Jocelyn%20Fall%202010.pdf (Accessed 2 August 2017).

Daniel, M., Devine, C., Gillespie, R., Pendry, E. and Zurawan, A. (2010) Helping new refugees integrate into the UK: Baseline data analysis from the Survey of New Refugees, Research Report 36, Analysis, Research and Knowledge Management, UK Border Agency.

Deaux, K. (2000) Surveying the landscape of immigration. *Journal of Community and Applied Social Psychology*, 10, 5: 421–431.

ECRI (2010) *The Council of Europe's Commission on Racism and Intolerance 2010 UK Country Report*, www.coe.int/t/dghl/monitoring/ecri/Country-by-country/United_Kingdom/GBR-CbC-IV-2010-004-ENG.pdf (Accessed 2 September 2017).

Erel, U. (2007) Constructing meaningful lives: Biographical methods in research on migrant women. *Sociological Research Online*, 12, 4, www.socresonline.org.uk/12/4/5/5.pdf (Accessed 14 April 2017).

Erikson, M. G. (2007) The meaning of the future: Toward a more specific definition of possible selves. *Review of General Psychology*, 1: 348–358.

Evans, O. and Murray, R. (2009) *The gateway protection programme: An evaluation*, London: Home Office.

Fletcher, S. (2007) Mentoring adult learners: Realizing possible selves. *New Directions for Adult and Continuing Education*, 114: 75–86.

Filges, T., Montgomery, E. and Kastrup, M. (2016) *The Impact of Detention on the Health of Asylum Seekers: A Systematic Review*. The Campbell Collaboration, www.campbellcollaboration.org/media/k2/attachments/Filges_Asylum_Protocol.pdf (Accessed 1 June 2017).

The Forum (2014) This is how it feels to be lonely: A report on migrants and refugees' experiences with loneliness in London. *The Forum*, http://migrantsorganise.org/wp-content/uploads/2014/09/Loneliness-report_The-Forum_UPDATED.pdf (Accessed 1 July 2017).

Frazier, L. K. and Hooker, K. (2006) Possible selves and adult development: Linking theory and research. In C. Dunkel and J. Kerpelman (eds) (1997) *Possible selves: Theory, research and applications*, New York: Nova Science, pp. 41–60.

Frazier, L. K., Hooker, K., Johnson, P. M. and Kaus, C. R. (2000) Continuity and change in possible selves in later life: A 5-year longitudinal study. *Basic and Applied Social Psychology*, 22, 3: 237–243.

Freedman, J. (2016) Sexual and gender-based violence against refugee women: A hidden aspect of the refugee 'crisis'. *Reproductive Health Matters*, 24, 47: 18–26.

Geller, W. (2015) *Rural young women, education, and socio-spatial mobility: Landscapes of success*, Lanham, MD: Lexington Books.

Gonzalez, L. M., Stein, G. L., Prandoni, J. I., Eades, M. P. and Magalhaes, R. (2015) Perceptions of undocumented status and possible selves among Latino/a youth. *The Counseling Psychologist*, 43, 8: 1190–1210.

Goodson, I. and Sikes, P. (2001) *Life history research in educational settings: Learning from lives*, London: Open University Press.

Grønseth, A. S. (2006) Experiences of tensions in re-orienting selves: Tamil refugees in Northern Norway seeking medical advice. *Anthropology & Medicine*, 13, 1: 77–98.

Griffiths, M., Rogers, A. and Anderson, B. (2013) *Migration, Time and Temporalities: Review and Prospect: COMPAS Research Resources Paper*, www.compas.ox.ac.uk/media/RR-2013-Migration_Time_Temporalities.pdf (Accessed 22 December 2017).

Hermans, H. J. M. (2001) Mixing and moving cultures require a dialogical self. *Human Development*, 44, 1: 24–28.

Hirsch, S. (2017) Racism, 'second generation' refugees and the asylum system. *Identities: Global Studies in Culture and Power.* 1–19.

Hitlin, S. and Elder, G. H. (2007) Time, self, and the curiously abstract concept of agency. *Sociological Theory*, 25: 170–191.

House of Commons (2017) *Asylum Statistics Briefing Paper Number SN01403*, 17 August 2017, http://researchbriefings.files.parliament.uk/documents/SN01403/SN01403.pdf (Accessed 2 December 2017).

Ibarra, H. (1999) Provisional selves: Experimenting with image and identity in professional adaptation. *Administrative Science Quarterly*, 44: 64–791.

Ipsos MORI (2010) A survey of refugees living in London. Report for the Greater London Authority, www.london.gov.uk/sites/default/files/gla_migrate_files_destination/A%20Survey%20of%20Refugees%20Living%20in%20London.pdf (accessed 23 March 2018)

Jaspal, R. (2015) Migration and identity processes among first-generation British South Asians. *South Asian Diaspora*, 7, 2: 79–96.

Jayaweera, H. (2010) *Health and Access to Health Care of Migrants in the UK*, www.better-health.org.uk/sites/default/files/briefings/downloads/health-brief19.pdf (Accessed 21 November 2017).

Landau, M. J., Oyserman, D., Keefer, L. A. and Smith, G. C. (2014) The college journey and academic engagement: How metaphor use enhances identity-based motivation. *Journal of Personality and Social Psychology*, 106, 5: 679–698.

Lewis, H., Craig, G., Adamson, S. and Wilkinson, M. (2008) *Refugees, Asylum Seekers and Migrants in Yorkshire and Humber 1999–2008: A Review of Literature for Yorkshire Futures*, www.migrationyorkshire.org.uk/userfiles/file/publications/YF-refugeesasylumseekersmigrantsreport1999-2008.pdf (Accessed 28 November 2017).

Markus, H. and Nurius, P. (1986) Possible selves. *American Psychologist*, 41: 954–969.

Markus, H. and Ruvolo, A. P. (1989). Possible selves: Personalized representations of goals. In L. A. Pervin (ed.) *Goal Concepts in Personality and Social Psychology*. Hillsdale, NJ: Lawrence Erlbaum, pp. 211–291

Markus, H. and Wurf, E. (1987) The dynamic self-concept: A social psychological perspective. *Annual Review of Psychology*, 39: 299–337.

Marx, K. (1963 [1852]) *The Eighteenth Brumaire of Louis Bonaparte*, New York: International Publishers.

McAdams, D. P. (1993) *Stories we live by: Personal myths and the making of the self*, New York: William Morrow and Company Inc.

McAdams, D. P. and McLean, K. C. (2013) Narrative identity. *Current Directions in Psychological Science*, 22, 3: 233–238.

Meara, N. M., Day, J. D., Chalk, L. M. and Phelps, R. E. (1995) Possible selves: Applications for career counseling. *Journal of Career Assessment*, 3: 259–277.

The Migration Observatory (2013) *Migration in the news: Portrayals of immigrants, migrants, asylum seekers and refugees in national British newspapers, 2010–2012*, Oxford: Migration Observatory, www.migrationobservatory.ox.ac.uk/wp-content/uploads/2016/04/Report-Migration_News.pdf (Accessed 2 October 2017).

Miller, R. L. (2000) *Researching life stories and family histories*, London: Sage Publications.

Morrice, L. (2011) *Being a refugee: Learning and identity: A longitudinal study of refugees in the UK*, Stoke-on-Trent: Trentham Books.

Morrice, L. (2013) Refugees in higher education: Boundaries of belonging and recognition, stigma and exclusion. *International Journal of Lifelong Education*, 32, 5: 652–668.

Nobel Women's Initiative (2016) *Women Refugees at Risk in Europe*, https://nobelwomensinitiative.org/wp-content/uploads/2016/03/Opening-Borders-Report_FINAL_WEB-1.pdf (Accessed 24 November 2017).

Oyserman, D., Ager, J. and Gant, L. (1995) A socially contextualized model of African American identity: Possible selves and school persistence. *Journal of Personality and Social Psychology*, 69, 6: 1216–1232.

Oyserman, D., Bybee, D., Terry, K. and Hart-Johnson, T. (2004) Possible selves as roadmaps. *Journal of Research in Personality*, 38: 130–149.

Oyserman, D. and James, L. (2009) Possible selves: From content to process. In K. D. Markman, W. M. P. Klein and J. A. Suh (eds) *Handbook of imagination and mental stimulation*, New York: Psychology Press.

Papadopoulos, I., Lees, S., Lay, M. and Gebrehiwot, A. (2004) Ethiopian refugees in the UK: Migration, adaptation and settlement experiences and their relevance to health. *Ethnicity and Health*, 9, 1: 55–73.

Phillimore, J., Ergün, E., Goodson, L. and Hennessy, D. (2007) *'They Do Not Understand the Problem I Have': Refugee Wellbeing and Mental Health*, www.lemosandcrane.co.uk/dev/resources/JRF%20-%20They%20do%20not%20understand%20the%20problem%20I%20have.pdf (Accessed 15 November 2017).

Phillimore, J., Goodson, L., Oosthuizen, R., Ferrari, E., Fathi, J., Penjwini, S. and Joseph, R. (2003) *Asylum seekers and refugees: Education, training, employment, skills and services in Coventry and Warwickshire*. Birmingham, UK: Centre for Urban and Regional Studies at the University of Birmingham with NIACE and BMG.

Pizzolato, J. E. (2007) Impossible selves: Investigating students' persistence decisions when their career-possible selves border on impossible. *Journal of Career Development*, 33: 201–223.

Platts-Fowler, D. and Robinson, D. (2011) *An Evaluation of the Gateway Protection Programme*. Sheffield: Sheffield Hallam University.

Refugee Council (2012) *The Experiences of Refugee Women in the UK*, www.refugeecouncil.org.uk/assets/0001/5837/Briefing_-_experiences_of_refugee_women_in_the_UK.pdf (Access 28 November 2017).

Refugee Council (2017) *Terms and Definitions: Glossary of Terminology Relating to Asylum Seekers and Refugees in UK*, www.refugeecouncil.org.uk/glossary (Accessed 22 July 2017).

Robjant, K., Hassan, R. and Katona, C. (2009) Mental health implications of detaining asylum seekers: Systematic review. *The British Journal of Psychiatry*, 194: 306–312.

Rossiter, M. (2007) Possible selves: An adult education perspective. *New Directions for Adult and Continuing Education*, 2007, 114: 5–15.

Shariatmadari, D. (2015) Swarms, floods and marauders: The toxic metaphors of the migration debate. *The Guardian*, www.theguardian.com/commentisfree/2015/aug/10/migration-debate-metaphors-swarms-floods-marauders-migrants (Accessed 4 January 2018).

Stevenson, J. and Willott, J. (2007) The aspiration and access to higher education of teenage refugees in the UK. *Compare: A Journal of Comparative Education*, 37, 5: 671–687.

Stevenson, J. and Willott, J. (2010) Refugees: Home students with international needs. Chapter in E. Jones (ed) *Internationalisation: The student voice*, London: Routledge.

Strahan, E. J. and Wilson, A. E. (2006) Temporal comparisons and motivation: The relation between past, present, and possible future selves. In C. Dunkel and J. Kerpelman (eds) *Possible selves: Theory, research, and application*, Hauppauge, NY: Nova Science Publishers, pp. 1–15.

United Nations General Assembly (1951) *Convention Relating to the Status of Refugees*, United Nations, Treaty Series, vol. 189, www.refworld.org/docid/3be01b964.html (Accessed 23 March 2018).

United Nations High Commissioner for Refugees (UNHCR) (2006) *UNHCR Master Glossary of Terms*, June 2006, Rev. 1, www.refworld.org/docid/42ce7d444.html (Accessed 1 December 2017).

United Nations High Commissioner for Refugees (UNHCR) (2013) *The Labour Market Integration of Resettled Refugees*, www.unhcr.org/5273a9e89.pdf (Accessed 23 November 2017).

United Nations High Commissioner for Refugees (UNHCR) (2016) *'Refugees' and 'Migrants': Frequently Asked Questions (FAQs)*, www.unhcr.org/afr/news/latest/2016/3/56e95c676/refugees-migrants-frequently-asked-questions-faqs.html (Accessed 1 December 2017).

United Nations High Commissioner for Refugees (UNHCR) (2017) *UNHCR Statistical Yearbook*, www.unhcr.org/uk/statistics/country/59b294387/unhcr-statistical-yearbook-2015-15th-edition.html (Accessed 30 November 2017).

Wambua, J. M. and Robinson, C. (2012) Possible selves and goal orientations of East African undergraduate students in the United States. In Z. Bekerman and T. Geisen (eds) *International handbook of migration, minorities and education*, Jerusalem: Springer.

Warfa, N., Bhui, K., Craig, T., Curtis, S., Mohamud, S., Stansfeld, S., McCrone, P. and Thornicroft, G. (2006) Post-migration geographical mobility, mental health and health service utilisation among Somali refugees in the UK: A qualitative study. *Health & Place*, 12, 4: 503–515.

Willott, J. and Stevenson, J. (2013) Attitudes to employment of professionally qualified refugees in the UK. *International Migration*, 51, 5: 120–132.

Index

Note: Page numbers in bold indicate tables. Notes are indicated by page numbers followed by n.

Abrams, L. S. 31
academic achievement: dyslexic students and 80; feared self and 121; possible selves and 112; strong possible selves and 20
accountancy: careers in 111, 115, 120; possible selves and 122–124; privileged social backgrounds and 114, 117; unequal access to 114, 118–119
acquisition metaphor of learning 61
acts 82, 104
acts of imagination 72–73
Adam, B. 46–47
agency: conflations and 49; families and 86; future self and 144; possible selves and 4; power and 144; refugee women and 142; structure and 4; theorisation of 48
Ager, J. 31
Aguilar, J. P. 31
Aimhigher 95
Appadurai, A. 97
Araújo, E. R. 46
Archer, M. 48–51, 53–54, 144
Arendt, H. 93
Arnett, R. C. 93
Article 26 131, 145n4
Ashley, L. 111, 114
Ashwin, P. 42–43
aspiration: career self and 116, 123; disruption of 123; educational 97; identity and 97–98; multidimensional concept of 97; possible selves and 100; problematic forces and 100; refugees and 127; respectability and 102–103, 106; widening participation and 96

asylum seekers: defining 128; dispersal policy for 133, 137; higher education and 145n2; mandated housing for 129; mental health needs of 130; poverty and 137; refused 128; resettlement of 132–133; trauma and 137
Australia: higher education in 94–95; widening participation in 94–95
autonomous reflexivity 50–51, 53

Bak, W. 30
Baker, W. 97
barriers: to higher education 81, 89, 139–140; to possible selves 78; structural 127, 142–143
Bathmaker, A. M. 4
Bauber, S. 87
behaviour 132
Being Human (Archer) 49
Bennett, A. 28, 47, 95
Berlant, L. 107
Bernstein, B. 42–44
Big Four Accounting Firms 111–112, 114, 116, 119–122, 124n1
Bourdieu, P. 3, 29, 97, 113, 115, 124
Bradley Review 95
Breen, R. 29
Brett, M. 95
Bruner, J. 96, 98
Burke, P. J. 28, 47, 100–102
Butler, J. 35–36
Bybee, D. 15, 30

Cameron, H. 81
Camfield, L. 97
Cantor, N. 18

capital: cultivation of 117–118, 121; future self and 117; internships as 114, 121; personal 111
Carawan, L. 87
career identity: aspiration and 116, 123; development of 122–123; personal capital and 111; possible selves and 111–113, 119–122; psycho-social aspects of 123; *see also* elite careers
career pathways 119–120
Charmaz, K. 63
classroom discourse: context-sensitive framework of 60–61, 68; meaning-making process 69–71; participation in 60–61, 68–69, 72; teacher-led 62
Clegg, S. 28, 96
cognition: language teaching and 59–60; as meaning-making 62; motivation and 132
cognitive psychology 1, 95
communicative reflexivity 50–51, 53
confidence 86–87, 117, 122, 133
confusion 87, 104
control: families and 86; possible others and 21; possible selves and 15; time management and 104
conversation analysis 64
Copestake, J. 97
Corbett, M. 3
Coward, F. 32
Crawford, C. 114
Crick, N. 93
critical hope 106–107
Crocker, J. R. 136
Cross, S. E. 20
Crozier, G. 101
cruel optimism 107–108
culture: educational success and 22; possible selves and 31; workplace 122, 124

Dark-Freudeman, A. 31
description: external language of 42–43; internal language of 42–43
Deshler, D. D. 30
Destin, M. 17
destination 79, 86–88
Dewey, J. 78
dialogue 101–102, 107
disability: possible selves and 89; social model of 80
Disability Discrimination Act 81
discrimination 81, 87, 137

discursive gap 43–45
dispersal policy 133, 137
Duberley, J. 111, 114
Duggan, S. 29
dyslexia: confidence and 87; defining 78, 80; diagnosis of 80–81, 87; discrimination and 87, 89; expectations and 83–84, 86; families and 80–89; learned helplessness and 87; life paths for 87–88; life trajectories and 87, 89; possible selves and 80–86; school disengagement and 81; screening for 80–81; siblings and 82, 87–89; social construct of 80; temporality and 78; understanding of 87
dyslexic healthcare students: interviews with 82; possible selves and 78, 82

Early, J. S. 19
education: individualisation in 107; subjects in 36; temporality and 27–28; *see also* higher education (HE)
educational linguistics: language learning 59; language teacher cognition in 59–61; language teaching in 59; teacher-student interactions in 60–61
educational subjectivities: defining 36; future orientation of 36; possible selves and 34–37
EFL *see* English as a Foreign Language (EFL)
Elder, G. H. 142
elite careers: gender and 113, 115; graduate recruitment processes for 114; mobilising resources for 111, 114–115, 117; possible selves and 111, 113, 115; preparation for 116–120, 123; race and 113, 115; socio-economic status and 113–114; unequal access to 111, 113–114, 118–119; *see also* career identity
embodied self 29, 49
emotional valence: positive/negative end-state 15–18; possible others and 21
employability: discourse of 28–29; temporality and 28; *see also* graduate recruitment processes
employment: elite careers and 111; higher education and 28, 34, 140; job applications and 112; privileged social backgrounds and 114; refugees and 127, 129, 137; refugee women and 129–130, 133; use of skills in 130

English as a Foreign Language (EFL): Slovakia 62–63; teacher development in 62–63
Equality Act 81
equity, in access to higher education 94–95
Equity Initiatives Framework (Bennett) 95
Erel, U. 134
Erikson, M. G. 3–5, 15–17, 30, 32
ethnicity 123
ethnography: grounded theory 63, 73; performance 78
Excitable Speech (Butler) 35

Falout, J. 21–22
family: agency and 86; dyslexia in 80–81; influence of 80; narratives 89; possible selves and 86–89; road maps and 86; role models in 88; self-esteem and 81, 87
feared self: academic achievement and 121; anxiety about 106; families and 88; insecure 141; lonely 141; motivation and 123; possible selves and 95, 112; poverty as 141; refugees and 127–128; refugee women and 135, 141; transitional life periods and 127
finance careers 115, 120
forced displacement: poverty and 137; refugees and 127, 129; violence and 137
Foucault, M. 35
fractured selves 135–137
Frazier, L. K. 131
Freire, P. 101, 107
Fryberg, S. 31
Frye, M. 97
Fukada, Y. 21–22
Fukuda, T. 21–22
future: anxiety about 106; concept of 46–48; orientations to 96; projected 102–104; social mobility narrative of 47; temporality and 45–49, 51, 53
future present 47
future self: agency and 144; barriers to 140; capitals and 117; career identity and 118–119, 122–123; construction of 124; development of new 140–141; ideal 112, 117–118, 120, 123; imagined 117–118, 120, 123; individual strategies for 144; power and 144; refugee women and 140; strategies for 127, 132, 144
future work self 118–119, 122–123

Gant, L. 31
gender: elite careers and 113, 115; possible selves and 31; respectability and 102; *see also* women
Giddens, A. 3, 48
goal-as-journey metaphor 132
goal-directed behaviour 132
goal-focused theory 14
goals: possible career selves and 113, 118, 123, 139; possible selves and 95, 112, 132; refugees and 127, 132–133, 139; student 13–14, 139
Godley, J. 17
Goffman, E. 97
Goldthorpe, J. H. 29
Gore, J. 95
graduate recruitment processes: mobility process in 112; packaging of personal capital in 111; possible selves and 112–113, 115; privileged social backgrounds and 114; rules of the game in 113
Gregg, P. 114
Griffin, M. A. 18–19
grounded theory ethnography 63, 73
Groves, C. 46–47
Guernica (Picasso) 93, 107

habitus 113, 115
Haggis, T. 42–43
Hamman, D. 32
Hansson, B. 17
Harré, R. 49
Harrison, N. 95
Hart-Johnson, T. 15
Harvey, A. 95
health professionals: actions to become 79–80; dyslexic 78, 82; motivation and 79–80
Heidegger, M. 102
higher education (HE): advising of refugees in 140; aspiration and 96–97; autonomous reflexivity and 50; barriers to 81, 89, 139–140; cultural preconceptions of 23; discrimination and 81; employability discourse in 28, 34; environment and 78; family narratives of 89; future orientation of 29; geographical mobilities and 3; ideological issue of 14, 23; participation in 2–3, 124n3; possible selves and 1–5; social class and 2–3; social mobility narrative of 47; student motivation in

13–18, 23; systemic inequalities in 27, 37; temporality and 28, 47; theory in 42–43, 48; tuition fees in 2
higher education (HE) and: dyslexic students 89; immigrants 127; minority ethnic students 31; refugees 130–131
Higher Education Participation and Partnerships Program (HEPPP) 95
high status careers 111, 113; see also elite careers
Hitlin, S. 142
Hock, M. F. 30
Hodkinson, P. 29
Hooker, K. 131
hope 106–107, 137
hoped-for selves 138–139
horizons for action 113, 122

ideal self 112, 117–118, 120, 123
identity: narrative 134; personal 49; social 49
identity formation 79
illegal migrants/immigrants 129
imagined selves 29–30
immigrants 129; see also migrants and migration; refugees
immigrant undergraduate students 127
immigrant women 127
impoverished self 128, 141
Indiatsi, J. 32
individualisation: disability and 89; in education 107; imagined futures and 104; self and 97
inequalities: in access to elite careers 111, 113–114; in higher education 27, 37, 47, 93; possible selves and 3–4; structural 47, 144; systemic 27, 32, 37
insecure self 141
internships 114, 116, 121

James, L. 140
James, R. 95
Jaspers, K. 23
Johnson, L. 32
journey metaphor 131–132

L2 learning 64
Lambert, M. 32
language learning: teaching and 59–60; whole-class interactions in 60–61, 64
language teacher cognition: analysis of 64–65; emerging acts of imagination 72–73; objectives of 61; possible selves and 59–60, 62, 65, 68, 71–73; reflection and 62, 70–72; representations of 62
learned helplessness 87
learning: acquisition metaphor of 61; participation metaphor of 59, 61–62
life paths 87–88
life tasks: defining 18; motivational power of 18–20; possible selves and 18–20
life trajectories 79, 87, 89
linear trajectories 112–113, 119, 123
lonely self 141
lost selves 137–138
Lundblad, S. 17

MacLeod, A. 17
Macmillan, L. 114
Manathunga, C. 47
Mäntylä, H. 46
Marginson, S. 2
Markus, H. 1, 14–18, 20–22, 28–31, 37, 44, 48, 51–53, 79, 95, 98, 112, 131, 144
Marx, K. 49
Mason, C. M. 19
meaning-making process 15, 69–71
Melhuish, E. C. 97
Mellor, K. 95
mental health 88, 130
mentoring programme: participatory methodology in 93, 98–99; possible selves and 95–96, 99–100; proper personhood and 104; story-sharing approaches in 96, 99; valuable-ness in 99; valuation in 100
Merton, R. 43
meta-reflexivity 50–51, 53
methodology: micro-narrative interviews 98–99; participatory 93, 98–99; praxis-based 93–94, 100–101; research-informed 93–94, 98; story-sharing approaches 96, 99; see also research methodologies
micro-narrative interviews 98–99, 101–102
middle-class backgrounds 114–117, 120, 123
migrants and migration: defining 129; discrimination and 137; forced displacement of 127–128, 137; temporality and 131; transition and 127; see also refugees
Miller, L. C. 21

minority ethnic students: career identity 116, 123; employment and 111; mobilities and 112; positive possible selves and 31
Mische, A. 98–99, 102, 104
Misiaszek, L. 101
mobilities: geographical 3; social 47, 50; social trajectories and 112
morphogenesis 50–51
motivation: aspects of 15–16; cognition and 132; defining 13; emotions in 17; self-concept and 14, 41; *see also* student motivation
Muniesa, F. 99
Munn, B. 95
Murphey, T. 21–22
Murphy, A. 3

Nalavany, B. 87
narrative: checking of 33; defining 145n8; future social interaction and 22; identity and 134; as mode of knowing 96; as personal myth 134; possible selves and 32–34, 134; self and 96, 98; social mobility 47; subjectivity and 34–36; theorisation of 33–35
narrative inquiry 78
narrative temporality 4, 32–34
Nathan, D. 97
Naylor, R. 95
need-focused theory 14
negative emotional valence 15
neoliberalism: agendas of 94, 100, 107; policy framing and 53
Niedenthal, P. 18
Niedenthal, P. M. 20
Novin, S. 17
Nurius, P. 1, 15–16, 18, 21, 28–31, 37, 44, 48, 51–53, 79, 95, 98, 112, 131, 144

ontological need 107
ought-to selves 135
outreach programmes 93, 95, 98, 106, 108
Oyserman, D. 15, 17, 30–31, 79, 140

Paired Peers project 111, 113
Papafilippou, V. 4
parents: aspirations of 88; dyslexic 80–81, 87; dyslexic children and 80, 82–84; perceptions of possible selves 86; as role models 88; students' possible selves and 18, 20
Parker, S. K. 18–19
participation metaphor of learning 59, 61–62
participatory methodology 93
past and future in the present 96
Pedagogical Methodology (PM) 101–102, 107
pedagogy: autonomous reflexivity and 50; employability discourse in 28; of ethics and care 100; goals and 61, 64, 68–70, 72
performance ethnography 78
performative subjectivity 35–36
Personal Development Planning (PDP) in HE 44–46, 48
personal identity 49
personalisation 107
personalism 98
personal myths 134
personhood 97–98, 104
phenomenology 102
Picasso, Pablo 93, 107
Pizzolato, J. E. 18, 30
positive emotional valence 15
positivist research 98
possible others: assumed behaviour of 21; concept of 21; defining 23n1; methodological approaches to 21; narratives of the future and 22; social interactions with 21–22
possible selves: ability to perceive 80; agency and 4; barriers to 78; behaviour and 132; careers and 111; controllability of 15, 21; destination of 79, 86–88; elaborated 30–31; embodied self and 29; evolution of 131–132; families and 78, 86–89; feared 88, 121, 123; fractured 135–137; hoped-for 138–139; life tasks and 18–20; life trajectories and 79; motivation and 13–20, 30, 41, 96, 112, 132; narrative and 32–34, 134; negative emotional valence of 15–18, 22; positive emotional valence of 15–18, 22; probability of 15; projected futures and 102–104; reality and 50; reflexivity and 51; salience of 15, 19, 22, 138–139; self-concept and 14–15, 20, 23, 79; self-esteem and 112; self-knowledge in 44; social cognition and 22; social construction of 31–32;

social context and 21–22, 79; social validation of 20–22; strategies for goals and 132; structure and 4; subjectivity and 32, 36; temporality and 78, 81, 112; valuation in 102–104, 107–108
possible selves: concept of 1–4, 28–30, 37–38, 79, 112; defining 14–15, 29–32; ideological assumptions and 23; sociologically informed notions of 41–42, 52–54; theorisation of 41–42, 51–54
poverty: aspirational 96–97; as a feared self 141; material 96; refugees and 129, 137–138, 141; subjectivity of 97
power: agency and 144; future self and 144; motivational 16–18, 20; refugees and 142; selfhood and 52–53; time and 28, 47
power relations 101–102
practice: embodied self and 49; praxis-based 93–94; research-informed 93–94, 98; teacher participation in 62; teacher reflection as 62, 70–72; teacher-student interactions as 63
Prince, D. 22, 36–37
privilege: elite careers and 114; perpetuation of 95; structuring power of 53
psychotherapy 30–31

race: elite careers and 113, 115, 123; higher education participation and 37; possible selves and 31
Rational Action Theory 29
Read, S. J. 21
reflexivity: autonomous 50–51, 53; communicative 50–51, 53; fractured 50; meta-reflexives 50–51, 53; morphogenesis and 50–51; possible selves and 51; temporality and 50–51, 53
refugees: aspirations of 127; defining 128; dispersal policy for 133, 137; education and training of; 130–131, 133; journey metaphor 131–132; recognition of qualifications of 139; resettlement of 127, 131–133; United Nations High Commissioner for (UNHCR) 128–129; *see also* migrants and migration
refugees and: entitlements 129; forced displacement 127; higher education 145n2; housing 137; National Asylum Support Service (NASS) 129–130; possible selves 127–128, 132, 137–138; poverty 137; structural barriers 143; temporality 127; trauma 130; unemployment 129–130; *see also* migrants and migration
refugee women: challenges of 139; education projects for 133, 137–138; fractured selves of 135–137; goal orientation of 139; hoped-for selves 138–139; mental health needs of 130; participant demographics 144; violence against 130
refugee women and: agency 142; future self 140; hope 137; lost selves 136–138; possible selves 128; poverty 137–138; power 142; sadness 136–138; structural barriers 142–143; trauma 136–137; unemployment 130, 133–134
research-informed practice 93–94, 98
research methodologies: narrative temporality 32–33; possible others and 21; possible selves and 4–5; *see also* methodology
resettlement 127, 131
respectability 102–103, 106
Ricoeur, P. 33–35
Rittel, H. 104
road maps 86, 132, 134, 143
Rossiter, M. 132

sadness 136–138
Sammons, P. 97
scenes 82
Schmidt, U. 17
Scholarios, D. 111, 114
Scholars at Risk 131, 145n3
school disengagement 81
Schumaker, J. B. 30
Schütz, A. 102
second language acquisition (SLA) 59
Segal, H. G. 32
self: constructive nature of 79; embodied 29, 49; environment and 49; fractured 135–137; hoped-for 138–139; lost 137–138; narrative of 96, 98; ought-to 135; survival 141–143; temporality and 1, 41, 44–45, 51; theories of 48; *see also* feared self; future self
self-concept: conceptions of the future and 23; cultural backgrounds and 22;

meaning-making and 15; motivation and 14–15; notions of 97; possible selves and 14–15, 20, 23, 79; self-schemata and 14
self-esteem 81, 87, 112
self-knowledge 44
self-schemata 14, 79
Setterlund, M. B. 20
Sfard, A. 61
Shahjahan, R. A. 47
siblings: dyslexia in 82, 87–89; as role models 88–89; support from 88; *see also* family
Siraj-Blatchford, I. 97
Skeggs, B. 97–98
Slovakia 62–63
Smith, S. 95
social class: career identity and 111; career inequalities and 113; higher education participation and 2–3, 37; middle-class backgrounds 114–117, 120, 123; mobilities of 3, 112; working-class backgrounds 115, 118, 123
social construct: of dyslexia 80; of possible selves 31–32
social context: communicative reflexivity and 50–51; identity formation and 79; possible selves and 21–22; social validation of 22
social environments 80
social groups: perceived membership of 20; refugees 128, 137
social identity 49
social interactions: narratives of 22; possible others and 21–22; possible selves and 20–21
social justice 102
social mobility: autonomous reflexivity and 50; narrative of 47
social spaces: inequalities in 124; possible selves and 112; structures of 112–113, 124
social trajectories 112
social validation: possible selves and 20, 22; student support and 18
Sommerlad, H. 111, 114
Sparkes, A. C. 29
Stevenson, J. 4, 31, 96
story-sharing approaches 96, 99
strategies: behavioral 141; future self and 127, 132, 144; goals and 132

Strauss, K. 18
structural barriers 127, 142–143
structural inequalities 47, 144
structure: agency and 4, 29, 32, 41, 43, 48, 101, 112; embodiment and 113; motivation and 14, 20; narrative 33, 36
student goals: motivation and 14; possible selves and 13; refugee women and 133, 139
student motivation: context of 17; goal-focused theory of 14; higher education and 13–14; life tasks and 18–20; need-focused theory of 14; possible selves and 13–20, 30, 96, 112; purpose of higher education and 23
students: dyslexic 80–86, 89; future orientation of 29–34; immigrant undergraduate 127; minority ethnic 31
student support: families and 82–89; influence on sense of purpose for 22–23; life tasks and 20; parents and 80, 82–84; positive possible selves and 18, 20; siblings and 88
subjectivity: educational 34–36; embodied self and 49, 107; narrative and 34–36; performative 35–36; possible selves and 32, 36; theorisation of 35
survival self 141–143
Sylva, K. 97
symbolic violence 93
systemic inequalities: higher education and 27, 37; identification of 32

Taggart, B. 97
Tchanturia, K. 17
teacher development (TD) 62–63
teacher-student interactions: analysis of 64–65; classroom context mode 60, 64; context-sensitive framework of 69; conversation analysis 64; Initiation–Response–Feedback (IRF) 60, 64; materials and skills mode 60; meaning-making process 69; practice of 63, 65, 68–69; systems mode 60; whole-class 60
temporality: conceptions of 46–47; education and 27–28; futures and 45–49, 51, 53; in higher education 47; narrative 4, 32–34; possible selves and 27, 78, 81, 112; reflexivity and 50–51, 53; refugees and 127, 135; self and 1, 41, 44–45, 51; spatial relations and 47; *see also* time

Terry, K. 15, 30
theories of the middle range 43, 45, 51–52, 54
theory: assemblage and 43; conflation in 48; discursive gap in 43–45; in higher education research 42–43, 48; language of description in 42–43; meaning-making process of 43; as process of theorisation 41; of the self 48
Tight, M. 42–43
time: dominant discourses of 47, 53; fluid experience of 46; imagined futures and 32, 46–47, 105–106; linear progression of 28, 46; power and 47; risks and 105–106; student use of 28; *see also* temporality
time future 28, 96
time management 46, 52, 54, 104–105
time present 96
timescapes 46
trajectories: linear 112–113, 119, 123; social 112; successful 113
transition 127
trauma 130, 136–137
Tutton, R. 104

unclear selves 140
undocumented immigrants 127
unemployment: refugees and 129–130; refugee women and 137; structural barriers and 7
United Kingdom: asylum seekers in 128–129; dyslexic students in 80; educational access in 81

valuation 94, 99–100, 102–104
valuable selves 99–100, 102–103

Vignoles, A. 114
Vygotsky, L. 49

Waller, R. 95
Walsh, S. 60, 64
Webber, M. 104
West, R. L. 31
Wherry, M. B. 20
Whitty, G. 95
wicked futures 94, 104–105
wicked problem 104
widening participation (WP): aspiration in 96; atheoretical nature of 95; deficit framings in 96, 98, 106; evaluation of 95; imagined futures and 98; national policy and 94–95; possible selves and 22; social justice and 102; symbolic violence in 93; unintended consequences of 93, 100
women: fractured selves 135–136; gender discourses and 102; immigrant 127; lack of employment for refugee 129–130; migrant 134; poverty and 137; refugee 127–128, 130, 133, 136–144; violence against 130; *see also* refugee women
Woodman, D. 29
Woolf, V. 94
working-class backgrounds 115, 118, 123
workplace culture 122, 124
WP *see* widening participation (WP)
Wurf, E. 22
Wyness, G. 114

Ylijoki, O. 46

Zhou, L. 32